FREUD'S THINKING

In this brief but comprehensive introduction to Freud's theories, Mikkel Borch-Jacobsen provides a step-by-step overview of his ideas regarding the unconscious, the cure, sexuality, drives, and culture, highlighting their indebtedness to contemporary neurophysiological and biological assumptions. The picture of Freud that emerges is very different from that of the fact-finding scientist he claimed to be. Bold conceptual innovations – repression, infantile sexuality, the Oedipus complex, narcissism, the death drive – were not discoveries made by Freud but speculative constructs placed on clinical material to satisfy the requirements of the general theory of the mind and culture that he was building. *Freud's Thinking* provides a final account of this mirage of the mind that was psychoanalysis.

A philosopher by training, Mikkel Borch-Jacobsen is Emeritus Professor of Comparative Literature at the University of Washington, USA, and an award-winning theorist and historian of psychoanalysis and psychiatry. He is the author or coauthor of some sixteen books translated into twelve languages, and coauthor, with Anne Georget, of the documentary *Branding Illness* (2011).

FREUD'S THINKING

An Introduction

MIKKEL BORCH-JACOBSEN

TRANSLATED BY
KATY MASUGA

Shaftesbury Road, Cambridge CB2 8EA, United Kingdom

One Liberty Plaza, 20th Floor, New York, NY 10006, USA

477 Williamstown Road, Port Melbourne, VIC 3207, Australia

314–321, 3rd Floor, Plot 3, Splendor Forum, Jasola District Centre, New Delhi – 110025, India

103 Penang Road, #05-06/07, Visioncrest Commercial, Singapore 238467

Cambridge University Press is part of Cambridge University Press & Assessment, a department of the University of Cambridge.

We share the University's mission to contribute to society through the pursuit of education, learning and research at the highest international levels of excellence.

www.cambridge.org
Information on this title: www.cambridge.org/9781009371131

DOI: 10.1017/9781009371117

First published 2023

A catalogue record for this publication is available from the British Library.

Library of Congress Cataloging-in-Publication Data
NAMES: Borch-Jacobsen, Mikkel, author.
TITLE: Freud's thinking : an introduction / Mikkel Borch-Jacobsen, University of Washington, Katy Masuga.
DESCRIPTION: Cambridge, United Kingdom ; New York, NY : Cambridge University Press, 2023. | Includes bibliographical references.
IDENTIFIERS: LCCN 2023007398 (print) | LCCN 2023007399 (ebook) | ISBN 9781009371131 (hardback) | ISBN 9781009371148 (paperback) | ISBN 9781009371117 (epub)
SUBJECTS: LCSH: Freud, Sigmund, 1856-1939. | Psychoanalysis–History.
CLASSIFICATION: LCC BF109.F74 B6648 2024 (print) | LCC BF109.F74 (ebook) | DDC 150.19/52–dc23/eng/20230415
LC record available at https://lccn.loc.gov/2023007398
LC ebook record available at https://lccn.loc.gov/2023007399

ISBN 978-1-009-37113-1 Hardback
ISBN 978-1-009-37114-8 Paperback

Contents

Introduction

"I thought it – so it must be true"

Sigmund Freud, quoted by Carl Gustav Jung[1]

Who was Sigmund Freud? A doctor? A psychologist? A philosopher?

Freud was not a philosopher. He had studied medicine in Vienna, before specializing in neuropathology and becoming a "nerve doctor" (today, we would say neurologist). We know that as a young man, he was very interested in philosophical questions and that during his studies, he enrolled in philosophy courses of the "brilliant" Franz Brentano (1838–1917). We also know that he projected, at that time, to obtain a double doctorate in Philosophy and Zoology. However, this early interest in philosophy soon gave way to an attitude that could well be described as resolutely antiphilosophical. In 1876, he joined the Institute of Physiology of Ernst von Brücke (1819–1892) as a research assistant (*Famulus*). Under the latter's influence, Freud adopted a militant positivism that remained his "spontaneous philosophy" until the end.

Freud was not a philosopher because he wanted to do science, just like his master Brücke and the other members of the prestigious Viennese School of Medicine: Carl von Rokitansky (1804–1878), Theodor Meynert (1833–1892), and Sigmund Exner (1846–1926). For all these people, science is defined, among other things, by its rejection of the philosophical way of thinking. Science sticks to facts, to experience, to observable data that it links and organizes patiently with the help of laws. Philosophy, on the contrary, proceeds a priori. It puts ideas before facts, and in doing so, it goes beyond experience, wandering in the clouds. It goes beyond, *meta*: philosophy, in the eyes of positivists, is by nature a metaphysics. In a letter addressed in 1927 to the philosopher and psychologist Werner Achelis

*Footnotes refer to the bibliography at the end of the volume. Translations have been modified where necessary.

[1] Charteris 1960.

(1897–1982), Freud specified as follows his "attitude toward philosophy (metaphysics)": "I believe that one day metaphysics will be condemned as a nuisance, as an abuse of thinking, as a survival from the period of the religious *Weltanschauung*."[2]

Admittedly, Freud left the physiology laboratory of his beginnings, and he also abandoned his first neurological research (on infantile paralysis, on aphasia) to turn to psychology, traditionally a branch of philosophy next to cosmology and theology. Psychoanalysis, which was the product of this change of orientation, was nonetheless a science in his eyes. In the *New Introductory Lectures on Psycho-Analysis*, he defines it without ambiguity as "a specialist science, a branch of psychology."[3] For him, science is not a matter of object or content but of method: "The intellect and mind are objects for scientific research in exactly the same way as any non-human things. Psycho-analysis has a special right to speak for the scientific *Weltanschauung* at this point ... Its special contribution to science lies precisely in having extended research to the mental field."[4]

Thus defined, the Freudian project is that of a scientific, dephilosophized, despiritualized psychology. It should be noted, it was also that of all the psychologists of the second half of the nineteenth century, from Wundt to Brentano, from Ebbinghaus to William James. For them, as for Freud, it was a question of completing the scientific revolution by extending the method of the natural sciences (*Naturwissenschaften*) to the things of the mind, the traditional domain of philosophy and ethics. Franz Brentano (the same one whose philosophy courses the young Freud had assiduously followed) declared in the opening of his influential *Psychology from an Empirical Standpoint*: "We must strive to achieve here what mathematics, physics, chemistry and physiology have already accomplished."[5] Théodore Flournoy (1854–1920), another pioneer of the "new psychology", was pleased that the government of Geneva had created for him a chair "in the faculty of sciences, rather than in that of letters where all the courses of philosophy are found; [it] has implicitly recognized (perhaps without knowing it) the existence of psychology as a particular science, independent of all philosophical systems, with the same claims as physics, botany, astronomy."[6]

Psychoanalysis, in the same way, is supposed to take over from philosophy by surpassing it, by replacing it with a true science of man. This is what Freud's often quoted statement means: "As a young man I knew no

[2] Freud 1960, 374–375. [3] Freud 1933a, 158. [4] Ibid., 159. [5] Brentano 1874, 2.
[6] Flournoy 1896, 1.

longing other than for philosophical knowledge, and now I am about to fulfill it as I move from medicine to psychology."[7] Scientific psychology (psychoanalysis) is not the continuation of philosophy; it is its truth. It unmasks its metaphysical or theological illusion. Feuerbach, whose *Essence of Christianity*[8] Freud had read when attending Brentano's lectures, asserted that theology had to be translated into anthropology. Freud, in the *Psychopathology of Everyday Life*, similarly demands that metaphysics be translated into metapsychology, into the "psychology of the unconscious."[9]

Freud has a name for the philosophical error: "speculation" (*Spekulation*). This is understood in a distantly Kantian sense: "Theoretical cognition is *speculative*", says Kant, "when it relates to an object or certain conceptions of an object which is not given and cannot be discovered by means of experience."[10] Speculation is a pure thought that exceeds possible experience and rambles beyond, *meta*. Freed from the constraints of experience, it is then free to simplify reality and to deduce it from some basic concepts (*Grundbegriffe*) or a priori principles. Practically every time he evokes philosophy, Freud reproaches it for its systematicity and its abstract coherence: "Philosophy is not opposed to science . . . it departs from it, however, by clinging to the illusion of being able to present a picture of the universe which is without gaps and is coherent."[11] Philosophy is a *Weltanschauung*, a conception of the world, that is to say "an intellectual construction (*Konstruktion*) that solves all the problems of our existence uniformly on the basis of one overriding hypothesis."[12] But Freud hates *Weltanschauungen*: "I must confess that I am not at all partial to the fabrication of *Weltanschauungen*. Such activities may be left to philosophers."[13]

To the totalizing speculation of philosophy, Freud opposes the fragmentary and provisional work of that "empirical science" that is psychoanalysis: "Psycho-analysis is not, like philosophies, a system starting out from a few sharply defined basic concepts, seeking to grasp the whole universe with the help of these and, once it is completed, having no room for fresh discoveries or better understanding."[14] Psychoanalysis fumbles around, letting itself be guided by experience, always ready to abandon its working hypotheses if necessary. (Conversely, in the *New Lectures*, he compares scientific work to the course of a psychoanalysis, with its false

[7] Freud 1985, 180. [8] Feuerbach 1841. [9] Freud 1901, 259. [10] Kant 1781, 355.
[11] Freud 1933a, 160. [12] Ibid., 158. [13] Freud 1926b, 96. [14] Freud 1923a, 253.

starts and its constant "withdrawal" of hypotheses.[15]) Psychoanalysis prides itself on being modest, in contrast to the arrogance of philosophers.

A passage from the essay "On Narcissism: An Introduction" sums up this negative epistemology:

> I am of the opinion that that is just the difference between a speculative theory and a science erected on empirical interpretation. The latter will not envy speculation its privilege of having a smooth, logically unassailable foundation, but will gladly content itself with nebulous, scarcely imaginable basic concepts, which it hopes to apprehend more clearly in the course of its development, or which it is even prepared to replace by others. For these ideas are not the foundation of science, upon which everything rests: that foundation is observation alone. They are not the bottom but the top of the whole structure, and they can be replaced and discarded without damaging it.[16]

"The foundation of science is observation (*Beobachtung*)." Freud echoes here the positivism of the physicist and philosopher of science Ernst Mach (1838–1916), who seems to be his main reference in the theory of knowledge. "For the scientist", Mach wrote, "it is quite a secondary matter whether his ideas fit into some given philosophic system or not, so long as he can use them with profit as a starting point for research. For the scientist is not so fortunate as to possess unshakeable principles, he has accustomed to regarding even his safest and best-founded views and principles as provisional and liable to modification through experience."[17] The concepts of the positivist are disposable, because only experience and observation count. They are, says Mach, "provisional fictions" that are used for convenience until better, more "economical" ones are found. Freud adds: the "basic concepts"[18] of psychoanalytical science are never more than "fictions,"[19] "speculative superstructures,"[20] "scientific constructions,"[21] "working hypotheses,"[22] "intellectual scaffolding,"[23] "conventions"[24] that are replaced as soon as they conflict with observation.

One will have noted the terms "basic concepts," "speculation," "construction": these are the same terms that Freud uses to talk about philosophy. Would psychoanalysis, therefore, also be a speculation? In fact, Freud often acknowledges the speculative character of his theories. One cannot, he says, do without hypotheses and heuristic constructions: "Even at the stage of description it is not possible to avoid applying certain

15 Freud 1933a, 174. 16 Freud 1914c, 77. 17 Mach 1905/1976, 9.
18 Freud 1915a, 117. 19 Freud 1900, 598; Freud 1926a, 194. 20 Freud 1925a, 32.
21 Freud 1917a, 142. 22 Freud 1915a, 124. 23 Freud 1938b, 159.
24 Freud 1915a, 117.

abstract ideas to the material in hand, ideas derived from somewhere or other but certainly not from the new observations alone."[25] Or again: "Without metapsychological speculation and theorizing – I had almost said 'phantasising' (*Phantasieren*) – we shall not get another step forward."[26] Yet, if Freud allows himself to play freely with ideas, just to see, it is because, as a good positivist, he posits that they will be corrected by experience anyway. This is what one might call the principle of conceptual selection: the facts are hard, stubborn, resistant, and only the theories that adapt to them survive (which supposes that the "facts", in psychoanalysis, are not influenced by the theories).

For Freud, then, there are two speculations, the bad and the good: the philosophical (the metaphysical), which goes beyond experience and bends reality to its *desiderata*; and the psychoanalytical (the metapsychological), which speculates under the control of experience and observation, in constant interaction with them.

However, Freud also sometimes criticizes philosophers for sticking too much to the observable. Psychoanalysis is a "psychology of the unconscious", i.e., a psychology of what does not present itself to consciousness. Strictly speaking, we can therefore not observe this unconscious; we can only postulate it. Now, "philosophers, who know no kind of observation other than self-observation, cannot follow [analysts] into that domain."[27] They are unable to accept that there is thought that is not conscious, that is not the object of a psychic experience or observation.

This is the second major reproach addressed to philosophers, tirelessly hammered throughout the work: "the majority of philosophers will hear nothing of 'unconscious mental processes'";[28] "they have identified the mental with the conscious and have proceeded to infer from this definition that what is unconscious cannot be mental or a subject for psychology";[29] "To most people who have been educated in philosophy the idea of anything psychical which is not also conscious is so inconceivable that it seems to them absurd and refutable simply by logic";[30] "The overwhelming majority of philosophers regard as mental only the phenomena of consciousness";[31] "The majority of philosophers . . . declare that the idea of something psychical being unconscious is self-contradictory."[32]

Why does Freud write "the *majority* of philosophers"? Because he knows perfectly well that he cannot write "*all* philosophers." Not only was the

[25] Ibid. [26] Freud 1937a, 225. [27] Freud 1925b, 217. [28] Freud 1905b, 266.
[29] Freud 1913a, 178. [30] Freud 1923b, 13. [31] Freud 1925b, 216. [32] Freud 1938b, 158.

idea of an "unconscious cerebration" commonplace in the neurophysiology of the second half of the nineteenth century, but many philosophers had taken it up, starting with Theodor Lipps (1851–1914) and Friedrich Nietzsche (1844–1900). In reality, behind the philosophical crowd evoked by Freud, there is *one* very specific philosopher: Franz Brentano. It was in the latter's *Psychology from an Empirical Standpoint* that Freud found the radical critique of "unconscious consciousness" that he later attributed to philosophers in general. The irony is that Brentano directed this critique against a "*philosophy* of the unconscious", that of Eduard von Hartmann (1842–1906), by opposing it to his own "empirical psychology" conceived as a "rigorous science". Like any other natural science, psychology was to be based on perception and experience, except that here it could only be a matter of self-perception in the first person (what Freud called "self-observation"): "Above all, however, [the] source [of psychology] is to be found in the inner perception of our own mental phenomena."[33] It is on this account that Brentano rejected the idea of "unconscious psychic acts": what is not consciously perceived cannot be the object of a truly empirical, scientific psychology. It can only be a philosophical speculation à la Hartmann.

No doubt Brentano would have consigned his ex-student's "unconscious" to the same philosophical trash bin, which probably explains why it is with him that Freud silently polemicizes each time he stigmatizes the error of philosophers, in the plural. By making Brentano's position the philosophical position par excellence, he opportunely diverts our attention from the fact that he himself philosophizes, speculates, transgresses the limits of empirical psychology.

Indeed, psychoanalysis presents itself without mystery as a "metapsychology," that is to say, according to Freud's own definition, a "psychology that leads behind consciousness"[34] – Brentano would have said: a psychology that goes beyond the empirical-perceptible-observable, a nonscientific psychology. What is the difference, then, between metapsychology and metaphysics? Freud may have translated the metaphysical into metapsychology, but the object of the latter is still *meta*, imperceptible, and unperceived: *un*conscious. The unconscious, the unique Thing of psychoanalysis, is as unknowable and unobservable as Kant's "thing in itself." The psychiatrist-philosopher Ludwig Binswanger (1881–1966) thus reports statements made by Freud in 1910: "He thought that just

[33] Brentano 1874, 29. [34] Freud 1985, 301–302.

as Kant postulated the thing in itself behind the phenomenal world, so he himself postulated the unconscious behind the conscious that is accessible to our experience, but that can never be directly experienced."[35]

Freud knew that he would be called a philosopher by his psychologist colleagues, since he was speculating on an unpresentable, "metapsychic" thing.[36] His great rival (and the ex-philosopher) Pierre Janet (1859–1947) put it bluntly: "Psycho-analysis is above all a philosophy ... perhaps interesting if it were presented to philosophers. Unfortunately, psycho-analysis wants to be a medical science at the same time."[37] So Freud is on the defensive on this point, and it's what explains his strange insistence on presenting himself as a philistine in philosophical matters. No, he claims, he had not read Arthur Schopenhauer (1788–1860), or only very late in life. No, he had not read Nietzsche either, because he had carefully "avoided"[38] him. To his disciple and future biographer Ernest Jones (1879–1958), who once asked him if he had read much philosophy, he replied: "Very little. As a young man I felt a strong attraction towards speculation and ruthlessly checked it."[39] Elsewhere, he states, on the contrary, that in his youth, he had little "taste for reading philosophical works."[40] A "constitutional incapacity" supposedly kept him away from it.[41]

The man "protests too much, methinks": no need for Shakespeare to understand that Freud leads us down the garden path. It is not only the case that he had read Schopenhauer, Nietzsche, and many other philosophers closely, whatever he may say. Much more fundamentally, it is that *he is, according to his own criteria, a philosopher himself*, since he speculates on an unconscious that no observation allows neither to prove, nor even to refute. And he knows it, even if his will to make science forbids him to admit it. Freud is an impeded, embarrassed, ashamed philosopher, a philosopher in denial.

Hence the contradictory criticisms of which he has been the object on the part of philosophers, some reproaching him for being too scientific and for "misunderstanding" the purely hermeneutic or existential character of his theory (Ludwig Binswanger, Karl Jaspers, Martin Heidegger, Jean-Paul Sartre, Jürgen Habermas, Paul Ricoeur), others of not being scientific enough (Adolf Grünbaum), or even of falling into pseudo-science (Karl Popper, Frank Cioffi) or aesthetic persuasion (Ludwig Wittgenstein).

[35] Binswanger 1957, 7–8. [36] Ibid. [37] Janet 1913, 51. [38] Freud 1925a, 60.
[39] Jones 1953, 32. [40] Freud 1914a, 15. [41] Freud 1925a, 59.

Neither a true science nor a true philosophy either, psychoanalysis occupies a hybrid and contradictory place in modern thought, an inexhaustible source of irritation and misunderstandings.

In what follows, I try to situate this placement, as close as possible to the texts.

CHAPTER 1

The Unconscious

It is often said that Freud discovered the unconscious. This is inaccurate, in several respects. Freud is neither the first nor the only one to have admitted the existence of unconscious psychic processes. Many others – writers, doctors, psychologists, philosophers – preceded him on this point. In reality, the Freudian unconscious is only one of the many unconsciouses in circulation during the second half of the nineteenth century. And this unconscious, Freud did not discover it as one discovers a buried treasure or the properties of a chemical compound. He constructed it in the very precise sense that this term has in his work: it is a heuristic hypothesis, a conjecture waiting for confirmation. A "speculation."

Hypnosis

The major event that opens the way to the idea of a psychic unconscious takes place in 1832, well before the first Freudian elaborations. It is the highlighting by Marshall Hall (1790–1857) of the reflex function of the spinal cord: cut the spinal cord of a snake between the second and third vertebrae, you will see that the stimulation of the reptile's body provokes violent movements even though an action of the brain is excluded. This means that these reflex-automatic movements are activated by the spinal cord independently of the brain and conscious volition. There is, in other words, an unconscious nervous activity.

Should we for that matter speak of an unconscious *psychic* activity? Hall himself saw in the reflex arc a purely mechanical (physiological) phenomenon, independent of the psychic sphere located in the brain. Others, on the other hand, will very quickly extend the reflex action to the higher areas of the nervous system, thus blurring the body/mind, physiological/psychic, unconscious/conscious division. This is the beginning of what the British psychiatrist Henry Maudsley (1835–1918) called the "physiology of mind,"[1] i.e., a resolutely neurophysiological approach for which the unconscious reflex action is the very foundation of psychic activity. For psychophysiologists, man is fundamentally a spinal automaton, a cerebral machine. From Spencer and Jackson to Wundt and Meynert, from Charcot and Ribot to Bernheim and Exner, everyone at the time agrees to think that conscious psychic activity (the ego) emerges from a background of unconscious automatisms that it inhibits, delays, and "represses," to use the term of the philosopher and psychologist Johann Friedrich Herbart (1776–1841). Conscious thought is a deferred reflex, a simple epiphenomenon (Ribot) of the fundamental automatisms. Which is what Nietzsche, a great consumer of psychophysiological literature, summarized thus: "The I-consciousness is the last to be added when an organism finishes growing, *almost* something superfluous ... The great principal activity is unconscious."[2]

How, then, did we go from Hall's spinal reflex to the idea of a "cerebral unconscious," to use Marcel Gauchet's term?[3] The impulse behind this extension of reflex activity to the cerebral hemispheres did not come, as one might expect, from a neuro-anatomical investigation but from the confrontation with the strange phenomena attributed by the Mesmerians to "animal magnetism" (today, we speak of "hypnosis"). Here again, the inaugural event can be dated with precision. In 1837, Baron Du Potet (1796–1881) arrived in London and created a sensation by giving public demonstrations of magnetism. He was followed four years later by his colleague Charles Lafontaine (1803–1888). These spectacular experiments immediately provoked controversy among British doctors, for how could the states of lethargy, cataleptic rigidity, and somnambulism induced by mesmerists be explained if one no longer believed in the action of a "magnetic fluid"? It was in this context that Thomas Laycock (1812–1876) published his famous *Treatise on the Nervous Diseases of Women*,[4] in which he proposes to see in the apparently involuntary and unconscious psychic acts of magnetized somnambulists the effects of a "cerebral" (and no longer only spinal) "reflex function,"[5] to which hysterical women would be particularly exposed.

At this stage, it is a purely speculative neurophysiology, but Laycock's hypothesis will nevertheless provide the model for countless theories of magnetism, hysteria, and so-called nervous diseases (the "neuroses") throughout the century. Just as Hippocrates' theory of hysteria (the

[1] Maudsley 1867. [2] Nietzsche 1881–1882, 461–462. [3] Gauchet 1992.
[4] Laycock 1840. [5] Laycock 1845; Laycock 1876.

wandering womb) had been used in the Renaissance to provide a medical explanation for demonic possession, the theory of the cerebral reflex and psychological automatism was to be used as a scientific explanation for hysteria and what the surgeon James Braid (1795–1860), in his *Neurhypnology* of 1843,[6] now called "neurohypnotism," or simply "hypnotism" (rather than "animal magnetism"). In all these puzzling phenomena, it is an "unconscious cerebration" that is supposed to be at work. The expression comes from the Scottish physician William Carpenter (1813–1885), and it will have a great success as the psycho-reflexological paradigm becomes more and more ubiquitous. In a more or less explicit way, fixed everywhere in people's minds is the great equation: hypnosis = hysteria = unconscious cerebration.

It is this unconscious – the cerebral unconscious – that provides Freud's starting point, at the crossroads of a conjectural neurophysiology and these extraordinary psychic phenomena that are hysteria and hypnosis. He encountered it for the first time in February 1880, when the Danish stage magnetizer Carl Hansen (1833–1897) came through Vienna. Freud later recounted in his autobiography how, as a young laboratory assistant at Brücke's, he had been convinced of the authenticity of the cataleptic rigidities caused by Hansen in the audience and, notably, how "scientific support was soon afterwards given to this view by Heidenhain."[7]

Rudolf Heidenhain (1834–1897), an eminent professor of physiology in Breslau, had indeed legitimized the phenomena of cataleptic rigidity caused by Hansen in a small book with a great impact, *The So-Called Animal Magnetism: Physiological Observations*.[8] The theory he put forward (a variant of Braid's) was straightforwardly neurophysiological: by staring at the shiny object held by Hansen, a cramp would form in the eye of the magnetized person, which would inhibit the higher functions and lead to a return to a purely reflexive, automatic, and unconscious psychic activity. Forty years after Du Potet and Laycock, history repeated itself in Germanic countries. The "so-called" animal magnetism was finally explained in a scientific, "physiological" way by recourse to the unconscious cerebration at work in every psyche.

Trained in neurophysiology at Brücke's, the young Freud could not but be impressed by the solution proposed by Heidenhain, all the more so as it was accompanied by an ambitious research program. Heidenhain declared that he had discovered, thanks to Hansen, a "new method of studying brain functions, which will be added as a third method next to anatomy

[6] Braid 1843. [7] Freud 1925a, 16. [8] Heidenhain 1880.

and vivisection."[9] Hypnosis was finally going to make it possible to directly explore the unconscious that Brentano had until then considered inaccessible to psychological observation! (Brentano, whose certainties had been shaken by Hansen's demonstrations, had immediately gone to Breslau to observe with his own eyes Heidenhain's hypnotic experiments.)

In a certain way, Freud remained faithful to this program until the end. Whenever he wanted to counter the objections of conscientialist philosophers like Brentano, it was hypnosis that he invoked: "I have often found that people who dispute the unconscious as being something absurd and impossible have not formed their impressions from the sources from which I at least was brought to the necessity of recognizing it. These opponents of the unconscious had never witnessed the effect of a post-hypnotic suggestion."[10] Freud repeats it in *The Ego and the Id* – these philosophers "have never studied the relevant phenomena of hypnosis and dreams, which – quite apart from pathological manifestations – necessitate this view."[11] Hypnosis, the royal road to the unconscious.

Hysteria

However, it was with the internist and neurologist Jean-Martin Charcot (1825–1893), whose teaching he followed in Paris from October 1885 to March 1886, that Freud was truly introduced to the problematic of the psychic-cerebral unconscious. This occurred through a confrontation with hysteria, a third term that came to be linked, unsurprisingly, to hypnosis and unconscious cerebration.

Charcot was a pioneer in neuropathology, a Napoleon of the central nervous system. At the Salpêtrière Hospital where he worked, he was the first to isolate multiple sclerosis, amyotrophic lateral sclerosis (Charcot's disease), syphilitic arthropathies, certain forms of aphasia, and many other neurological disorders. When Freud arrived in Paris, Charcot had been working for fifteen years on the clinical picture of hysteria, a protean disease characterized at the time by a multitude of somatic symptoms – paralysis, anesthesia, contractures, convulsions, various sensory disorders. For Charcot, there was no doubt that it was a neurological disease in its own right, although the post-mortem examination of patients never allowed the detection of the slightest lesion or tumor responsible. It is what was called at the time a "neurosis," i.e., a disorder that was attributed a priori to a dysfunction of the nervous system (a "functional" or

[9] Ibid., 58. [10] Freud 1905d, 162. [11] Freud 1923b, 13.

"dynamic" lesion, Charcot proposed) in the hope of being able to demonstrate it one day.

The clinical picture of hysteria observed by Charcot was multifarious and complex, as shown by the spectacular photographs of the *Iconography of the Salpêtrière*,[12] but the theory behind it was very simple. It was a combination of predisposing constitutional factors (the "nervous diathesis") and triggering factors (the "agents provocateurs"). Under the influence of the doctrine of degeneration in vogue at the time, Charcot saw hysteria as an innate nervous disorder transmitted through heredity (the "neuropathic family" theory). This predisposition to hysteria was supposed to remain latent, like a dormant virus, or be awakened by some occasional cause – illness, alcoholism, physical or psychological shock, annoyance (the list is long).

Charcot was led to this theory of provoking agents by the disconcerting ease with which he could make hysterical symptoms appear and disappear by pressing on certain body zones (the "hysterogenic zones") or by exposing his patients to agents known as "aesthesiogenic," because they increased sensitivity, such as metals, magnets, electricity, or certain sound vibrations (gongs, tuning forks). Better still, these aesthesiogenic agents, to which Charcot was introduced by Dr. Victor Burq (1822–1884), a Mesmerian of the old school, would cause a strange torpor in patients from which they would wake up without remembering what happened during their trance. This was hypnosis, which Charcot discovered at the very heart of the experimental device he had set up to study hysteria. Very logically, he deduced that the hypnotic state thus provoked was nothing other than the latent hysterical state, the "nervous diathesis" waiting to be reactivated. To study hypnosis experimentally was, therefore, to study hysteria, and vice versa. Hysteria = hypnosis: Charcot went back all over again to the equation launched by Laycock. All that was missing was the third term, "the unconscious."

Quite naturally, the neurologist Charcot made the link with the psycho-reflexological paradigm. If the hysteric-hypnotized person acts like a somnambulist, if he/she blindly obeys the hypnotist's suggestions, it is obviously because he/she is moved by a purely reflex psychic activity. Under the conscious self, the unconscious cerebration: the "nervous diathesis" of the hysteric is finally nothing other than a pathological propensity to this psychological automatism that we usually inhibit. Here, for example, is Charcot's description of the cataleptic state of "grand hypnotism,"

[12] Bourneville and Regnard 1878.

during which the subject adopts a statue-like rigidity and keeps all the poses that the hypnotist gives or suggests to him/her:

> The suggested idea or group of ideas will be isolated, outside the control of that vast collection of personal ideas, accumulated and organized long ago, which constitutes consciousness properly so called, the *ego*. That is why the movements that translate these acts of unconscious cerebration to the exterior are distinguished by their automatic, purely mechanical character. This is truly, in all its simplicity, the *machine man* dreamt of by De la Mettrie that we have then before our eyes.[13]

This machinic unconscious is governed by what Hippolyte Bernheim (1840–1919), Charcot's colleague and rival from Nancy, announced at the same time to be the law of "ideo-dynamism": in the absence of the moderating action of "the upper stage of the brain" on "the lower stage (I call this the part of the brain devoted to the faculties of imagination, to cerebral automatism),"[14] ideas are spontaneously transformed into action (ideomotor reflex), into sensation (ideosensorial reflex), into emotion (ideosensitive reflex). This accounts for what Bernheim called "suggestibility," the normal regime of brain activity that he put at the foundation of hypnosis: "Every suggested and accepted idea tends to become action ... Every cerebral cell activated by an idea activates the neural fibers necessary to realize that idea."[15]

Trauma

When Freud arrived in Paris, Charcot was applying this set of reflexological hypotheses to what he called "traumatic hysteria." This was a group of disorders of neurological appearance that followed shocks or physical accidents (particularly railway collisions, which were much on people's minds at the time). Some neurologists believed that these paralyses and anesthesias were the result of microscopic spinal lesions ("railway spine") caused by mechanical shock. Others attributed the symptoms to a "nervous shock," i.e., a functional disturbance of the nervous system due to the fright caused by the accident. For Charcot, however, there was no doubt: it was a question of "hysteria, nothing but hysteria."[16]

Charcot posited that the victims were people predisposed to hysteria whose "nervous diathesis" had been awakened by the shock. Just as paralysis can be produced experimentally in hysterics by the application

[13] Charcot 1887, 290, translation modified. [14] Bernheim 1891, 67. [15] Ibid., 45.
[16] Charcot 1887, 221.

of a magnet or a hypnotic procedure (e.g., gaze fixation), it can be triggered in real life by a traumatic shock acting as an "agent provocateur." As proof, Charcot managed to suggest under hypnosis the return of a paralysis of the left arm that had first appeared spontaneously in the patient Pinaud following a fall from a scaffold. Charcot's conclusion (or rather hypothesis, speculation): "In this respect it may be inquired whether the mental condition occasioned by the emotion, by the Nervous Shock experienced at the moment of the accident ... is not the equivalent in a certain measure, in subjects predisposed as Porcz[enska] and Pin[aud] were, to the cerebral condition which is determined in 'hysterics' by hypnotism."[17]

In both cases, Charcot wrote, there is a real "clouding of the ego,"[18] a "dissociation of the mental unity, of the ego."[19] Shocked, the subject faints, so to speak. He/she is no longer an "ego"; he/she becomes (again) a psychic automaton, a sleepwalker. Any sensation experienced at the time of the shock (a sensation of numbness, for example) acts from then on as a "traumatic suggestion," by "auto-suggestion."[20] It becomes embedded in the psyche as a "fixed idea"[21] separate from the other groups of associations (of the ego) and is realized in the mode of reflex automatism proper to the "unconscious or sub-conscious cerebration,"[22] exactly as if the subject were executing a suggestion given by a hypnotist: "That idea, once installed in the brain, takes sole possession and acquires sufficient domination to realize itself objectively in the form of a paralysis."[23]

In 1892, Charcot illustrated this theory with a diagram that is reminiscent of the "topographies" of the psychical apparatus that Freud would later draw in *The Ego and the Id* and *New Introductory Lectures on Psychoanalysis*. In the center of a circle, the conscious "Ego." All around, a second circle populated by "sealed off previous ideas but not constituting a concrete ego." Then, inside this circle, a denser circle: **I**, "The Unconscious [*L'Inconscient*], 2nd ego in the making," coagulating around **F**, "The fixed idea that paralyzes." Finally, an arrow starting from **I** represents the paralyzing effraction of the fixed idea **F** in the Ego, under the effect of the "Force of revival." In short: the hysterical symptom (paralysis, in this case) is a reflex production of the unconscious on which the conscious Ego has no control because of the dissociation of the psyche. The unconscious is like a "2nd ego" that does as it pleases.

"The Unconscious." This is obviously the term that Freud will translate into German as "das Unbewusste." It was at Charcot's that the young

[17] Ibid., 305. [18] Ibid., translation modified. [19] Ibid., 383, 387 note 1.
[20] Ibid., 307, 384. [21] Ibid., 310. [22] Ibid., 387. [23] Ibid., 305.

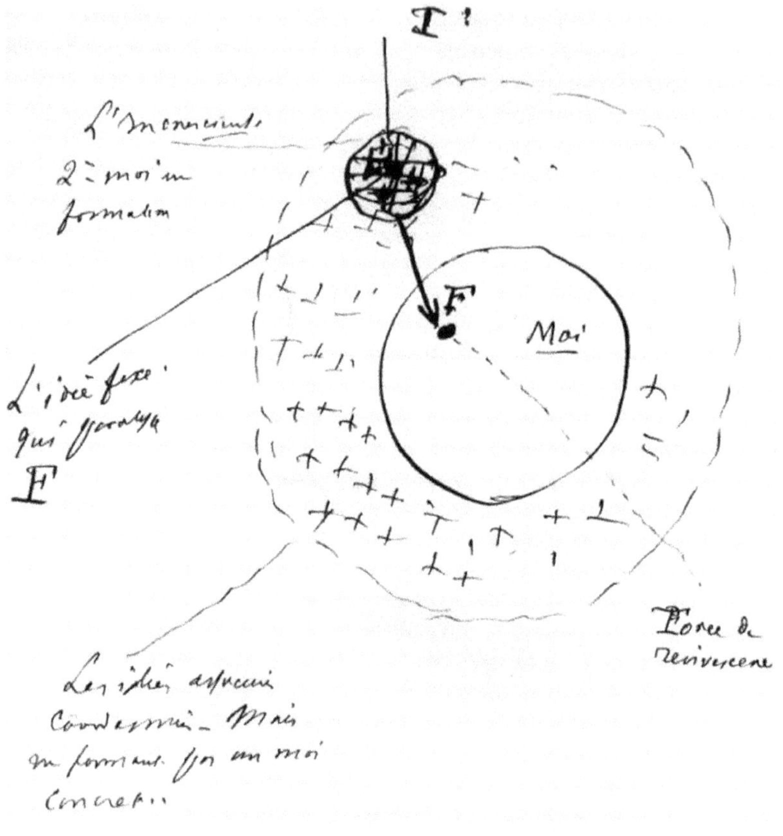

Figure 1. Jean-Martin Charcot's diagram of the unconscious, 1892, © Sorbonne Université – Bibliothèque Charcot.

neurologist learned to speak of the unconscious as a psychic place populated by ideas ("representations," *Vorstellungen*, he said in philosophical German) likely to be realized in the form of neurotic symptoms beyond the control of the conscious self. The nature of these ideas and the mechanism of their formation may later have changed considerably for Freud, but he will never abandon this fundamental, founding scheme.

The very first lectures of Charcot that Freud attended on arriving in Paris dealt with a case of traumatic hysteria (Charvet, a sawmill worker who suffered from hip pain following an accident at work). The theory of "hystero-traumatism" that Charcot developed again on this occasion immediately fascinated Freud. The day after the second lecture devoted to Charvet, on November 24, 1885, he wrote to his fiancée that Charcot was turning all his ideas upside down. On the spot, he abandoned the neurological research in which he was engaged and suggested to Charcot that he translate into German volume III of his *Lectures on Diseases of the Nervous System*, in which the Master put forward for the first time his theory of traumatic hysteria. Freud became a disciple of Charcot.

Back in Vienna, he worked to make Charcot's ideas known and to defend them. He kept in touch with Charcot by letter about patients from the Viennese Jewish upper class whom he treated under the Master's supervision: Anna von Lieben, Elise Gomperz, Franziska von Wertheimstein. Most importantly, he developed a hypnotherapeutic technique directly inspired by the Charcotian theory of traumatic hysteria. At the end of December 1887, he announced to his friend, the Berlin ear, nose, and throat specialist Wilhelm Fliess (1858–1928), that "during these past weeks I have thrown myself into hypnosis and have achieved all sorts of small but noteworthy successes."[24] In the encyclopedia article "Hysteria," written at the same time, he describes his hypnotherapeutic method more precisely, comparing it favorably with that of Bernheim, which consisted in directly suggesting the disappearance of the symptom under hypnosis:

> It is even more effective if we adopt a method first practiced by Josef Breuer in Vienna and lead the patient under hypnosis back to the psychical prehistory of the ailment and compel him to acknowledge the psychical occasion on which the disorder in question originated. This method of treatment is new, but it produces successes which cannot otherwise be achieved. It is the method most appropriate to hysteria, because it precisely imitates the mechanism of the origin and passing of these hysterical disorders.[25]

Freud, strangely enough, attributes his method to his friend and mentor Josef Breuer (1842–1925). This is an allusion to the "talking cure" of Bertha Pappenheim (better known by the pseudonym "Anna O."), a young woman whom Breuer had treated in 1881–1882 for severe hysteria. Breuer had found that he could make his patient's symptoms temporarily disappear by asking her to recount under hypnosis the "fantasies" and annoyances that had triggered them. This was the beginning of what Breuer and Freud would later call in their *Studies on Hysteria* (1895) the "cathartic method."[26] However, contrary to what they would claim at the time, this treatment had not allowed the patient to be cured, who finally

[24] Freud 1985, 17. [25] Freud 1888a, 56, translation modified. [26] Breuer and Freud 1895.

had to be interned in a private clinic. So it was not this "success" that Freud had in mind when he referred to the positive results obtained with his young treatment method but rather the "small but noteworthy successes" he mentioned to Fliess. In fact, his method was initially very different from Breuer's. Breuer had exploited Bertha Pappenheim's autohypnotic states to make her *remember* the events that were supposed to be the cause of her symptoms. Freud, on the contrary, induced hypnosis in his patients to make them *forget* their traumatic memories, to erase them from their memory.

The idea, which was very simple, was to desuggest the "traumatic suggestion" of which Charcot spoke. Freud was not the only one to have had this idea, for we also find it at the same time in Janet and Joseph Delboeuf (1831–1896): since hysterical symptoms are due to ideas ("reminiscences") that have become embedded in a dissociated, unconscious part of the psyche under the effect of a hypnotic shock, why not use hypnosis to gain access to "the unconscious" and erase by suggestion the pathogenic idea, as if the trauma had never happened? This is what Freud called, as soon as 1889, the "causal treatment"[27] of hysteria, contrasting it with the purely symptomatic treatment of Bernheim: it is only by suppressing the unconscious cause of the symptoms that hysteria can really be cured.

This point is crucial, because this is exactly how Freud will always distinguish psychoanalysis from hypnosis and, more generally, from other forms of psychotherapy disqualified as purely "suggestive." The continuity between Charcot's traumatic-dissociative theory and the psychoanalysis of the mature period is, on this point, very striking.

Repression

From 1887 to the end of 1892, Freud induced hypnosis in his patients in order to "expunge," "extinguish," "wipe out," "suggest away" their traumatic memories. These are the terms he used in the case history of "Frau Emmy von N." in *Studies on Hysteria*, which refers to Fanny Moser, a wealthy Swiss aristocrat whom he treated for anxiety symptoms in 1889 and 1890. This is the same technique he used with "Frau Cäcilie M." (Anna von Lieben) and most of his "nervous" patients of the time (including those suffering from manic-depressive psychosis or melancholic depression, such as Mathilde Schleicher and probably also Pauline

[27] Freud 1889, 100.

Silberstein). You hypnotize the patient, you find the traumas (about forty in the space of nine days for Fanny Moser, hundreds over several years for Anna von Lieben), you erase them. Amnesia upon awakening. The traumas range from the most dramatic (witnessing the sudden death of one's husband) to the most trivial (being frightened by a toad), passing through minor vexations or disappointments in love. In 1891, Freud compared his hypnotic method to the technique of electrically "extirpating" unwanted memories imagined by Edward Bellamy in his science fiction novel *Dr. Heidenhoff's Process.*[28] Brainwashing, in short. The psychic unconscious that Freud manipulates obviously continues to be thought of by him as a mechanical, automatic-reflex brain, in the manner of Charcot and others.

At the end of the day, Freud had to face the facts: his process did not work. The treatments either stalled or failed. Anna von Lieben, Elise Gomperz, and Fanny Moser did not get better; Mathilde Schleicher had to be committed; Pauline Silberstein threw herself off the third floor of her therapist's building. At first, Freud thought that this was because he was not always able to put his patients into deep somnambulism with posthypnotic amnesia (this was the case with Anna von Lieben). But other patients (Fanny Moser, Elise Gomperz) had no difficulty in falling into somnambulism and forgetting everything that was asked of them, without, however, their condition improving. The therapeutic failure could therefore not be explained by a technical deficiency; it was the whole theory on which hypnotic therapy was based that had to be revised.

On the face of it, Freud was thus complying with the strictest positivist requirement, as formulated by Ernst Mach: if the facts contradict your theory, change your theory. As a matter of fact, Freud changed his theory many times afterwards, according to the difficulties he encountered in his practice. This flexibility and heuristic inventiveness is admirable, but it should be noted that it most often took the form of an adjustment of the original theory. In reality, Freud never abandoned a theory; he modified it to explain its deficiencies, especially in therapy. In this sense, his multiple and ingenious conceptual innovations are less paradigm shifts (Thomas Kuhn) or epistemological breaks (Gaston Bachelard) than "auxiliary ad hoc hypotheses" in the sense of Karl Popper (1902–1994), i.e., revisions intended to save the theory and to immunize it against its refutation. Freud's thought does not progress by experimental verification/falsification but by theoretical overkill.

[28] Bellamy 1880.

In the case at hand, Freud could have concluded from his therapeutic failures that the traumatic-dissociative theory of hysteria proposed by Charcot was invalid. Instead, he asked himself why his patients did not recover. In 1892, he thought he had found the answer: it was because they *did not want* to heal, because a "force" stood in the way of therapy. This is the theory of the hysterical "counter-will," which Freud developed in an article he published at the end of 1892, "A Case of Successful Treatment by Hypnosis. With Some Remarks on the Origin of Hysterical Symptoms through 'Counter-Will.'"[29]

Two years earlier, in his article "Psychical (or Mental) Treatment," Freud had already remarked in passing that "the power of suggestion is contending against the force which created the symptoms, and maintains them."[30] A "resistance" (*Widerstand*), he wrote, is opposed to suggestions and therefore to healing.[31] It is this resistance that he theorizes now in his 1892 article, with respect to an anonymous patient (in reality, his wife, Martha Bernays) in whom he had succeeded in making an occasional hysterical symptom disappear through hypnosis.

Any "representation" (any idea), Freud posits, inevitably gives rise to a "contrast representation" (*Kontrastvorstellung*), i.e., the opposite idea. If I form a project, for example, I will also have the idea of what can be opposed to this project: "It won't work," "I can't do it," etc. Usually, these negative and distressing ideas are inhibited, repressed by the "healthy representative life," but in neurosis, they take over. In the case of neurasthenia (what we would call nowadays depression), they are consciously *associated* with expectations and projects, giving rise to the pessimism, anxiety, and weakness of will characteristic of this illness. In the case of hysteria, on the other hand, there is *dissociation* of consciousness, so that the contrasting idea escapes the conscious will and sets up as an independent "counter-will." The patient is divided, in conflict with him/herself. He/she wants to get well but his/her nonconscious part does not want to, hence the "daemonic characteristic" that so often characterizes hysteria.[32]

So far, nothing very new compared to the Charcotian theory, except that Freud formulates it in the terms of Herbart's "mechanics of representation" (*Vorstellungsmechanik*), where ideas interact (merge, reinforce, inhibit, or repress) in a dynamic way. The dissociation of consciousness continues to explain the incapacity of the voluntary self to control the contrasting idea. However, Freud no longer thinks that this is a simple

[29] Freud 1892–1893. [30] Freud 1890, 301. [31] Ibid., 300.
[32] Freud 1892–1893, 122–126, translation modified.

effect of the traumatic shock. The dissociation, he suggests, is willed, in that it is precisely the will to "suppress" (*unterdrücken*) the contrasting idea that creates the division of the field of consciousness. The more one wants to ignore, forget, or erase such a painful idea, the more it becomes autonomous, the more it paradoxically escapes the conscious will and is realized in a reflex fashion in the form of physical symptoms. The hysterical "counter-will" is the product of an antagonistic will, of a psychic conflict between groups of irreconcilable representations.

In support of his theory, Freud significantly invokes the obscenity of the hysterical delusions of the nuns of the Middle Ages or of well-bred young people (the first appearance, it should be noted, of the theme of sexuality): "It is the suppressed – the laboriously suppressed – groups of ideas that are brought into action in these cases, by the operation of a sort of counter-will, when the subject has fallen a victim to hysterical exhaustion. Perhaps, indeed, the connection may be a more intimate one, for the hysterical condition may perhaps be *produced* by the laborious suppression."[33]

"It is the effort of suppression that causes hysteria": Freud has just silently replaced the Charcotian model of dissociation of consciousness with a brand new "psychical mechanism." If hysterics get sick, it is because they do not want to know about certain ideas or memories – because they "repress" them. The term comes from Herbart's psychology and is initially used by Freud as a simple equivalent of "suppression," "inhibition," or "defense." In the "Psychical Mechanism of Hysterical Phenomena: Preliminary Communication" written at the same time with Breuer, we read that the psychic trauma at the origin of hysterical symptoms corresponds to something "which the patient wished to forget, and therefore intentionally repressed from his conscious thought and inhibited and suppressed."[34]

Very quickly, however, repression will become the prototype, if not the generic concept, of all the specific defense mechanisms enumerated later by Freud – rejection, projection, transference, denial, etc. "The essence of repression lies simply in turning something away, and keeping it at a distance, from the conscious."[35] It is in this sense that Freud writes in 1914 that "The theory of repression is the corner-stone on which the whole structure of psycho-analysis rests."[36] The concept of repression, as it is first outlined in the article "A Case of Successful Treatment by Hypnosis," is indeed at the foundation of the new theory of the psychic unconscious proposed by Freud. The psychic unconscious, as he often

[33] Ibid., 126. [34] Breuer and Freud 1895, 10. [35] Freud 1915e, 147. [36] Freud 1914a, 16.

reminds us, certainly has a "wider compass" than the repressed, which is only "a part"[37] (this is what we would call today the cognitive unconscious). The fact remains that the unconscious that psychoanalysis deals with is essentially the repressed unconscious and that this is what distinguishes it from the "unconscious or sub-conscious cerebration" that Charcot and others spoke about. The latter was certainly inhibited and controlled (at least normally) by the conscious self; it was not *constituted* by this distancing. The unconscious in the sense of the young Freud, on the other hand, is formed of ideas, thoughts, "representations" of which the conscious self does not want to know anything because they are painful, shameful, forbidden, dangerous, and which from then on "are stored up and enjoy an unsuspected existence in a sort of shadow kingdom, till they emerge like bad spirits and take control of the body, which is as a rule under the orders of the predominant ego-consciousness."[38]

The Psychical Apparatus

The Freudian unconscious is a "dynamic" unconscious, that is to say it results from an antagonism between opposite psychic forces, will against "counter-will," each one trying to supplant the other, preventing it, bypassing it, compromising with it, etc. This is how Freud distinguished his conception of the unconscious from that of Janet, the other great heir of Charcot's dissociative theory: "We do not derive the psychical splitting from an innate incapacity for synthesis on the part of the mental apparatus; we explain it dynamically, from the conflict of opposing mental forces and recognize it as the outcome of an active struggling on the part of the two psychical groupings against each other."[39]

For the rest, the Freudian unconscious remains very close to the unconscious cerebration of its predecessors, from which it inherits many features. In particular, the contrast between the conscious and the unconscious continues to be thought by Freud on the model of the reflex/inhibition pair, the foundation of all neuro-psycho-physiological constructions of the time. If the unconscious is so "daemonic," so intractable, it is because it is governed by a purely reflex, irreflective, immediate, uninhibited psychic activity. As for the conscious, it is never anything else than a deferred, delayed, inhibited – repressed – reflex.

This persistence of the psycho-reflexological model is evident in the metapsychological texts where Freud tries to situate the unconscious and

[37] Freud 1915f, 166. [38] Freud 1892–1893, 127. [39] Freud 1910a, 26.

the conscious within what he significantly calls the "psychical apparatus," as if it were a machine or an instrument. Chapter VII of *The Interpretation of Dreams*, which broadly follows the "Project for a Scientific Psychology" or "Psychology for Neurologists" of 1895, from the very first describes the psyche (the central nervous system) as a conductive apparatus whose function is to evacuate as quickly as possible the excitation (the electrical nerve impulse) that flows through it. At one end (*Pcpt*), the apparatus perceives external or internal stimuli that lead to innervations and "turns it on," so to speak; at the other end (*M*), it "opens the locks [*die Schleusen*] to motor activity" through which the excitation will be evacuated.[40] S/R, stimulus/response. One will, of course, have recognized the familiar schema of the reflex arc, which Freud had inherited from his masters Brücke, Exner, and Meynert: "This, however, does no more than fulfill a requirement with which we have long been familiar, namely that the psychical apparatus must be constructed like a reflex apparatus. *Reflex processes remain the model of every psychical function.*"[41]

This was already stated by the "Project," which saw in the reflex the manifestation of the "primary function of the nervous system," namely, the discharge (*Entlastung*, *Entbindung*) of the quantities of excitation in excess in order to return to a state of inertia or at least of psychic "constancy": "Reflex movement is now intelligible as an established method of this giving-off [of quantity]: the principle [of inertia] provides the motive for reflex movement."[42] If the unconscious reflex remains for Freud "the model of every psychical function," it is because it corresponds to what he considers to be the most fundamental tendency of the psychical apparatus: to avoid the displeasure linked to the increase of quantities of nervous excitation in the system by evacuating them as quickly as possible. This is what Freud calls from 1900 the "pleasure principle" (or, more exactly, the "unpleasure principle"), to which he adds a "reality principle" that tempers and postpones the immediate discharge in order to take into account the conditions imposed by the external world.

The pleasure principle governs the so-called primary psychic processes, whose "chief characteristic . . . is that the whole stress is laid upon making the cathecting energy [the excitation] mobile and capable of discharge."[43] The excitation then passes from one representation to another ("cathects" them) without regard for reality or logic, the important thing being to arrive as quickly as possible at the discharge: hallucination of a previous

40 Freud 1900, 537, translation modified. 41 Ibid., 538, emphasis added.
42 Freud 1895, 296. 43 Freud 1900, 597.

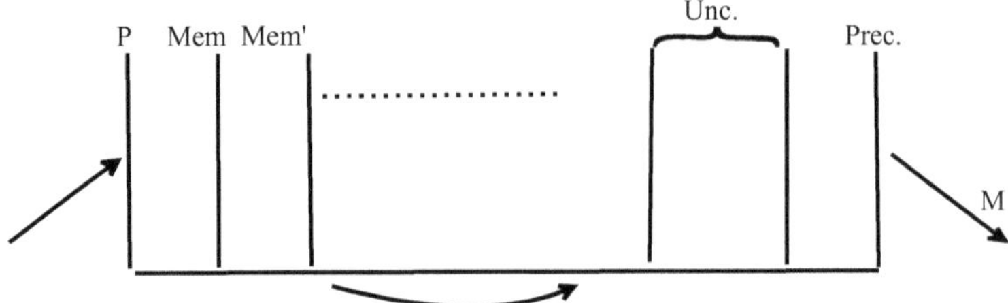

Figure 2. Diagram of the psychical apparatus in *The Interpretation of Dreams*

"experience of satisfaction" in the absence of the real object, over-cathexis of certain representations (condensation), displacement of the excitation along associative chains, etc. The reality principle, on the other hand, governs the "secondary processes," which defer the discharge by inhibiting it and, at the same time, make the energy pass from the "free" state to the "bound," stable, quiescent state: waking thought linked to the ego and to "reality testing," attention, judgment, reasoning, voluntary action, etc.

To this "economic" difference between the two regimes of energy circulation (fast/slow) corresponds a "topographical," spatial distinction, inside the psychical apparatus. Freud imagines three systems or "agencies" staggered in the order followed by the intracerebral excitation: the unconscious (*Ucs*), the preconscious (*Pcs*), and the conscious (*Cs*), the latter being closely linked to perception (*Pcpt*) and situated at the motor extremity *M*. The representations or "memory traces" (*Mem*) that form the unconscious have "no access to consciousness *except via the preconscious*,"[44] a "critical agency" that "stands like a screen between [the unconscious] and consciousness,"[45] and filters them, inhibits them, "censors" them before they lead to the motor discharge.

We see that the spatial extension of the apparatus and its division into agencies correspond rigorously to the temporal delay that is imposed by censorship on the immediate discharge of primary processes. We find again the classic scheme of the "physiologies of mind" of the time. On the one hand, we have an unconscious cerebration that is purely reflex ("ideo-dynamic" in Bernheim's sense) and does not admit any delay between the idea and its realization, between the wish and its fulfillment. As Freud will always repeat, the unconscious knows neither time nor contradiction, nor

[44] Ibid., 541. [45] Ibid., 540.

doubt, nor the difference between thought and reality.[46] On the other hand, we have the "upper stage of the brain," as Bernheim put it, which inhibits and controls this reflex activity by binding it, by slowing it down, and thus opens up the *time* for reflection. Thought, logic, judgment, voluntary action, "all this is only introduced by the work of the censorship between the Ucs and the Pcs."[47] All this is only repressed, deferred, slowed down, distended, put at a distance, *spaced* reflex.

Freud accentuates even more the proximity between his psychical topography and the "physiologies of mind" of his contemporaries by combining his neurophysiological hypotheses with evolutionary postulates, notably, the law of the recapitulation of phylogenesis by ontogenesis of the famous biologist and Darwinian propagandist Ernst Haeckel (1834–1919): "When I described one of the psychical processes occurring in the mental apparatus as the 'primary' one, what I had in mind was not merely considerations of relative importance and efficiency; I also intended to choose a name which would give an indication of its chronological priority."[48] Primary, unconscious processes are also more primitive, older than secondary processes. They date from childhood, and "behind this childhood of the individual we are promised a picture of a phylogenetic childhood – a picture of the development of the human race, of which the individual's development is in fact an abbreviated recapitulation influenced by the chance circumstances of life."[49] In this sense, the staggering of agencies inside the psychical apparatus recapitulates spatially the cognitive evolution of the species, a bit like the neocortex involved in the higher functions developed, it is said, after and on the other layers of the cortex. From *Pcpt* to *M*, the arrow of the intracerebral excitation *progresses*; it goes from the inferior/primitive/unconscious to the superior/evolved-civilized/conscious. When, for one reason or another, it is repressed at the level of the preconscious (which happens, according to Freud, when we are asleep), it goes backwards and *regresses* towards the unconscious. This regression is simultaneously topographical, temporal, and formal, "for what is older in time is more primitive in form and in psychical topography lies nearer to the perceptual end."[50] In the unconscious, we continue to think like the newborn that we were or like the primitive men and other animals from which we descend, on the mode of instinctive, reflex, prelogical, hallucinatory immediacy.

[46] Freud 1915f, 186–187. [47] Ibid., 186. [48] Freud 1900, 603. [49] Ibid., 548.
[50] Ibid.

"In the unconscious": up to what point should we take this topography of the psyche seriously? Do the "psychical localities" of which Freud speaks[51] correspond to specific zones of the brain, to cortical or subcortical centers whose comparative anatomy could determine their place in evolution? The answer is negative, both in *The Interpretation of Dreams* and in the metapsychological essay of 1915 on "The Unconscious": "I shall carefully avoid the temptation to determine psychical locality in any anatomical fashion";[52] "Our psychical topography has *for the present* nothing to do with anatomy."[53] As a student in Vienna of the neuroanatomist Meynert and himself a specialist in the anatomy of the brain (to which he devoted an encyclopedia article[54]), Freud knew that he could not correlate his psychical "agencies" and "processes" with brain regions. So, like whenever he leaves the realm of empirical observation, he resorts to an epistemological commodism and conventionalism à la Ernst Mach. The psychical apparatus that he imagined is never, he writes, anything but a heuristic and revisable "fiction,"[55] destined to account for phenomena such as neurosis or dreams: "We are justified, in my view, in giving free rein to our speculations so long as we retain the coolness of our judgement and do not mistake the scaffolding for the building. . . . all that we need is the assistance of provisional ideas";[56] "It will, however, be useful to remind ourselves that as things stand our hypotheses set out to be no more than graphic illustrations."[57]

And yet, what is thus imaged or fictionalized is nothing other than the central nervous system. Why else would Freud use the language of neurophysiology? Why would he insist so much that "Psyche is extended; knows nothing about it"?[58] If the topography has "for the present" nothing to do with anatomy, it is because *one day* the latter will necessarily throw light on the former. For the neurologist that Freud is, there is no doubt about it: "Research has given irrefutable proof that mental activity is bound up with the function of the brain as it is with no other organ."[59]

We would be completely wrong if we wanted to make of metapsychology "that leads behind consciousness" a pure psychology disengaged from neuro-physio-biology. Both in its language and in its intention, the Freudian topography is a neuroanatomy in hollow, a neuroscience awaiting confirmation, just as Charcot's hysterical "neurosis" was a neurological disorder awaiting anatomical localization. In this sense, it has the

[51] Ibid., 536. [52] Ibid. [53] Freud 1915f, 175, Freud's emphasis. [54] Freud 1888b.
[55] Freud 1900, 598. [56] Ibid., 536. [57] Freud 1915f, 175. [58] Freud 1938a, 300.
[59] Freud 1915f, 174.

same ambiguous epistemological status as all the reflexological constructs that followed one another from Laycock to Charcot and beyond to account for hypnosis, hysteria, and nervous illnesses. It is a conjectural neurophysiology, a speculative machine intended to explain the apparently involuntary and compulsive behavior of neurotics by attributing it to a putative, because unobservable, psychic unconscious.

Interpretation

Indeed, how do we know the unconscious? Certainly not by observation, since it is "for the present" inaccessible to the scalpel of the anatomist or the microscope of the physiologist. "As far as their physical characteristics are concerned, [the unconscious psychical states] are totally inaccessible to us: no physiological concept or chemical process can give us any notion of their nature."[60] The unconscious is therefore strictly unknowable since it is not the object of any experience, never appears, nor becomes phenomenal.

This is why Freud often compares it to Kant's "thing in itself." Ludwig Binswanger remembers a conversation with him:

> On one occasion I referred to the statement he [Freud] had made during a Wednesday meeting that "the ... unconscious is metapsychic, we simply posit it as real," meaning, of course, that we acted *as if* the unconscious were something real, like the conscious. Being a true scientist, Freud said nothing about the nature of the unconscious, precisely because we know nothing certain about it; rather, we merely deduce it from the conscious. He thought that just as Kant postulated the thing in itself behind the phenomenal world, so he himself postulated the unconscious behind the conscious that is accessible to our experience, but that can never be directly experienced.[61]

One will notice the ambiguity of this "as if" entrusted to Binswanger. On the one hand, Freud seems anxious to maintain the conjectural and fictional character of his theory, insisting on the impossibility of presenting the Thing of the unconscious. But, on the other hand, and in the same gesture, he invites us to do "as if the unconscious were a reality," by transgressing the limit he has just drawn between hypothesis and observation, theory and empiricism, "metapsychics" and psychology, noumenon and phenomenon. This transgression is exactly what Kant called speculation. Freud, on the other hand, calls it construction or, again, *interpretation*.

[60] Ibid., 168. [61] Binswanger 1957, 7–8, Binswanger's emphasis. See also Freud 1915f, 171.

Let us ask ourselves again how we know the unconscious. As the 1915 article "The Unconscious" explains, it can only be known by becoming conscious, that is, by disappearing at the very moment it appears: "How are we to arrive at a knowledge of the unconscious? It is of course only as something conscious that we know it, after it has undergone transformation or translation into something conscious."[62] But how does this transposition or translation take place, which transforms the thing in itself of the unconscious into an observable phenomenon? How do we know, for example, that the hysteric unconsciously wants what he/she does not consciously want? How do we know that the dreamer fulfills in the unconscious a wish that is never formulated in the "manifest content" of the dream of which he/she is conscious? Only thanks to the interpretations of the psychoanalyst who, with the help of rules of transformation called displacement, condensation, projection, identification, reversal into the opposite, symbolism, etc., translates the symptoms and the patients' dreams into unconscious thoughts that are unknown to them.

The rest of the article "The Unconscious" explains it again very clearly: "Psycho-analytic work shows us every day that translation of this kind is possible. In order that this should come about, the person under analysis must overcome certain resistances – the same resistances as those which, earlier, made the material concerned into something repressed by rejecting it from the conscious."[63] The unconscious thus appears nowhere else than in the interpretations of the analyst who *says* that there is something to be translated where the main interested parties know nothing about it and even strongly doubt it: "Your symptom, Madam, symbolizes an unmentionable memory"; "Your dream, Miss, is a rebus whose latent meaning is as follows"; "Your slip of the tongue, Sir, indicates that you nourish a desire for your father's death."

This idea of an indirect access to the unconscious by way of interpretation is specific to Freud, and it is this idea that really differentiates his theory of the unconscious from that of his predecessors. It seems to have originated with certain statements made by Anna von Lieben, a very important patient whom Freud called his "teacher" (*Lehrmeisterin*).[64] She was known for her wit and in *Studies on Hysteria*, where he refers to her as "Frau Cäcilie M.," Freud describes how she always found a way to explain the emergence of this or that symptom with a bon mot. If she had facial neuralgia, it was because she had received an insult like "a slap in the face." If she had heart pain, it was because an incident had "stabbed her to the

[62] Freud 1915f, 166. [63] Ibid. [64] Freud 1985, 229.

heart." If she had a hallucination in which she saw Breuer and Freud hanging (*pendus* in French) on two trees, it was because both had refused her morphine: "One's the *pendant* [match] of the other," etc.[65]

Anna von Lieben was apparently the only patient to explain her symptoms in this way,[66] but Freud nevertheless took her witticisms and puns seriously. If the symptoms of hysteria are so often incomprehensible, he theorized, it is because they represent their unconscious cause in a "symbolic" form.[67] Not being able to externalize directly because of the repression, the hysterical "counter-will" does it in an indirect, diverted, figurative way. The symptoms of hysteria are metaphors or bodily "conversions" and the task of the doctor is henceforth to find their literal meaning. At the school of his preceptress, Freud the neurologist became an interpreter, a hermeneutist, a decipherer of symbols, rebus, and witticisms – in a word, a psychoanalyst. Soon, he would apply this same symbolic reading grid to the symptoms of other neuroses, to the delusions of psychoses, to sexual "perversions," then to dreams, to slips of the tongue, to missed acts, to jokes, to art, to literature, to myths, to society, to culture. Everywhere hidden meaning, clandestine signs, messages of the unconscious to be deciphered. Looking back twenty-five years later on the path taken, Freud summarized in one word: "Psychoanalysis was then first and foremost an art of interpreting."[68]

The unconscious, in itself unknowable, is known to us thanks to the interpretations of the analyst. In the end, there is no other access to the unconscious, no other proof of its existence. In this sense, psychoanalytical theory as a whole is based on the interpretations proposed by Freud and his successors; it is a speculative neuro-physio-biology backed by a hermeneutic. But then, who can tell us if these interpretations are correct? How can we be sure that they are not arbitrary constructions, empty speculations, unverifiable hypotheses? How can we be sure, even, that *there is* this unconscious of which Freud speaks to us? How, in other words, can we validate Freud's psychoanalytical theory?

[65] Breuer and Freud 1895, 181. [66] Ibid., 180. [67] Ibid., 5, 178 ff. [68] Freud 1920, 18.

CHAPTER 2

The Analytic Cure

Freud always knew that his theory was extraordinarily fragile and depended on his ability to convince his patients, colleagues, and readers of the legitimacy of his interpretations. His entire work can be read as a long pro domo plea designed to forestall the objections of skeptics and to counter the rival interpretations of his colleagues. Constantly, Freud argues, pleads, defends, justifies (a section of his article on the unconscious is entitled "Justification for the Concept of the Unconscious"). How, indeed, can one prove the accuracy of an interpretation if one cannot produce the original text or its author?

Justifications for the Unconscious

Freud frequently invokes the narrative coherence brought by his interpretations to the patients' accounts or, more generally, to the canvas of a neurosis. This could be called the "puzzle argument," initially used by Freud to prove the authenticity of infantile sexual traumas supposed to be the cause of hysteria:

> It is exactly like putting together a child's picture-puzzle: after many attempts, we become absolutely certain in the end which piece belongs in the empty gap; for only that one piece fills out the picture . . . In the same way, the contents of the infantile scenes turn out to be indispensable supplements to the associative and logical framework of the neurosis, whose insertion makes its course of development for the first time evident, or even, as we might often say, self-evident.[1]

This argument, which Freud will take up almost word for word in his 1923 "Remarks on the Theory and Practice of Dream-Interpretation,"[2] is clearly rhetorical. It pleads the narrative plausibility/probability (Aristotle's

[1] Freud 1896b, 205. [2] Freud 1923c, 116.

eikos) to win us over: the analyst convinces us (and convinces him/herself) because his/her interpretation organizes the clinical data into a coherent, logically and aesthetically satisfying whole. This is what Ludwig Wittgenstein (1889–1951) called the "charm" of psychoanalysis,[3] the source of its persuasive character.[4] The problem, of course, is that the plausible does not lead to the true. It is not because a story is good that it reflects reality. Freud himself recognizes this in his book *Moses and Monotheism*: "Not even the most tempting probability is a protection against error; even if all the parts of a problem seem to fit together like the pieces of a jig-saw puzzle, one must reflect that what is probable is not necessarily the truth and that the truth is not always probable."[5] The fact that an interpretation is extraordinarily convincing does not prove its correctness (this is the difference, Wittgenstein would say, between an aesthetic explanation and a causal explanation).

But what if the patient him/herself accepts the analyst's interpretations? "You are right, Doctor, I must have seen my parents making love *a tergo* when I was one and a half years old." Doesn't this validate the hypotheses put forward by the therapist-researcher? As a matter of fact, Freud never refrained from invoking the assent of one or other of his patients to support his constructions, sometimes even going so far as to present these assents as factual confirmations (see the case histories of the "Wolf Man" and the "Rat Man"). However, he was always careful not to make the patient the arbiter of his interpretations, and for good reason: this would have contradicted his theory. Patients, by definition, do not have access to their unconscious and therefore cannot be considered reliable witnesses. Whether they accept or refuse the interpretations proposed to them, their testimony is a priori suspect since *they do not know what they are saying.* They cannot, therefore, be taken at their word. Here, as elsewhere, confession is not proof.

There remains, then, the "pragmatic argument":[6] the interpretation is correct if it works, if the symptom disappears. This is the argument most often invoked by Freud and it is in line with the theory. Indeed, we remember that Freud described his method from the beginning as a "causal"[7] and "radical"[8] treatment, in that it is supposed to deactivate the unconscious idea of which the symptom is the effect. It follows that the

[3] Malcolm 1958, 44–45; Wittgenstein 1966, 24–25, 43. [4] Wittgenstein 1966, 27.
[5] Freud 1939, 17. [6] Woodworth 1917, 194.
[7] Freud 1889, 100; Freud 1891, 113; Freud 1892, 177. [8] Breuer and Freud 1895, 17.

disappearance of the symptom signals the disappearance of the cause and thus proves the correctness of the symbolic interpretation put forward by the doctor. It is in this sense that Freud writes, concerning the traumatic "scenes" supposed to be the cause of hysteria, that "in a number of cases therapeutic evidence of the genuineness of the infantile scenes can also be brought forward. ... my expectation is that a complete psycho-analysis implies a radical cure of the hysteria."[9]

Conversely, therapeutic failure invalidates incorrect interpretations: if it doesn't work, it must be wrong. It is this argument that led the philosopher Adolf Grünbaum to object to Karl Popper (1902–1994) that Freudian theory is not "unfalsifiable," as the latter would have it, because it makes risky predictions and defines the conditions under which it can be refuted. In a passage from the *Introductory Lectures on Psycho-Analysis*, Freud, indeed, explains that the analyst should not be afraid to propose risky interpretations to the patient, because they will necessarily be swept away if they are incorrect: "After all, [the patient's] conflicts will only be successfully solved and his resistances overcome if the anticipatory ideas he is given tally with what is real in him. Whatever in the doctor's conjectures is inaccurate drops out in the course of the analysis; it has to be withdrawn and replaced by something more correct."[10] This famous argument, which Grünbaum suggested calling the "Tally Argument" and of which he makes the foundation of Freudian epistemology,[11] amounts to postulating that the unconscious (the "psychical reality") is an objective reality, as such indifferent to the expectations, "anticipatory ideas," and speculations of the psychoanalyst. The patient only recovers if the theory corresponds to this reality, and recovery (or not) therefore provides an infallible criterion for judging the validity (or not) of the analyst's interpretations and constructions.

The argument is seductive, but it is in fact based on a circular reasoning coupled with a logical error. On the one hand, it presupposes what is to be proved (the reality of the unconscious). On the other hand, it falls into the well-known fallacy of *post hoc, ergo propter hoc* ("as a result of that, therefore because of that"). As Freud's contemporaries pointed out very early on, there is nothing to say that the successful cures he invoked (which in fact were very rare) were not due to other causes, for example, to suggestion or to what we would call today the placebo effect. The British psychiatrist Bernard Hart (1879–1966) wrote:

[9] Freud 1896b, 206. [10] Freud 1916–1917, 452. [11] Grünbaum 1985, Chapter 2, B.

> In the history of medicine many structures have been built upon the fallacy of *post hoc propter hoc* ... It is of course true that satisfactory results are achieved by psychoanalysis, but it is equally true that satisfactory results are achieved by many, indeed by all, other methods of psychotherapy, and by a multitude of methods which lie altogether outside the walls of medicine. ... We must hence conclude that the argument from therapeutic results cannot provide the independent confirmation of psychoanalytic validity of which we are in search.[12]

To this objection, Freud always answered with the analytical "experience" (*Erfahrung*). This is what we might call the "argument from practice," which amounts to reiterating the Tally Argument as many times as necessary (and which justifies, by the way, the accusation of irrefutability made by Popper):

> What is advantageous to our therapy is damaging to our researches. This is the objection that is most often raised against psycho-analysis, and it must be admitted that, though it is groundless, it cannot be rejected as unreasonable. If it were justified, psycho-analysis would be nothing more than a particularly well-disguised and particularly effective form of suggestive treatment and we should have to attach little weight to all that it tells us about what influences our lives, the dynamics of the mind or the unconscious. ... These accusations are contradicted more easily by an appeal to experience than by the help of theory. Anyone who has himself carried out psycho-analyses will have been able to convince himself on countless occasions that it is impossible to make suggestions to a patient in that way.[13]

So it is less the cure in itself than the slow working through (*Durcharbeiten*) of the cure and the painful "overcoming" of the resistances opposed to the analyst's interpretations that ultimately convinces. But again, how is this hard-won conviction proof? Is the fact that the patient finally accepts the interpretations after having resisted them for a long time a guarantee of their correctness? Perhaps it is simply an effect of the therapist's influence, or even pressure, or of the patient's complacency?

It is therefore impossible to come to a decision. We are running in circles; there is no escaping the analysis' endless circularity. Will we have better luck by staying there? Let's follow Freud's recommendation and enter his office to see if the analytic "experience" will decide in the end, as promised by the character of Nestroy quoted in "Constructions in Analysis": "It will all become clear in the course of future developments."[14]

[12] Hart 1929, 79, 81. [13] Freud 1916–1917, 452. [14] Freud 1937b, 265.

Free Association

We remember that Freud initially hypnotized his patients to erase and desuggest their traumatic "reminiscences." What he was aiming at was oblivion and that is why, during this whole period (1887–1892), Freud tried to obtain in his patients a deep somnambulism with post-hypnotic amnesia. However, from the moment he attributed the dissociation of consciousness and the persistence of the symptoms to a desire to forget (repression), it goes without saying that the objective could no longer be amnesia, since it was this that the patients were actually supposed to be suffering from. As Freud writes in the case of "Miss Lucy R." in *Studies on Hysteria*, it is "a deliberate repression from consciousness which rendered the ... memory ... pathogenic."[15] It is therefore this will to forget, this resistance to recollection, that must be fought, instead of unwittingly reinforcing it with hypnosis. Later on, one of the main criticisms that Freud was to make of the hypnotic procedure was that it hid "the resistance with which the patient clings to his disease and thus even fights against his own recovery."[16]

Logically, Freud's aim was now to facilitate the *recollection* of the repressed memory. This is the principle of the "cathartic method" described by Breuer and Freud in their "Preliminary Communication" of 1893. This method, they write, subjects the pathogenic memory "to associative correction by introducing it into normal consciousness (under light hypnosis) or by removing it through the physician's suggestion, as it is done in somnambulism accompanied by amnesia."[17] We can see that, at this date, the authors are still hesitating between removing the traumatic memory by means of suggestion under hypnosis and bringing it back to consciousness. But two years later, in the chapter of *Studies on Hysteria* devoted to "The Psychotherapy of Hysteria," Freud settles the matter: the treatment does not "consist in extirpating (*exstirpieren*) – something psychotherapy is not able to do this for the present – but in causing the resistance to melt and in thus enabling the circulation to make its way into a region that has hitherto been cut off."[18] Note in passing the hydraulic metaphor: it is a matter of making the unconscious memory conscious by *liquefying* the obstacle that opposes the *flow* of the excitation along the associative chains and its cathartic discharge or "abreaction" through the "*locks* to motor activity."

[15] Breuer and Freud 1895, 113. [16] Freud 1905b, 261. [17] Breuer and Freud 1895, 17.
[18] Ibid., 291.

During a stay in Nancy in 1889, Freud had seen how Hippolyte Bernheim managed to overcome the apparent post-hypnotic amnesia of his subjects by placing his hand on their foreheads (a very classic "magnetic pass") and by asking them to remember what had transpired during their trance. Freud decided to proceed in the same way with his patients, asking them to remember the origin of their symptoms: "You will think of it under the pressure of my hand. At the moment at which I relax my pressure you will see something in front of you or something will come into your head [an *Einfall*]. Catch hold of it. It will be what we are looking for. Well what have you seen or what has occurred to you?"[19]

This is the "pressure procedure" (*Druckprozedur*), which will soon become the method of "free association" (*freie Assoziation*) or of "freely occurring ideas" (*Methode der freien Einfälle*). Freud seems to have used this technique for the first time in the autumn of 1892 with his patients "Elisabeth von R." (real name Ilona Weiss) and "Lucy R." Regarding the latter, Freud tells us that her treatment took place "in a state which may in fact have differed very little from a normal one,"[20] which has led many to think that Freud abandoned hypnosis for the method of free associations in the waking state as early as this date. In reality, the *Druckprozedur* from which the free association method emerged was intended to provoke a state of "light hypnosis." In "Manuscript H" sent to Wilhelm Fliess in 1895, Freud speaks of "concentration hypnosis" (*Konzentrationshypnosis*),[21] and in *Studies on Hysteria*, he compares his procedure to a "momentarily intensified hypnosis" as well as to the well-known hypnotic technique of fixing attention on a crystal ball.[22]

Under his insistent "pressure," his patients seem to have gone through a modified state of consciousness characterized by visual "scenes" of a hallucinatory type, great emotional expressiveness, and an increase in ideo-motor and ideo-sensory activity in Bernheim's sense. Judging from letters to Fliess in 1897, some of them even engaged in very theatrical "reproductions" of the traumatic scene that would not have been out of place at Charcot's Salpêtrière.[23] Freud would later claim to have abandoned hypnosis around 1896,[24] but in reality, it was only very gradually that he stopped inducing hypnotic states in order to obtain the emergence of ideas that were not filtered by censorship. Heinrich Treichl, the grandson of Baroness Marie von Ferstel, even states in his *Memoirs* that Freud

[19] Ibid., 110. [20] Ibid., 107. [21] Freud 1985, 109. [22] Breuer and Freud 1895, 271.
[23] Freud 1985, 226, 288. [24] Freud 1905b, 261.

was still using hypnosis in the treatment of his grandmother, which had begun at the end of 1899.[25]

Whether or not Freud used a hypnotic technique to bring out the incidental ideas and spontaneous associations of his patients is in fact relatively insignificant, since the project is the same in both cases: to facilitate access to the psychic unconscious. This was already the hypnotic project of Heidenhain, Charcot, and many others. But whereas for them and for the first Freud it was a kind of psychological vivisection performed without the patient being conscious, the aim now was to take advantage of the patient's hypnoid state to make *him/her* become aware of his/her unconscious. Thus defined, the project is that of a paradoxical introspection of unconscious or subliminal psychic states intended to circumvent the impossibility for the subject to consciously access the nonconscious.

In this respect, Freud could draw inspiration from Joseph Delboeuf's analysis of his personal dreams[26] or from the "introspective hypnotism" practiced at the time by researchers such as August Forel (1848–1931), Eugen Bleuler (1857–1939), or Oskar Vogt (1870–1959), who had all published observations of hypnotic states in the first person.[27] Forel summarized this research as follows:

> The object of psychology is the study of so-called psychic functions of our brain by direct introspection . . . Those cerebral functions which do not fall into the ordinary field of attention of our consciousness in a waking state or its memories escape direct introspective psychology. But modern studies have made us increasingly aware that a large part of the cerebral functions called unconscious possess an introspective shimmering which we can surprise in certain circumstances, and one designates this fact by the term "subconscious," a term which for good reason is being increasingly adopted.[28]

It is this "introspective shimmering" that the *Druckprozedur* and free association attempt to capture, by short-circuiting the censorship that usually opposes the entry of repressed ideas into consciousness. About the *Druckprozedur*, Freud writes in *Studies on Hysteria*: "The advantage of the procedure lies in the fact that by means of it I dissociate the patient's attention from his conscious searching and reflecting – from everything, in short, on which he can employ his will – in the same sort of way in which

[25] Treichl 2003, 67–68. [26] Delboeuf 1885. [27] Mayer 2001. [28] Forel 1910, 308.

this is effected by staring into a crystal ball, and so on."[29] It is a question, in other words, of favoring as much as possible a mode of involuntary, automatic, reflex thought – what André Breton (1896–1966), faithful interpreter of Freud, will call in his first "Manifesto of Surrealism" the "actual functioning of thought."[30] In *The Interpretation of Dreams* of 1900, Freud likewise explains that his method (which he does not yet call free association) aims at making "involuntary ideas" emerge:

> What is in question, evidently, is the establishment of a psychical state which, in its distribution of psychical energy (that is, of mobile attention), bears some analogy to the state before falling asleep – and no doubt also to hypnosis. As we fall asleep, "involuntary ideas" emerge, owing to the relaxation of a certain deliberate (and no doubt also critical) activity which we allow to influence the course of our ideas while we are awake.[31]

This is why the analyst asks the patient to lie down on a comfortable couch, so as to *anesthetize* the censorship, to *numb* the consciousness and the will, halfway between wakefulness and sleep. "This arrangement," Freud writes in 1913, "has a historical basis; it is the remnant of the hypnotic method out of which psycho-analysis was evolved."[32] In this sense, free association on the couch is a hypnosis without hypnosis and without a hypnotist, a psychological automatism in a semi-vigil state. The patient is invited to say whatever comes into his/her head, without regard to logic, propriety, or morality: this is the famous "fundamental rule" of the psychoanalytic treatment, which replaces hypnotic induction and from which Freud hopes for a spontaneous revelation of the unconscious.

Freud often insists that this method does not impose anything on the subject, as did the hypnotic-suggestive process. It "does not seek to add or to introduce anything new, but to take away something, to bring out something," like Leonardo's sculptor who "proceeds *per via di levare*, since it takes away from the block of stone all that hides the surface of the statue contained in it."[33] It is in this sense that the association of ideas is said to be "free": "the method of free association has an advantage over the earlier method. It exposes the patient to the least possible amount of compulsion [*Zwang*] . . . it guarantees to a great extent that no factor in the structure of the neurosis will be overlooked and that nothing will be introduced into it by the expectations of the analyst."[34]

[29] Breuer and Freud 1895, 271. [30] Breton 1924b, 26. [31] Freud 1900, 102.
[32] Freud 1913b, 133. [33] Freud 1905b, 261. [34] Freud 1925a, 41.

Resistance

The problem, of course, is that the marble *resists* the sculptor's chisel. The sculptor has to work hard to bring out the statue he/she has in mind, and it is exactly the same for the analyst who tries to make the patient aware of his/her inner "statue." Very quickly, Freud had to face the fact that his new method did not allow direct access to unconscious primary processes. While it was supposed to "melt" the censorship between the unconscious and the conscious, he noticed a reluctance on the part of patients to let themselves go. In *Studies on Hysteria*, he describes the thousand and one breaches of the fundamental rule that they commit: they cannot concentrate, nothing comes to their mind, they are distracted by the neighbor's piano, they have difficulty describing the images that arise in their mind, they reason too much, they become secretive, etc. Or they break the contract with the therapist outright, like the paranoid patient mentioned in "Manuscript H" sent to Fliess in January 1895. Freud was convinced that her delusion of persecution was linked to a sexual attack committed on her a few years earlier by a tenant:

> I talked to her twice; in concentration hypnosis got her to tell me everything to do with the lodger; in reply to my pressing inquiries about whether something "embarrassing" had actually happened, I received the most decided negation as an answer; and – saw her no more. She sent me a message to say that it upset her too much. Defence! That was obvious. She wanted not to be reminded of it and consequently intentionally repressed it.[35]

This is the phenomenon of resistance. The term comes from Bernheim, who used it to refer to the resistance put up by the subjects to the hypnotist's suggestions.[36] For Freud, it names the resistance put up by patients to the analyst's interpretations and, more generally, to the treatment proposed to them. Anything that hinders the elucidation of symptoms and the progress of the cure is henceforth considered as resistance to the cure. It is that "which finally brings the [analytic] work to a halt."[37] The patient falls asleep on the couch? Resistance. He/she arrives late for his/her session or cancels an appointment due to the flu? Resistance. He/she has nothing to say, or does not remember the dream he/she had last night? Resistance. "[T]he person who initially was such a good, noble human being becomes mean, untruthful, or obstinate, a malingerer – until

[35] Freud 1985, 109. [36] Bernheim 1888, 52–54. [37] Freud 1985, 274.

I tell him so and thus make it possible for him to overcome this character."[38]

Nothing is innocent in the patient's behavior; everything must be interpreted, dissected, suspected. The treatment, which was initially an analysis (an interpretation) of symptoms, now becomes an analysis of the resistances in opposition to this analysis – or what amounts to the same thing, an analysis of the resistances in opposition to the analyst's theory. Indeed, it is the analyst who posits that there is some unconscious memory or wish behind the patient's behavior and symptoms. When the patient refuses to admit this, he/she therefore refuses to confirm the analyst's theory. The treatment becomes, by the same token, a scientific controversy, as one of the protagonists rejects the hypotheses put forward by the other about him/her. This is what is meant by "analysis of resistance": the analyst must constantly fight with the patients to convince them and make them admit his/her theory. "Since this insistence involved effort on my part and so suggested the idea that I had to overcome a resistance, the situation led me at once to the theory that by means of my psychical work I had to overcome a psychical force in the patients which was opposed to the pathogenic ideas becoming conscious (being remembered)."[39]

Once again, one will have noticed the circular character of Freud's reasoning: resistance to the theory validates the theory that predicts the resistance. As Freud's colleagues and critics pointed out very early on, the controversy that is the cure has no chance of ending since it takes the form of an analysis of resistance to analysis. No objection from the patient can end the dispute, because it will necessarily be interpreted as a desire to avoid the unpleasant truth uncovered by the analyst: "The 'No' uttered by a patient after a repressed thought has been presented to his conscious perception for the first time does no more than register the existence of a repression and its severity."[40] The same applies to the objections of colleagues, which are also deciphered as "resistances to psycho-analysis."[41] To Fliess, Freud wrote: "[I] am contending with hostility and live in such isolation that one might imagine I had discovered the greatest truths."[42] And to Carl Gustav Jung (1875–1961): "My inclination is to treat those colleagues who offer resistance exactly as we treat patients in the same situation."[43]

[38] Ibid. [39] Breuer and Freud 1895, 268. [40] Freud 1905c, 58. [41] Freud 1925b.
[42] Freud 1985, 179. [43] Freud and Jung 1974, 18.

In the end, it is the whole of humanity that resists psychoanalysis:

> Thus the strongest resistances to psycho-analysis were not of an intellectual kind but arose from emotional sources. This explained their passionate character as well as their poverty in logic. The situation obeyed a simple formula: men in the mass behaved to psycho-analysis in precisely the same way as individual neurotics under treatment for their disorders. . . . [this] was at once alarming and consoling: alarming because it was no small thing to have the whole human race as one's patient, and consoling because after all everything was taking place as the hypotheses of psycho-analysis declared that it was bound to.[44]

Once he had admitted that the patient necessarily resists his/her recovery in order not to have to face his/her unconscious, Freud would never deviate from this line again: objections to psychoanalysis confirm its predictions. These predictions and hypotheses are therefore in no way "risky" in Popper's sense, since nothing, in fact, can contradict them. The contradiction is foreseen by the theory, which is therefore rigorously irrefutable. Even the absence of therapeutic results cannot be invoked against it, contrary to what Freud admitted when he put forward his Tally Argument. Faced with his therapeutic failures, his plea will always be the same: if the patient has not been cured, it is because they have not accepted the solution proposed by the analyst, because they have resisted the truth of the unconscious. *Therapeutic failure proves the theory*, even better than the cure, which can always hide a ruse of resistance.

The "Dora" Case

The first properly psychoanalytic case history published by Freud, the famous "Dora" case, is the account of such a failure. The exact title is "Fragment of an Analysis of a Case of Hysteria," as if to better underline the unfinished nature of the treatment. It has often been asked why Freud chose this case to illustrate his new psychotherapeutic method, rather than a clear therapeutic success. The answer is probably that he had none at his disposal, and that rather than invoking what were in fact very temporary successes (as he and Breuer had done in *Studies on Hysteria*), he found it more convincing, paradoxically, to insist on the resistance he encountered in his work. One is more likely to believe someone who confesses his/her failures than a braggart who boasts too much about his/her successes. To which should be added that counterintuitive or paradoxical explanations

[44] Freud 1925b, 221.

have, as Wittgenstein put it, a singular "charm": "It is charming to destroy prejudices."[45]

Indeed, Freud does not at any time give himself the positive role in this story – quite the contrary. The young Ida Bauer (the real name of "Dora") had been brought to him by her father, Filipp Bauer, due to behavioral problems linked to a scabrous family dynamic. Ida had twice been subjected to undue advances by a family friend, Hans Zellenka ("Herr K." in the case history), whose wife was also having an affair with Filipp Bauer. In the second incident, Ida had slapped Zellenka hard and complained to her father. Zellenka was asked to explain his actions, but he denied them and accused Ida of erotic obsession and mythomania. Rather than question the delicate balance of their ménage à trois, Filipp Bauer had accepted his explanations. Humiliated and outraged at being sacrificed on the altar of family tranquility, Ida had demanded in vain that her father break off all relations with the Zellenkas, threatening suicide. After an argument during which she had fainted, her father had finally dragged her to Freud, "in spite of her reluctance,"[46] to be cured of her hysterical behavior.

Contrary to what the father obviously hoped for, Freud recognized the validity of Ida's accusations. However, he did not question the diagnosis of mental illness made by Hans Zellenka and Filipp Bauer. The aversion Ida felt when Zellenka kissed her in the first incident was, in his opinion, clearly hysterical, because a girl of that age (Ida was thirteen and a half) would normally have felt pleasure from "the pressure of the erect member."[47] Ida had *repressed* her love for Hans Zellenka and converted the excitement she felt in her clitoris into oral disgust. All of Ida's organic disorders (asthma, appendicitis, dragging leg) were likewise deciphered as symbolic expressions of her desire for Zellenka and, more deeply, for her own father. Thus, her periods of asthmatic aphonia corresponded to Zellenka's absences and expressed the regret of not being able to speak to her loved one. Her coughing expressed the desire to feel in her throat the organ of her father, the original love object for which Zellenka served as a substitute. Her asthmatic dyspnea mimicked the panting of her father copulating with her mother. Her "alleged . . . appendicitis"[48] fulfilled the fantasy of giving birth to Zellenka's child.

Freud was very satisfied with his interpretations. As soon as he had finished the article, he wrote to Fliess: "It is the subtlest thing I have written so far and will put people off even more than usual."[49] Dora, for

[45] Wittgenstein 1966, 24. [46] Freud 1905c, 23. [47] Ibid., 30. [48] Ibid., 101.
[49] Freud 1985, 433.

her part, rejected the interpretations of her analyst with as much determination as she had rejected those of Zellenka and her father. She refused, in other words, to be considered sick. One day, after Freud tried to convince her that her dragging leg symbolized the "faux pas" she unconsciously wished to commit with Zellenka, she informed him that their session was to be the last. Freud replied that she was dismissing him like a servant – like the servant she was jealous of because she had had an affair with Zellenka: "Now I know your motive for the slap in the face with which you answered Herr K.'s proposal. It was not that you were offended at his suggestions; you were actuated by jealousy and revenge."[50] After listening politely to him, Ida Bauer took leave of her analyst and . . . did not return. Freud's comment: "Her breaking off so unexpectedly, just when my hopes of a successful termination of the treatment were at their highest . . . this was an unmistakable act of revenge on her part. Her purpose of self-injury also profited by this action."[51] And a little further: "she took her revenge on me as she wanted to take her revenge on him [Herr K.], and deserted me as she believed herself to have been deceived and deserted by him."[52]

A year later, Ida returned to Freud for a painful facial neuralgia (let us not forget that Freud was a neurologist). Freud was pleased to note that this neuralgia had begun shortly after Ida had read in the newspaper the announcement of his appointment as Professor. Clearly, Ida was punishing herself for leaving him by "slapping" herself, just as she had slapped Hans Zellenka.

> Her alleged facial neuralgia was thus a self-punishment – remorse at having once given Herr K. a box on the ear, and at having transferred her feelings of revenge on to me. I do not know what kind of help she wanted from me, but I promised to forgive her for having deprived me of the satisfaction of affording her a far more radical cure for her troubles.[53]

From this last remark, one can deduce that Freud considered Ida still to be ill but that he could not (or did not wish to?) give her help since she continued to refuse it. The neuralgia was her punishment for rejecting the analyst's interpretations. These were, therefore, retroactively verified by the persistence of the symptoms (circular reasoning, once again).

We can see that the failure of the treatment is not for Freud an incentive to revise his hypotheses but, on the contrary, a confirmation of their validity. Ida Bauer had no chance of having her protests heard, because they were interpreted a priori as proof of her hysterical neurosis. Even her

[50] Freud 1905c, 106. [51] Ibid., 109. [52] Ibid., 119. [53] Ibid., 122.

refusal to continue the treatment was turned against her. While by this act she was, in short, affirming that she was sane and did not need analysis, Freud saw it as resistance to recovery. But was she ill in the first place?

Freud's "Dora" has become for generations of psychoanalysts the paradigm of the Hysteric. The real Ida, on the other hand, showed no signs of neurosis or psychic instability in her adult life. The psychoanalyst Kurt Eissler (1908–1999), who had interviewed her relatives at length in the early 1950s, confirmed this in a letter to Anna Freud (1895–1982): "Apparently the information I got from Dora[Ida Bauer]'s cousin two years ago is correct and she never developed serious neurotic or psychotic symptoms after her treatment by Freud."[54] Freud presented the treatment of "Dora" as an abject failure, but one can legitimately wonder if there was anything to be cured.

Transference

In the coda of the case history, one will have noticed the strangely personal tone adopted by Freud: Dora had left him, she had inflicted a slap in the face on him, she had taken revenge on him as she had done with Herr K. – and he himself savors his revenge when she returns to him with her pathetic "alleged facial neuralgia." The disagreement about the analyst's interpretations is not only theoretical; in Freud's writing, it takes the form of a real showdown between two people. In this arena, all blows are allowed: "No one who, like me, conjures up the most evil of those half-tamed demons that inhabit the human breast, and seeks to wrestle with them, can expect to come through the struggle unscathed."[55]

This arena is that of the *transference* on the analyst. In his concluding comment, Freud in fact attributes the failure of the treatment to the fact that he had not been able to flush out the transference that Dora was operating from Herr K. on him:

> it is only by means of this factor that I can elucidate the peculiarities of Dora's analysis. Its great merit, namely, the unusual clarity which makes it seem so suitable as a first introductory publication, is closely bound up with its great defect, which led to its being broken off prematurely. I did not succeed in mastering the transference in good time.[56]

According to Freud, transference consists of a displacement: the patient puts the doctor in the place of another person and behaves towards him/

[54] Eissler 1952. [55] Freud 1905c, 109. [56] Ibid., 118.

her as he/she would towards that person. In *Studies on Hysteria*, Freud mentions the case of a patient (most likely Elise Gomperz) who, at the end of a hypnosis session, had experienced a strong erotic desire for him and had become frightened by it, thereby hindering the treatment. Rather than attributing this scabrous episode to his "own irresistible personal attraction,"[57] Freud saw it as a "false connection," a transference to his *present* person of a *past* desire for another man. To use a slightly later Freudian terminology, the patient had "repeated," "acted out," instead of remembering:[58]

> The wish which was present was then, owing to the compulsion to associate which was dominant in her consciousness, linked to my person, with which the patient was legitimately concerned ... Since I have discovered this, I have been able, whenever I have been similarly involved personally, to presume that a transference and a false connection have once more taken place.[59]

Hence, Freud continues, a resistance to treatment since the patients stop cooperating at the point "where apparently personal relations were concerned and where the third person coincided with the figure of the physician."[60] We have seen that it is the same explanation that is put forward in the "Dora" case: by rejecting *Freud's* treatment, Dora in fact rejects the advances of *Herr K.* From this point of view, the resistance to analysis quite naturally takes the form of a *transference resistance* since the "no" in opposition to the interpretations is also a "no" in opposition to the person of the analyst who proposes these interpretations. The analysis of resistance becomes, by the very fact, an *analysis of transference*. For Freud, everything now revolves around the relation to the analyst, deciphered as the symptom of a "transference-neurosis."[61]

As a result, no objection made by the patient can be taken seriously any longer because it will be interpreted in affective terms, as the somnambulistic repetition of a previous relationship. If the patient argues, if he/she becomes irritated by the analyst's insistence on imposing his point of view, if he/she adopts a hostile attitude towards the analyst, if he/she stops the treatment, it is because he/she is making a "negative transference" and reproducing with the analyst an older conflict with this or that relative, this or that friend, this or that love relationship. Inversely, if the patient systematically accepts all the analyst's interpretations, if he/she brings to each session "corroborative dreams,"[62] if he/she idolizes the analyst, it is because he/she is developing a "positive transference," or even a

[57] Freud 1925a, 27. [58] Freud 1914b. [59] Breuer and Freud 1895, 303. [60] Ibid., 304.
[61] Freud 1914b, 154. [62] Freud 1923c, 115.

"transference-love"[63] that is actually directed at another person. This obedience is no less a resistance, because it is a "hypocritical yes,"[64] a complacency that hides the refusal to heal.

We remember that this is the reproach that Freud also addressed to hypnosis and, in fact, he now sees in the amorous transference the key to "the mysterious element that was at work behind hypnotism":[65] "It is true . . . that there is usually a sort of blind dependence and a permanent bond between a patient and the physician who has removed his symptoms by hypnotic suggestion; but the scientific explanation of all these facts is to be found in the existence of 'transferences' such as are regularly directed by patients on to their physicians."[66] He returns to this twenty years later in his autobiographical presentation:

> In every analytic treatment there arises, without the physician's agency, an intense emotional relationship between the patient and the analyst which is not to be accounted for by the actual situation. . . . This transference – to give it its short name – soon replaces in the patient's mind the desire to be cured . . . We can easily recognize it as the same dynamic factor which the hypnotists have named "suggestibility," which is the agent of hypnotic rapport and whose incalculable behaviour led to difficulties with the cathartic method as well.[67]

Starting with the "Dora" case, Freud saw the transference as the major obstacle to analysis, the one around which the trial of strength between the patient and the analyst is decided, but also and simultaneously its most powerful auxiliary:

> In psycho-analysis . . . all the patient's tendencies, including hostile ones, are aroused; they are then turned to account for the purposes of the analysis by being made conscious, and in this way the transference is constantly being destroyed. Transference, which seems ordained to be the greatest obstacle to psycho-analysis, becomes its most powerful ally, if its presence can be detected each time and explained to the patient.[68]

The analyst has to "destroy," "liquidate," "dissolve" the transference, that is to say, to show the patient that his/her resistance to the interpretations and constructions that the analyst proposes to him/her are not addressed to the therapist but to such and such a beloved or hated figure of his/her unconscious. But how is the analyst going to succeed if the patient refuses, if he/she is not convinced by the analyst's hypotheses – if the

[63] Freud 1915b. [64] Freud 1937b, 262. [65] Freud 1925a, 27. [66] Freud 1905c, 117.
[67] Freud 1925a, 42. [68] Freud 1905c, 117.

patient tells him/her, for example: "Doctor, I refuse that you reduce my objections to a 'negative transference' on your person"; "I do not give you the right to say that my decision to stop listening to your nonsense is only a repetition of the slap I gave to Herr K."; or like Jung in his famous break-up letter with Freud: "I would, however, point out that your technique of treating your pupils like patients is a blunder. I am namely not in the least neurotic – touch wood!"?[69]

Freud's answer to this question was always the same: one must use transference against transference, exploiting the ascendancy it provides to make the patient accept the correctness of the proposed interpretations. Already in *Studies on Hysteria*, Freud made the "influence" due to the transference the very mainspring of the treatment of certain patients. Unlike others who shun treatment, these

> have decided to put themselves in [the analyst's] hands and place their confidence in him – a step which in other such situations is only taken voluntarily . . . with these other patients, I say, it is almost inevitable that their personal relation to him will force itself, for a time at least, unduly into the foreground. It seems, indeed, as though an influence of this kind on the part of the doctor is a sine qua non to a solution of the problem.[70]

This positive transference is what Freud called five years earlier the *glaübige Erwartung*, the "faithful" or "hopeful expectation" that he put at the time at the basis of the therapeutic effectiveness of hypnotic suggestion: the patient trusts his/her doctor, obeys his/her suggestions, puts blind faith in his/her theories, etc. In a word, he/she is "suggestible," as Bernheim said. Freud, in his *Introductory Lectures on Psycho-Analysis*, credits Bernheim with being the first to put his finger on this phenomenon: "His suggestibility was nothing other than the tendency to transference, somewhat too narrowly conceived, so that it did not include negative transference. . . . And it must dawn on us that in our technique we have abandoned hypnosis only to rediscover suggestion in the shape of transference."[71]

As such, it is this "credivity" (Bernheim)[72] that characterizes positive transference that Freud relies on to overcome negative transference, i.e., the resistances opposed by the patient to the analyst's interpretations. A bit like in martial arts, it is a question of using the strength of the opponent to turn it against them, using the ascendancy and authority conferred by the transference to dissolve the latter. In "Beyond the Pleasure Principle,"

[69] Freud and Jung 1974, 535. [70] Breuer and Freud 1895, 266. [71] Freud 1916–1917, 446.
[72] Bernheim 1888, second part, Chapter 1; Bernheim 1891, 35, 71

Freud describes how analysis has become over the years an analysis of resistances: "The art consisted now in uncovering these as quickly as possible, in pointing them out to the patient and in inducing him by human influence – this was where suggestion operating as 'transference' played its part – to abandon his resistances."[73]

We can see, of course, the problem with this kind of assertion. For if transference is only a new name for ex-"suggestibility," how can we distinguish analysis from suggestion, or even from an enterprise of indoctrination? How can we guarantee the correctness of the analyst's interpretations when the patient's conviction is extorted by "suggestion operating as 'transference'"? Freud's answer:

> It is perfectly true that psycho-analysis, like other psychotherapeutic methods, employs the instrument of suggestion (or transference). But the difference is this: that in analysis it is not allowed to play the decisive part in determining the therapeutic results. It is used instead to induce the patient to perform a piece of psychical work – the overcoming of his transference resistances.[74]

> In every other kind of suggestive treatment the transference is carefully preserved and left untouched; in analysis it is itself subjected to treatment and is dissected in all the shapes in which it appears. At the end of an analytic treatment the transference must itself be cleared away; and if success is then obtained or continues, it rests, not on suggestion, but on the achievement by its means of an overcoming of internal resistances, on the internal change that has been brought about in the patient.[75]

The analyst uses patients' transference (their suggestibility) to bring them to overcome their transference (their suggestibility). The argument is subtle and serves to distinguish psychoanalysis advantageously from other psychotherapies. Does this solve the problem of the validation of psychoanalytic interpretations and constructions? We don't know, for when are the patients supposed to overcome their transference, i.e., their suggestibility? When they accept the suggestions (the interpretations) that the analyst makes to them? Or when they reject them? In the first case, we will not know if they accept the solution proposed by the analyst because they have overcome their transference or because they are still entangled in it. In the second case, we will not know either if they reject the authority of the analyst because they have finally freed themselves from their transference or on the contrary because they continue to resist it. All this is

[73] Freud 1920, 18. [74] Freud 1925a, 43. [75] Freud 1916–1917, 453.

undecidable and, in practice, it is the analyst who decides and declares that the transference is dissolved (or not) and the patient cured (or not).

"It will all become clear in the course of future developments," Freud promised, but, in fact, we are not much further ahead than before. The end of the analysis does not provide any criteria for determining whether the patient has been desuggested or rather indoctrinated. As a result, nothing guarantees that the confirmations of the hypotheses put forward by the analyst are not simply an effect of these, i.e., an artifact of psychoanalytic theory itself. Nothing, except the analyst's word.

Self-Analysis

But, then, how to guarantee this word itself? In Freudian terms: how can we be sure that the analyst has had access to the patient's unconscious and has not been influenced by his/her own unconscious motivations, by his/her own "counter-transference"? It was to answer this thorny question that Freud, in 1910, required every beginning psychoanalyst to engage in a *self*-analysis:

> We have noticed that no psycho-analyst goes further than his own complexes and internal resistances permit; and we consequently require that he shall begin his activity with a self-analysis and continually carry it deeper while he is making his observations on his patients. Anyone who fails to produce results in a self-analysis of this kind may at once give up any idea of being able to treat patients by analysis.[76]

Freud himself had carried out a self-analysis in the autumn of 1897, in order to treat what he then called "my little hysteria . . . greatly accentuated by my work."[77] It was during this therapeutic self-analysis that he had found in himself the phenomenon of "being in love with my mother and jealous of my father,"[78] in other words, what he would later call the "Oedipus complex." Started in earnest at the beginning of October 1897, this self-analytical exploration seems, however, to have been extremely brief and even, in the eyes of the main person concerned, rather disappointing. How, indeed, to overcome one's *own* resistance? Six weeks later, Freud concluded with a very lucid statement of failure: "My self-analysis remains interrupted. I have realized why I can analyze myself only with the knowledge obtained objectively (like an outsider). True self-analysis is impossible; otherwise there would be no [neurotic] illness.

[76] Freud 1910b, 145. [77] Freud 1985, 261. [78] Ibid.

Since I am still contending with some kind of puzzle in my patients, this is bound to hold me up in my self-analysis as well."[79]

Yet it was this impossible self-analysis that Freud initially demanded of his collaborators in the psychoanalytic movement. To the question of how one becomes a psychoanalyst, he answered in 1909: "by studying one's own dreams."[80] In other words: "Follow my example." Problems soon arose. As each analyst availed him/herself of his/her own self-analysis, there was soon a cacophony of divergent interpretations. Where Freud had found Oedipus, others found Electra. Where he insisted on the paternal complex, others insisted on the maternal complex. Where he had discovered infantile sexuality, others discovered "organ inferiority." Where he said "libido," others said "aggression drive" or "will to power." It is no coincidence that this was also the time of the great disputes between Freud, Jung, Alfred Adler (1870–1937) and Wilhelm Stekel (1868–1940). Insofar as the ultimate criterion for the validity of psychoanalytic interpretations was self-analysis, each could invoke his/her own to delegitimize that of the others and accuse the rivals of projecting their own unanalyzed complexes onto the theory or of acting out a badly liquidated transference. There was no way to settle the interpretive conflicts that were tearing the psychoanalytic movement apart.

To remedy this situation, Jung proposed in 1912 that all future analysts should be analyzed by another analyst – in short, that they should undergo a training analysis. Freud followed suit in his "Advice to Physicians on Analytical Treatment" of the same year:

> I count it as one of the many merits of the Zurich school of analysis that they have laid increased emphasis on this requirement, and have embodied it in the demand that everyone who wishes to carry out analyses on other people shall first himself undergo an analysis by someone with expert knowledge . . . But anyone who has scorned to take the precaution of being analysed himself . . . will easily fall into the temptation of projecting outwards some of the peculiarities of his own personality, which he has dimly perceived, into the field of science, as a theory having universal validity.[81]

In theory, the training analysis was supposed to guarantee that the interpretations of the analysts were not deformed by their "dim" personal equation, that is to say, by their neurosis. In practice, it guaranteed that everyone interpreted in the same way as Freud or as those of his disciples whom he had analyzed. By operating a hermeneutic standardization,

[79] Ibid., 281. [80] Freud 1910a, 32. [81] Freud 1912, 116–117.

training psychoanalysis provided, in short, an institutional answer to an aporia impossible to solve at the theoretical level. The problem was that this answer immediately gave rise to a new difficulty: what about Freud? If every analyst drew his/her hermeneutical authority from his/her training analysis, where did Freud draw his? As long as psychoanalysts were supposed to train themselves, Freud's self-analysis was not a problem. This was no longer the case now that the rules of the game had changed, because Freud had not been analyzed by anyone. Then who could guarantee that his analysis had been complete?

This problem came to a head at the time of the conflict with Jung, the very man who had been at the origin of training psychoanalysis. Freud having boiled down their theoretical differences to the "father complex" that Jung was supposed to harbor towards him, Jung finally retorted that he had no diagnosis to receive from someone who had not been analyzed – from a neurotic:

> You see, my dear Professor, so long as you hand out this stuff I don't give a damn for my symptomatic actions; they shrink to nothing in comparison with the formidable beam in my brother Freud's eye. I am namely not in the least neurotic – touch wood! I have namely *lege artis et tout humblement* let myself be analysed, which has been very good for me. You know, of course, how far a patient gets with self-analysis: *not* out of his neurosis – just like you.[82]

How to respond to this? Upset by Jung's "impudence," Freud informed him that the one who constantly cries that he is normal "gives ground for the suspicion that he lacks insight into his illness. Accordingly, I propose that we abandon our personal relations entirely."[83] However, it was his disciple Sándor Ferenczi (1873–1933) who found the final word. More lucid than Freud, Ferenczi saw that there was no point in symmetrically reproaching Jung for what he reproached Freud for. In a letter to Freud dated December 26, 1912, he advocated frankly affirming the *exceptional* character of the self-analysis of the first analyst:

> You are probably the only one who can permit himself to do without an analyst . . . If you had the strength to overcome in yourself, without a leader (*for the first time in the history of mankind*), the resistances which all humanity brings to bear on the results of analysis, then we must expect of you the strength to dispense with your lesser symptoms. The facts speak decidedly in favor of this. But what is valid for *you* is not valid for the rest of us. Jung has not achieved the same self-mastery as you.[84]

[82] Freud and Jung 1974, 535. [83] Ibid., 539. [84] Freud and Ferenczi 1993, 449.

This will henceforth be the official position of the psychoanalytic movement: self-analysis is impossible, *except* for Freud. Self-analysis, which initially had been no more than a self-observation that could be replicated by anyone, was transformed, from argument to argument, into a literally extraordinary enterprise, reserved for Freud alone. Just as the establishment of training analysis had been a way to put an end to the interpretive conflicts inherent to psychoanalysis, so the elevation of Freud's self-analysis to a status of exception allowed to close the controversies about the didactic power (the hermeneutical power) itself. For training analysis to work, one analyst, and *only one*, had to be shielded from being analyzed in turn. The self-analysis of the founder thus became the keystone of psychoanalytic theory, without which it would immediately collapse in a chaos of rival and undecidable interpretations. To all those, patients or colleagues, who disputed his interpretations, Freud could now oppose his indisputable and rigorously solitary experience of the unconscious. Self-analysis, in this sense, provided the ultimate validation of psychoanalytic theory, in the form of what can only be called an argument from authority. As Ferenczi wrote in the same letter to Freud: "Everyone must be able to tolerate an authority over himself from whom he accepts analytic correction."[85] This authority was Freud.

[85] Ibid.

CHAPTER 3

Sexuality

What does resistance resist? We know Freud's answer: the unveiling of a sexual desire. We remember that from the first formulation of the theme of repression, in his article on the hysterical "counter-will," he evoked the obscenity of the hysterical delusions of nuns or of well-bred young people: what the will "suppresses" and that resurfaces in such an impulsive way in the hysterical "counter-will" is something unacceptable for the conscious ego, and this unacceptable something is first and foremost sexuality.

But which one? It is clear that, at the beginning, Freud speaks of an adult, genital, heterosexual, one could almost say conjugal sexuality. Let's remember that the time when he began to theorize hysteria as a product of repression was also the time when he urged his female patients from Viennese high society to recall under hypnosis things that they "wished to forget, and therefore intentionally repressed from [their] conscious thought and inhibited and suppressed."[1] In the context of this very bourgeois clientele, it is not surprising that he was able to obtain intimate secrets, confessions of illicit desires or of amorous jealousy. From this point of view, *Studies on Hysteria* can be read as a faithful survey of Victorian sexuality. As Breuer bluntly writes in the theoretical part of *Studies on Hysteria*:

> Sexual traumas also occur in the later course of many marriages. The case histories from whose publication we have been obliged to refrain include a great number of them – perverse demands made by the husband, unnatural practices, etc. I do not think I am exaggerating when I assert that the great majority of severe neuroses in women have their origin in the marriage bed.[2]

It was confidences of this type, obtained in the secrecy of the medical practice, that led Breuer and Freud to return to the old sexual theory of

[1] Breuer and Freud 1895, 10. [2] Ibid., 246.

female hysteria (the word comes from the Greek *ustera*, uterus), which was, however, firmly rejected by Charcot and most of the authorities of the time.[3] As for neurasthenia and anxiety neurosis, Freud attributed them equally to a frustrated sexuality – masturbation for the first and interrupted coitus for the second. This is the contrast between what he calls "actual neuroses" (neurasthenia and anxiety neurosis), caused by a "disorder of [the patient's] contemporary sexual life" and whose mechanism is somatic (intoxication by substances of the sexual metabolism), and the "neuro-psychoses of defence" (hysteria, obsessional neurosis, paranoia), caused by "important events in [the patient's] past life" and whose mechanism is psychic.[4] In any case, the sexuality that is incriminated in all these neuroses remains, at the time of *Studies on Hysteria*, an adult and "normal," even if frustrated, repressed, Victorian sexuality.

The Seduction Theory

Things soon evolved, however, under the influence of the method of psychic investigation used by Freud during this period (the *Druckprozedur*). The more he pressed his patients to remember sexual traumas, the more he got. Anna von Lieben (the "Cäcilie M." of *Studies on Hysteria*) found hundreds of them, at an average rate of two per day: "For nearly three years after this she once again lived through all the traumas of her life – long-forgotten, as they seemed to her and, some, indeed, never remembered at all – accompanied by the acutest suffering and by the return of all the symptoms she ever had."[5] And the more the "reminiscences" of the patients accumulated, the more they went back in time. Here again, it seems that it was Anna von Lieben who showed the way. In a letter to August Forel, Breuer retraced the path that had led him and Freud to insist on the role of sexuality in neuroses: "Freud was greatly surprised when ... sexual abnormalities (coit.[us] interrupt.[us], etc.) were with ever greater frequency and certainty found to be the cause ... We were no less doubtful and surprised when analyses of severe cases of hysteria (e.g. of 'Cäcilie M.' in the book) led us further back in childhood."[6]

The implication of this going back in time is obvious: the hysterics had undergone sexual traumas during childhood, *before puberty*. It was, in other words, sexual attacks that had taken place in a "pre-sexual" period. This is the beginning of the famous "seduction theory"

[3] Ibid., note 1. [4] Freud 1896a, 149. [5] Breuer and Freud 1895, 70. [6] Forel 1968, 396.

(*Verführungstheorie*), which would be better called "theory of statutory rape" (this is the meaning of the word *Verführung* in this precise context). It was on October 8, 1895, while he was writing the third part of the *Project*, that Freud formulated it for the first time for his friend Wilhelm Fliess: "I am on the scent of the following strict precondition of hysteria, namely, that a primary sexual experience (before puberty), accompanied by revulsion and fright, must have taken place; for obsessional neurosis, that it must have happened, accompanied by *pleasure*."[7] In both cases, Freud explains, the memory of an event whose meaning was not understood at the time by the child becomes traumatic by deferred action (*nachträglich*) during puberty and therefore gives rise to massive repression.

Please note the expression "I am on the scent": this etiology is still only a hypothesis on the respective roles of displeasure and pleasure in the two neuroses, hysterical and obsessional. But a month later, Freud announces that he has already had a first clinical confirmation of his new theory: "Today I am able to add that one of the cases gave me what I expected (sexual shock – that is, infantile abuse in male hysteria!)."[8] Then things accelerate. Three months later, in his "Further Remarks on the Neuro-Psychoses of Defence" of February 1896, Freud publicly reported no less than thirteen cases of hysteria confirming his new etiology.[9] The lecture "The Aetiology of Hysteria," delivered two months later, brings this number to eighteen cases where, according to Freud, "I have been able to discover this connection in every single symptom, and, where the circumstances allowed, to confirm it by therapeutic success."[10] Freud does not hesitate to generalize: "I therefore put forward the thesis that at the bottom of every case of hysteria there are *one or more occurrences of premature sexual experience*, occurrences which belong to the earliest years of childhood but which can be reproduced through the work of psychoanalysis in spite of the intervening decades."[11]

An additional hypothesis is added the following month: the "presexual sexual shock,"[12] whose posthumous return during puberty provokes the pathological defense, took place in the case of hysteria *before the age of four*. Why is this? Because the hysterical symptom consists of a somatic conversion, and it is therefore necessary to imagine that the traumatic scene dates from a time when it could not be "translated into verbal images."[13] The logical consequence of this conjecture is that the sexual attack must have been particularly perverse, frankly pedophilic, and could only have been

[7] Freud 1985, 141. [8] Ibid., 149. [9] Freud 1896c. [10] Freud 1896b, 199.
[11] Ibid., 203. [12] Freud 1985, 144. [13] Ibid., 188.

perpetrated without arousing the attention by someone in the immediate family circle – a governess or a close relative, *including the father*.

Confirmations were not long in coming. From December 1896 onwards, Freud evoked in rapid succession a whole series of traumatic "scenes" of extreme perversity. It was also on this date that he read and annotated extensively the ninth edition of *Psychopathia Sexualis* by the psychiatrist Richard von Krafft-Ebing (1840–1902), an impressive repertory of deviant forms of sexuality.[14] On January 3, 1897, he wrote to Fliess that the cases described by Krafft-Ebing corroborated his discoveries: "The agreement [of my material] with the perversions described by Krafft[-Ebing] is a new, valuable reality confirmation."[15]

The symmetry is indeed striking. In the letter to Fliess of December 6, 1896, we read the following about a patient: "she remembered in her unconscious a scene in which (at the age of 4) she watched her papa, in the throes of sexual excitement, licking the feet of a wet nurse."[16] A few days later, on December 17, 1896: "Will you believe that the reluctance to drink beer and to shave was elucidated by a scene in which a nurse sits down *podice nudo* [with bare buttocks] in a shallow shaving bowl filled with beer in order to let herself be licked, and so on?"[17] "*Habemus papam*!" Freud exclaims, playing on the Latin: "We have a pope / We have the papa."[18] On January 11, 1897, he discovers that one of his hysterical patients had been abused by his uncle during debaucheries "in some of which his little sister (less than a year old) participated (*beteiligt*)."[19] The next day, he reports that one patient has convulsive attacks because he was subjected to a "*lictus* [licking] (or finger) in the anus" by his governess at the age of two, another because he was subjected to similar treatment by his father before the age of one.[20]

In one of the most astonishing developments of this quest for confirmations, Freud even finds scenes of perversions perpetrated by a secret satanic sect. Some of Krafft-Ebing's remarks having rekindled Freud's interest in the witch-hunts of the Middle Ages,[21] he notices that the accounts of diabolical debauchery extorted by the inquisitors bear an uncanny resemblance to the "scenes" of his patients,[22] and he deduces, by symmetry, that the satanic cults and abuses alleged under torture must also have been *real*. It is on this occasion that he develops for the first time the idea that hysteria is the "negative" (i.e., the inverted, repressed form) of perversion. On January 24, 1897, he writes to Fliess:

[14] Krafft-Ebing 1894. [15] Freud 1985, 219. [16] Ibid., 213. [17] Ibid., 218.
[18] Ibid., 220. [19] Ibid., 222. [20] Ibid., 223. [21] Swales 1983. [22] Freud 1985, 227.

> I am beginning to grasp an idea: it is as though in the perversions, of which hysteria is the negative, we have before us a remnant of a primeval sexual cult (*Sexualkultus*) which once was – perhaps still is – a religion in the Semitic East (Moloch, Astarte). . . . I dream, therefore, of a primeval devil religion whose rites are carried on (*deren Ritus sich . . . fortsezt*) secretly, and understand the harsh therapy of the witches' judges.[23]

Here again, the confirmations pile up. On January 17, 1897, it is one of his most faithful patients, Emma Eckstein, who provides one: "Eckstein has a scene where the diabolus sticks needles into her fingers and then places a candy on each drop of blood."[24] A week later, on January 24, new confirmation: "Imagine, I obtained a scene about the circumcision of a girl. The cutting off of a piece of the labium minor (which is even shorter today), sucking up the blood, after which the child was given a piece of the skin to eat."[25]

Throughout the year 1897, the confirmations follow one another. As the scandalous "paternal etiology"[26] becomes ever more pregnant in his mind, Freud dreams one night that he has incestuous feelings towards his own daughter, Mathilde. He sees this as further proof: "The dream of course shows the fulfillment of my wish to catch a *Pater* [father] as the originator of neurosis and thus puts an end to my ever-recurring doubts."[27] Even his father, Jakob Freud, turns out to be a pedophile: "Unfortunately, my own father was one of these perverts and is responsible for the hysteria of my brother . . . and those of several younger sisters."[28]

Then Freud leaves on vacation. On his return, on September 21, 1897, he announces to Fliess "the great secret that has been slowly dawning on me in the last few months. I no longer believe in my *neurotica* [theory of the neuroses]."[29] Why this sudden and abrupt turnaround, when he had been satisfied until then with the evidence he had obtained? One thing is certain: it is not because Freud had become aware of facts refuting (falsifying) his theory, because nothing could contradict the reality of "scenes" going back to an age before any possible memory (one of them was supposed to have taken place at eleven months[30]). But nothing could corroborate them either and this is what Freud seems to have realized, as if sobered up after a long speculative binge. The reasons he gives in his letter for abandoning his theory are all reasons to *doubt* the confirmations he had been intoxicated with – that is, in no particular order: 1. the absence of infantile scenes in psychoses, where they should in theory surface

[23] Ibid. [24] Ibid., 224–225. [25] Ibid., 227. [26] Ibid., 237. [27] Ibid., 249.
[28] Ibid., 230–231. [29] Ibid., 264. [30] Ibid.

spontaneously because of the absence of defense; 2. the statistical implausibility of the paternal etiology, for how can one admit that there are so many pedophile fathers, "not excluding my own"?;[31] 3. the total absence of conclusive therapeutic results (whereas Freud had publicly stated the opposite); and finally, 4. the impossibility of distinguishing, in the alleged abuses, between "truth and fiction that has been cathected with affect."[32]

This last reason is decisive and shows that Freud must have had doubts from the start, because it was impossible in this situation to distinguish truth from falsehood, reality from fantasy, fact from hypothesis. This is exactly what the internist Adolf von Strümpell (1853–1925) had already pointed out in a "vicious review" of *Studies on Hysteria* that had much irritated Freud:[33] "I cannot suppress my doubts either as to whether what is extracted from hypnotized patients by questioning always correspond to reality. I fear that in these circumstances some hysterics give free rein to their fantasy (*Phantasie*) and invent stories."[34] But now Freud admits that he too has doubts. The unconscious that he tracks down is like that "evil genius, at once exceedingly potent and deceitful" of which Descartes spoke, which ruins all certainty and forces universal doubt.[35] But as in Descartes, it is also in this very doubt that Freud finds his certitude: let the unconscious deceive me as much as it likes; it will never bring it about that it is not, since it *wants* to deceive me. *Ergo*, "fiction that has been cathected with affect" *is*. It is what Freud will soon call the "psychical reality" of the unconscious, distinct from "material reality":

> We are tempted to feel offended at the patient's having taken up our time with invented stories ... It remains a fact that the patient has created these phantasies (*Phantasien*) for himself ... The phantasies possess *psychical* as contrasted with *material reality*, and we gradually learn to understand that *in the world of the neuroses it is psychical reality which is the decisive kind.*[36]

Immediately after having indicated in his letter that "one cannot distinguish between truth and fiction that has been cathected with affect," Freud continues in brackets: "(Accordingly, there would remain the solution that the sexual fantasy invariably seizes upon the theme of the parents.)"[37] This "solution" is obviously the psychoanalysis of maturity, as it emerged from the rubble of the seduction theory. It can be summarized in three points: 1. what are repressed in the unconscious are not real sexual traumas but *fantasies* expressing ("fulfilling") a desire that they take

[31] Ibid. [32] Ibid. [33] Ibid., 170. [34] Strümpell 1896, 160.
[35] Descartes 1644, 76, translation modified. [36] Freud 1916–1917, 367–368.
[37] Freud 1985, 264–265.

place; 2. these fantasies are *Oedipal* and revolve around the parents; 3. they refer to a *perverse infantile sexuality.*

At least this is how Freud always described his abandonment of the seduction theory later on. In his historical-autobiographical recapitulations, he never fails to tell us how he had momentarily taken at face value the memories of sexual abuse and incestuous perversions that his patients reported to him, before realizing that they were in fact fantasies expressing unconscious infantile-Oedipal desires. It is in this reversal that we usually see the inaugural moment of the Freudian "epistemic rupture": first the hysterical deception, then the conceptual reversal that reveals at once the truth of lies, the reality of fiction, the logic of fantasy.

Thus, in "On the History of the Psycho-Analytic Movement":

> Influenced by Charcot's view of the traumatic origin of hysteria, one was readily inclined to accept as true and aetiologically significant the reports made by patients (*Berichte der Kranken*) in which they ascribed their symptoms to passive sexual experiences in the first years of childhood – to put it bluntly, to seduction. When this aetiology broke down under the weight of its own improbability and contradiction in definitely ascertainable circumstances, the result at first was helpless bewilderment . . . If hysterical subjects trace back their symptoms to traumas that are fictitious, then the new fact which emerges is precisely that they create such scenes in phantasy (*phantasieren*), and this psychical reality requires to be taken into account alongside practical reality. This reflection was soon followed by the discovery that these phantasies were intended to cover up the auto-erotic activity of the first years of childhood . . . And now, from behind the phantasies, the whole range of a child's sexual life came to light.[38]

Same account in the autobiographical presentation of 1925:

> Under the influence of the technical procedure which I used at that time, the majority of my patients reproduced (*reproduzierten*) from their childhood scenes in which they were sexually seduced by some grown-up person. With female patients the part of seducer was almost always assigned to their father. I believed these communications (*Mitteilungen*), and consequently supposed that I had discovered the roots of the subsequent neurosis in these experiences of sexual seduction in childhood. . . . When I had pulled myself together, I was able to draw the right conclusions from my discovery: namely, that the neurotic symptoms were not related directly to actual events but to wishful phantasies . . . I had in fact stumbled for the first time upon the Oedipus complex, which was later to assume such an

[38] Freud 1914a, 17–18.

> overwhelming importance, but which I did not recognize as yet in its disguise of phantasy.[39]

This account is well known to all readers of Freud, but its simplicity is deceptive. Now that the full set of letters to Fliess has been published, we can get a better idea of Freud's thought process during this crucial period, as well as its complexity. In particular, it is clear that Freud did not simply *discover* fantasy, the Oedipus, and infantile sexuality as a result of the collapse of the seduction theory, as if it were simply a matter of removing the deceptive veil that had previously concealed them. Not only was Freud already speculating freely on all these themes before the abandonment of *neurotica* (so that his theoretical turnaround is the effect rather than the cause of these new ideas) but these were conjectures and hypotheses that he floated before any corroboration. As Freud wrote to Fliess encouraging him to publish his theories, "even if they are only conjectures": "We cannot do without people who have the courage to think something new before they can demonstrate it."[40]

Fantasy

Let's take fantasy (*Phantasie*). Freud made it an important element of his seduction theory as early as May 1897, at the height of his quest for "scenes" of pedophile abuse. At the beginning, it is only a question of granting the obviously fanciful character of certain scenes, while preserving the reality of the initial scene. These imaginary scenarios that the patients tell (themselves) are fantasies, fictions, fabrications that should be discarded in order to access the real scene, the real memory: "They are protective structures, sublimations of the facts, embellishments of them, and at the same time serve for self-relief."[41] But immediately thereafter, Freud adds something that changes everything: "A second important piece of insight tells me that the psychic structures which, in hysteria, are affected by repression are not in reality memories – since no one indulges in memory activity without a motive – but *impulses* that derive from primal scenes."[42] It is these endogenous impulses (*Impulse*) coming from within the body that are embellished and dramatized by fantasies, rather than the memory of the traumatic irruption of an exogenous sexuality, coming from outside.

39 Freud 1925a, 33–34; see also Freud 1933a, 120. 40 Freud 1985, 155. 41 Ibid., 239.
42 Ibid.

We can see that Freud is already on the point of making fantasy the expression of internal impulses (or to put it better, of drives, *Triebe*), which will obviously be the solution adopted a few months later when the theory of exogenous seduction is abandoned. Moreover, it is in the notes attached to this same letter of May 2, 1897 (Draft L) that Freud puts forward for the first time the idea that the dream is a wish-fulfillment (*Wunscherfüllung*), which will be the central thesis of *The Interpretation of Dreams* published two and a half years later. In passing, he notes shorthand that "the formation of fantasies ... closely resembles the formation of dreams ... A relationship among dreams, fantasies, and reproduction [reliving of scenes by patients]."[43] At the end of the month, Draft N, appended to the letter of May 31, 1897, extends this mechanism to the formation of neurotic symptoms in a dazzling synthesis that renders the *neurotica* obsolete in advance: "Remembering is never a motive but only a way, a method. The first motive for the formation of symptoms is, chronologically, libido [sexual desire, *libido sexualis*]. Thus symptoms, like dreams, are *fulfillments of a wish*."[44]

From a protective fiction interposed between the real pedophile abuse and the symptom, the fantasy has thus become, in a few weeks, the expression (the representation) of a drive, the fulfillment of the sexual desire (libido) that is hidden behind the neurosis. In short, the fantasy is the ultimate "psychical reality" of the unconscious, which Freud will henceforth track down behind dreams, symptoms, bungled actions, slips of the tongue, repetitive behaviors, works of art, and literature.

But what does this psychical reality consist of? *Phantasie*, in German, means imagination in the sense of fantasy, reverie, creation of a world of unreal images. It is therefore a visual phenomenon or appearance ("As sight is the most highly developed sense, the name *phantasia* [imagination] has been formed from *phaos* [light] because it is not possible to see without light"[45]). Even if fantasy sometimes includes auditory elements, it is essentially a visual scene, a waking dream where the subject imagines (itself in) such and such a situation.[46] It is clear that Freud, from the outset, thought of fantasy and dream on the same model. In both cases, in fact, we have visual images in which "a thought, and as a rule a thought of something that is wished, is objectified ... is represented as a scene, or, as it seems to us, is experienced."[47] This is what Freud illustrates in *The Interpretation of Dreams* with the daydream of Mr. Joyeuse, Daudet's poor

[43] Ibid., 242. [44] Ibid., 251. [45] Aristotle 1831–1870, De anima, III, 3, 429a, 1–5.
[46] Freud 1908. [47] Freud 1900, 534.

hero, who while wandering the streets of Paris fantasizes that he has obtained a job and is *presently* at his office: "Thus the dream (*Traum*) makes use of the present tense in the same manner and by the same right as the day-dream (*Tagtraum*). The present tense is the one in which wishes are represented as fulfilled."[48]

In this respect, according to Freud, fantasy and dreams are linked to unconscious primary processes in that they regress to a more immediate, reflex mode of thought, where there is no delay between the wish and its hallucinatory presentation. (Bernheim, in the same way, placed the "faculties of imagination" in which the dream participates on the side of the "cerebral automatism."[49]) We could therefore say that these visual representations are like the very stuff of the unconscious, and indeed this is what Freud will explicitly state in his metapsychological article "The Unconscious," where he distinguishes the "thing-presentation (*Sachvorstellung*)" from the "word-presentation (*Wortvorstellung*)" linked to consciousness: "the conscious presentation comprises the thing-presentation plus the word-presentation belonging to it, while the unconscious presentation is the thing-presentation alone."[50] Or again, in *The Ego and the Id*: "Thinking in pictures . . . stands nearer to unconscious processes than does thinking in words, and it is unquestionably older than the latter both ontogenetically and phylogenetically."[51] What Freud often calls "unconscious thought," "wishful thinking (*Wunschgedanke*)," or "dream-thought (*Traumgedanke*)" is not a thought in the strict sense of the word; it is an image, an imagination.

But then, how to visualize, how to imagine this image if it is unconscious? If it does not appear, does not phenomenologize itself in consciousness? Freud indeed speaks very early on of *unconscious* fantasies, and this is why psychoanalysts sometimes translate *Phantasie* as "phantasm," in order to distinguish it from daydream or subliminal fantasy. Already in Draft N, which dates from the end of May 1897, Freud writes: "Symptom formation by identification is linked to fantasies – that is, to their repression in the Ucs. [unconscious]."[52] It is, of course, these unconscious fantasies – the "primal scene" of parental coitus, the seduction or castration fantasy, the "family romance" of the neurotic, etc. – of which psychoanalysis always speaks, much more than of the innocent daydreams or of the manifest imagery of the night dream. Yet, unlike the latter, unconscious fantasies are invisible. Freud conceives them as wish dreams hidden behind

48 Ibid., 535. 49 Bernheim 1891, 66–68. 50 Freud 1915f, 201, translation modified.
51 Freud 1923b, 21. 52 Freud 1985, 251–252.

the "facade" of the dream or daydream, but the fact is that no one has ever seen them: they are the analyst's constructions, obtained by interpretation of the night or waking dream.

Freud, in this sense, constantly and imperceptibly shifts from one meaning of the word fantasy to another, inviting us to confuse unconscious scenes imagined by him with scenes imagined consciously by the subject. Fantasy is a slippery, amphibological, mixed concept:

> On the one hand, they [the "fantasies of normal people as well as of neurotics"] are highly organized, free from self-contradiction, have made use of every acquisition of the system Cs. and would hardly be distinguished in our judgement from the formations of that system. On the other hand they are unconscious and are incapable of becoming conscious. Thus qualitatively they belong to the system Pcs. [preconscious], but factually to the Ucs. Their origin is what decides their fate. We may compare them with individuals of mixed race who, taken all round, resemble white men, but who betray their coloured descent by some striking feature or other, and on that account are excluded from society and enjoy none of the privileges of white people.[53]

One must, therefore, always ask oneself, when reading Freud, which fantasy is he talking about exactly – the conscious fantasy or the unconscious fantasy? The daydream confessed by the patient or the scenario conjectured by the analyst? The picture formed in the mind's eye or the invisible "other scene"? This question is crucial with regard to Freud's rejection of his seduction theory. After all, what are these fantasies of perverse and/or incestuous abuse whose "psychical reality" he supposedly discovered by abandoning his belief in their "material reality"? Were they conscious? This is what Freud suggests in his historical recapitulations when he writes that he was initially deceived by patients' accounts (*Berichte*), communications (*Mitteilungen*), and invented stories (*erfundenen Geschichte*) of sexual abuse in early childhood. Anyone who reads these famous passages inevitably gets the impression that the patients had misled him by presenting these scenes as memories of real traumatic events, when in fact they were fictions from their *Phantasie*. However, one need only go back to the texts of the time to realize that this is a retrospective simplification of the seduction theory. In reality, far from patients spontaneously confiding in Freud the horrible sexual attacks of which they had been victims, most of the time, they were indignant when *he* evoked such a hypothesis. It was then necessary for him, as he himself stated, to fight

[53] Freud 1915f, 190.

their resistance step by step and to tear out of them "piece by piece" the *unconscious* memory of the sexual scene.

Let us read, for example, the article "The Aetiology of Hysteria": "Before they come for analysis the patients know nothing about these scenes. They are indignant as a rule if we warn them that such scenes are going to emerge. Only the strongest compulsion (*Zwang*) of the treatment can induce them to embark on a reproduction of them."[54] Or again in "Heredity and the Aetiology of the Neuroses":

> how is one to arm oneself against the tendency to lies and the facility of invention which are attributed to hysterical subjects? I should accuse myself of blame-worthy credulity if I did not possess more conclusive evidence. The fact is that these patients never repeat these stories spontaneously, nor do they ever in the course of a treatment suddenly present the physician with the complete recollection of a scene of this kind. One only succeeds in awakening the psychical trace of a precocious sexual event under the most energetic pressure of the analytic procedure, and against an enormous resistance. Moreover, the memory must be extracted from them piece by piece, and while it is being awakened in their consciousness they become the prey to an emotion which it would be hard to counterfeit.[55]

The letters to Fliess from the same period give a very concrete idea of this resistance. Read the description of the case of "Miss G. de B.," a patient whom Freud was trying to convince that she had been forced as a child to perform fellatio on her father:

> When I thrust the explanation at her, she was at first won over; then she committed the folly of questioning the old man himself, who at the very first intimation exclaimed indignantly, "Are you implying that I was the one?" and swore a holy oath to his innocence. She is now in the throes of the most vehement resistance, claims to believe him, but attests to her identification with him by having become dishonest and swearing false oaths. I have threatened to send her away and in the process convinced myself that she has already gained a good deal of certainty which she is reluctant to acknowledge.[56]

In most cases, as Freud would later acknowledge, the patient did not remember the scene, even after he had reconstructed it for him/her: "Indeed, telling and describing his repressed trauma to him did not even result in any recollection of it coming into his mind."[57] And in the few cases where the patients came, "under the most energetic pressure of the

[54] Freud 1896b, 204. [55] Freud 1896a, 153. [56] Freud 1985, 220–221.
[57] Freud 1913b, 141.

analytic procedure," to visualize or "reproduce" (relive) fragments of the scene, they denied them the status of true recollection:

> While they are recalling these infantile experiences to consciousness, they suffer under the most violent sensations . . . and, even after they have gone through them once more in such a convincing manner, they still attempt to withhold belief from them, by emphasizing the fact that, unlike what happens in the case of other forgotten material, they have no feeling of remembering the scenes.[58]

That the patients did not remember spontaneously or even at all the scenes of perversion and incestuous rape that Freud was trying to get them to confess is, of course, consistent with the doctrine he professed about neuroses, both before and after the abandonment of his *neurotica*. An immediate recollection of the repressed cause of the symptoms would have been a complete anomaly and a scathing refutation of the theory. But why, then, did Freud later claim that his patients had brought him their reminiscences on a platter? It must be because it was difficult for him to admit that it was *he* who had imagined/conjectured all these perversions, *he* who had pressed his patients to find them in their unconscious. As he wrote quite candidly in 1925: "I do not believe even now that I forced (*aufgedrängt*) the seduction-fantasies on my patients, that I 'suggested' them."[59] By presenting his own hypotheses and conjectures as spontaneous accounts of the patients, he was, in short, absolving himself of any responsibility in this embarrassing affair. Moreover, and above all, he gave substance and reality to his speculations, despite their erroneous character. Once transformed into fabulations and fantasies of the patients, his interpretations acquired a "psychical reality," instead of returning to the nonexistence of false or falsified ideas. As a result, Freud could now state that he had observed (heard) something rather than nothing.

This is what is usually called the "discovery" of unconscious fantasy, but one may wonder what was actually discovered on this occasion. For if the patients did not spontaneously report *scenes* of seduction, where did Freud ever observe (hear) their *fantasies* of seduction? These so-called unconscious fantasies were just as speculative as the scenes of sexual abuse that Freud postulated earlier. Once one discards the narrative illusion created by Freud's retrospective account, one is forced to conclude that his patients had no more incestuous fantasies than they had memories of sexual abuse. At least, they did not have them consciously "before they came for analysis."

58 Freud 1896b, 204. 59 Freud 1925a, 35.

That they had them unconsciously is, again, an assumption or interpretation that the patients themselves mostly rejected with indignation.

The Oedipus

We remember that Freud, when announcing to Fliess the collapse of his seduction theory, added: "(Accordingly, there would remain the solution that the sexual fantasy invariably seizes upon the theme of the parents)." In other words: instead of accusing the parents, and in particular the father, of monstrous pedophilic acts, let us rather see if it was not the children who wanted to be raped by them. What Freud would later describe as the sudden uncovering of the Oedipus complex once the scales had fallen from his eyes is at first only a theoretical reframing, an ad hoc hypothesis created in order to save the *neurotica* from sinking by modifying its premises (and exonerating its theorist). In reality, Freud had already been thinking for several months about what he called the "family romance," i.e., the set of fantasies revolving around the parents.[60] In Draft N, sent to Fliess at the end of May 1897, we read:

> Hostile impulses against parents (a wish that they should die) are also integrating constituents of neuroses . . . It seems as though this death wish is directed in sons against their fathers and in daughters against their mothers. A maidenservant makes a transference from this by wishing her mistress to die so that her master can marry her. (Observation: Lisel's dream relating to Martha and me.)[61]

This is the very first appearance of the Oedipal theme in Freud's writings, but it should be noted that the "observation" on which Freud bases himself is not an observation at all. It is in fact the *interpretation* of a dream of Lisel, the Freud children's governess, who apparently dreamt that she married her boss after the death of *Frau Professor*. The idea of matricidal desire is introduced by Freud, not by Lisel herself, nor by her dream. It is therefore, at this stage, pure conjecture. The same applies a fortiori to this other fragment of Draft N, in which we see Freud speculating freely on the origin of the incest taboo:

> "Holy" is something based on the fact that human beings, for the benefit of the larger community, have sacrificed a portion of their sexual liberty and their liberty to indulge in perversions. The horror of incest (something impious) is based on the fact that, as a result of communal sexual life (even

[60] Freud 1985, 248. [61] Ibid., 250.

> in childhood), the members of a family remain together permanently and become incapable of joining with strangers. Thus incest is antisocial – civilization consists in this progressive renunciation. Contrariwise, the "Overman."[62]

We have here a lightning anticipation of a theme that Freud will develop many times later in the great "cultural" texts of his maturity, that of the conflict between the Oedipal sexual drives and civilization. As he will repeat in the "Three Essays on the Theory of Sexuality," the child is obliged before puberty to renounce the closest sexual objects because of the "barrier against incest" (*Inzestschranke*), itself required by the social demand of exogamy: "Respect for this barrier is essentially a cultural demand made by society. Society must defend itself against the danger that the interests which it needs for the establishment of higher social units may be swallowed up by the family."[63] However, when he formulates this idea for the first time, Freud is not talking about the incestuous desires of the child but about the antisocial perversion of the paternal "Overman." The theme of Oedipus initially appears in Freud's work through a theorization of the perversion that he still attributes to "seductive" fathers, conceived as the vestige of an endogamous sexuality practiced in a pre-social (pre-civilized) era of the human species. It will be necessary to add to this evolutionary hypothesis that of the recapitulation of phylogenesis (evolution of the species) by ontogenesis (embryogenesis and development of the individual) for the idea to emerge of a perverse and incestuous sexuality *of the child*, contained before puberty by the horror of incest.

What is striking in this first breakthrough of the Oedipal theme is its openly speculative, almost philosophical character. As Freud announces to Fliess in the letter that accompanies Draft N, "I know these are only premonitions ... Another presentiment tells me, as though I already knew – but I know nothing at all – that I shall very soon uncover the source of morality."[64] It is clear that Freud leaves here the field of the clinic and of psychology (even if it is "meta") to embark on vast (meta)biological hypotheses on the evolution of the human species. This is not by chance. The years during which he elaborated the seduction theory were also those during which he was engaged in an intense intellectual collaboration with his friend Fliess, whose theories were expressly biological and evolutionary. Far from seeing Fliess as a mere sounding board for his own hypotheses, Freud was so impressed by his ideas that he hailed him as a "Kepler of

[62] Ibid., 252, translation modified. [63] Freud 1905a, 225. [64] Freud 1985, 249.

biology"[65] from whom he expected the "physiological" foundation of his own psychological theories. On December 4, 1896, precisely when he was engaged in his hunt for the perverted fathers, he wrote to him: "I am dealing with something that cements your work to mine, places my structure on your base."[66]

What base was this? An ear, nose, and throat specialist by training, Fliess was an ambitious theorist, author of articles and books that had earned him a certain recognition from his contemporaries. Having observed a regular swelling of the nasal mucosa during menstruation and, conversely, the disappearance of dysmenorrhea (painful periods) following the cocainization of said mucosa, Fliess postulated a particular reflex relationship between the nose and the female genital apparatus, and, more generally, between the sense of smell and sexuality. This theory was based on phylogenetic considerations, as the sense of smell and sexual attraction were linked, according to Ernst Haeckel, in our animal ancestors.[67] Insofar as he had succeeded in suppressing neurasthenic symptoms in some of his male patients by applying cocaine to the "genital spots," erectile (Freud would soon say "erotogenic") zones of the nasal mucosa, Fliess deduced that the same reflex relationship between the nose and the genital zone existed in men and that neurasthenia had a sexual (masturbatory) etiology – an idea he shared with Freud.

In a book published in 1897 with Freud's encouragement and help,[68] Fliess had amplified these observations into a vast theory on the role of biorhythms in human life that admitted, besides the female menstrual cycle of twenty-eight days, another group of male periodic phenomena recurring every twenty-three days. These two sexual cycles referred phylogenetically to the rhythm of the tides undergone by our ascidian ancestors: "Yes, the wonderful accuracy with which the time of 23 or 28 whole days is kept, allows for the assumption of a deep engagement of astronomical conditions on the creation of organisms."[69]

These cycles coexisted in every individual, according to what Fliess called our "bisexual disposition," taking up an idea already evoked by Darwin about the same ascidians.[70] By this he meant not so much an original sexual duality (hermaphroditism) as a *mono*sexuality that differentiates itself later: "both [periodic processes] are present in *man and woman* – only with different emphasis."[71] The combination of the male and female cycles, which gave rise to all sorts of complicated calculations, was

[65] Ibid., 320. [66] Ibid., 204. [67] Haeckel 1874, 656–657; Bölsche 1926 (1898), 149.
[68] Fliess 1897. [69] Ibid., IV. [70] Darwin 1871, I, 207. [71] Fliess 1897, IV.

supposed to determine all the events of our biological existence, from the day we are born to the day we die, including teething, infantile enuresis, variations in sexual desire, illnesses, migraines, and so on. According to Fliess, the cycles manifested themselves in the form of periodic "thrusts" (*Schübe*) and "drives" or "impulses" (*Triebe*).

Freud took these ideas very seriously. The smallest events in the life of the Freud family, from his wife's menstruation to the fluctuations of his own libido to the death of his father, were interpreted in the light of the Fliessian "periods" and offered to the Berlin friend as confirmations of his theories. Now, as the historian of Darwinism Frank Sulloway[72] has shown, Fliess' biogenetic theory implied not only a kind of vast pansexualism, since the whole of biological existence was punctuated by (bi)sexual cycles, but also the presence of an infantile sexuality insofar as these biorhythms were supposed to be transmitted to the child by the mother from the time of life in utero. Among the periodic phenomena of this type, Fliess listed the spontaneous erections of male babies, the diarrhea accompanying teething, nocturnal enuresis, defecation, as well as the cyclical "impulse" of young children to suck (*Trieb zum Lutschen oder Ludeln*), which he linked to the sucking of the mother's breast and in which he saw an "equivalent of masturbation."[73] As he wrote, all these impulses are in fact "of a sexual nature."[74]

According to Fliess, there was therefore an oral, anal, and urethral infantile sexuality, concentrated on nongenital organic zones: this was the biological foundation on which Freud wanted to place his psychological construction. This explains why he was so interested, during the months preceding the abandonment of the seduction theory, in perverse "impulses" and their phylogenetic origins. This also explains why he ended up scrapping his beloved *neurotica*. The latter was predicated on the idea of a traumatic irruption of adult perverse sexuality in a "presexual", i.e., sexually innocent, childhood. However, such a hypothesis became untenable once one admitted an endogenous infantile sexuality. Freud could not fail to realize this, hence his theoretical reversal. In this sense, we can say that Fliess' biogenetic theory simply shattered Freud's psychogenetic theory. As he was to summarize it later in "My Views on the Part Played by Sexuality in the Aetiology of the Neuroses," "accidental influences have been replaced by constitutional factors and 'defence' in the purely psychological sense has been replaced by *organic* 'sexual

[72] Sulloway 1992. [73] Fliess 1897, 185 n. [74] Ibid., 198.

repression.'"[75] The "impulses," that is to say the drives and instincts inherited from the history of the species, have come to replace the trauma postulated by Charcot.

Following the example of Darwin, who had studied the mental and behavioral development of his son William,[76] Fliess kept a diary in which he observed the day-to-day evolution of his son Robert, born on December 29, 1895. He had noted that the baby had had a spontaneous erection while his mother was naked, about which he had, of course, informed Freud. For his part, Freud complained that he could not carry out an identical investigation on his daughter Anna, born on December 3, 1895, because, he said, "the womanfolk [Martha Freud and the governess] do not support my research."[77] His self-analysis, begun immediately after the announcement of the abandonment of the seduction theory, was to provide him with an opportunity to compensate for this lack of objective data by going back anamnestically to his own childhood.

On October 3–4, 1897, Freud informed Fliess of the first results of his introspective investigation. His "prime originator" of neurosis and "teacher in sexual matters" had been an old woman who took care of him as a baby, and above all:

> the old man [Freud's father] plays no active part in my case . . . then later (between two and two and a half years old) my libido toward *matrem* was awakened, namely, on the occasion of a journey with her from Leipzig to Vienna, during which we must have spent the night together and there must have been an opportunity of seeing her *nudam* (you inferred the consequences of this for your son long ago, as a remark revealed to me).[78]

Here, then, Freud opportunely finds in his early childhood something to confirm the theory of his friend. The "little hysteria" he complained about was not due to his father's perversion but to his own incestuous libido. Note, however, the conjectural nature of this confirmation: Freud does not say that he remembers seeing his mother naked and having an erection but only that the occasion "must" have presented itself. In other words, things *must* have taken place as Fliess' theory predicted.

However, two weeks later, Freud already made a striking generalization: "A single idea of general value dawned on me. I have found, in my own case too, [the phenomenon of] being in love with my mother and jealous of my father, and I now consider it a universal event in early childhood."[79] The proof being the universal effect produced by the tragedy *Oedipus Rex*:

[75] Freud 1906, 278, my emphasis. [76] Darwin 1877. [77] Freud 1985, 230. [78] Ibid., 268.
[79] Ibid., 272.

> If this is so, we can understand the gripping power of *Oedipus Rex* . . . the Greek legend seizes upon a compulsion which everyone recognizes because he senses its existence within himself. Everyone in the audience was once a budding Oedipus in fantasy (*Phantasie*), and each recoils in horror from the dream fulfillment here transplanted into reality, with the full quantity of repression which separates his infantile state from his present one.[80]

The Oedipus complex is now in place, as well as the program of psychoanalysis "applied" to art and literature, as Freud immediately follows up with a comparison between Sophocles' play and Shakespeare's *Hamlet.* "Hamlet the hysteric," who hesitates to avenge his father by killing the man who, by means of murder, took the place by his mother's side, is like the inhibited negative of the perverse Oedipus who kills his father and marries his mother. He is the product of Shakespeare's *repressed* fantasy: literature is a variant (distorted, sublimated, socially acceptable) of the universal Sophoclean scenario.

Three years later, in *The Interpretation of Dreams*, the universality of incestuous and patricidal "psychical impulses" is presented as an established fact, based on Freud's "experience, which is already extensive" and corroborated by the Greek legend.[81] Did Freud, meanwhile, receive confirmation of his hypothesis from certain patients? It is possible. But insofar as these Oedipal fantasies would have been obtained using the same method that Freud had already used to obtain "scenes" of incestuous attacks, one does not see why they would be more conclusive than those. The truth is that the theory of the Oedipus complex was not the product of an inductive generalization from clinical observations and spontaneous confessions of patients. As the chronology of the correspondence shows, it was an a priori synthesis of highly speculative ideas inspired by Fliess' biogenetic theories, which Freud then "confirmed" in his self-analysis with the help of an interpretation of two works of literature, before then finding them universally in the dreams and symptoms of his patients.

This is what Karl Popper called, with great cruelty, the "Oedipus effect":

> Those "clinical observations" which analysts naïvely believe confirm their theory cannot do this any more than the daily confirmations which astrologers find in their practice. [Footnote:] Years ago I introduced the term "*Oedipus effect*" to describe the influence of a theory or expectation or prediction *upon the event which it predicts* or describes: it will be remembered that the causal chain leading to Oedipus' parricide was started by the oracle's prediction of this event.[82]

[80] Ibid. [81] Freud 1900, 260 ff. [82] Popper 1963, 37–38.

Infantile Sexuality

The same applies to the "discovery" of infantile sexuality. Freud, in his later recapitulations, tells us that this sexuality "came to light" once he understood that the scenes of perversion alleged by his patients were in fact wishful fantasies expressing drives dating from childhood. But Freud, as we have seen, had already been convinced by Fliess of the existence of an endogenous infantile sexuality *before* the abandonment of the seduction theory, so that the collapse of the latter is rather the effect of the new theoretical insight than its cause.

On December 6, 1896, nearly a year before the formal abandonment of *neurotica*, Freud announced to Fliess that the specific cause of hysteria was a *perverse* sexual attack:

> It seems to me more and more that the essential point of hysteria is that it results from *perversion* on the part of the seducer, and *more and more* that heredity is seduction by the father. Thus an alternation emerges between generations:
>
> 1st generation – perversion
> 2nd generation – hysteria, and consequent sterility
>
> ... Accordingly, hysteria is not repudiated sexuality but rather *repudiated perversion.*[83]

Hysteria is the daughter of perversion in that it is its negative, its repression.

We can see that under the theme of the father's perversion, that of the child's "inherited" perversion is already pointing. This is confirmed in the following paragraph, in direct reference to Fliess' "periods" and "genital spots" (in other words, erotogenic zones):

> Furthermore, behind this lies the idea of abandoned *erotogenic zones*. That is to say, during childhood, sexual release (*sexuelle Entbindung*) would seem to be obtainable from a great many parts of the body, which at a later date are able to release only the 28[-day, feminine] anxiety substance and not the others. In this differentiation and limitation [would thus lie] progress in culture, and moral as well as individual development.[84]

In this crucial and visibly speculative passage, Freud tries to explain in a biogenetic (Fliessian) way the psychological phenomenon of repression postulated by him at the level of the clinic of neuroses. For, in fact, why is sexuality repressed if it is at the very foundation of all life? Why does it

[83] Freud 1985, 212. [84] Ibid.

trigger anguish and not pleasure once puberty arrives? From an evolutionary point of view, Freud could no longer be satisfied with appealing to moral and social prohibitions, as he had done until then. It was still necessary to explain these prohibitions in a socio*biological* way, by rooting them in the evolutionary history of the species. It is to this requirement that corresponds the explanation outlined by Freud: sexuality is repressed because it is originally perverse and emanates from nongenital bodily zones that have been abandoned in the course of the evolution of the species.

To understand this quasi-shorthand reasoning, one must understand that Freud, here as elsewhere, implicitly relies on Ernst Haeckel's famous "biogenetic law," of which he and Fliess were fervent advocates. According to this theory that was extremely influential at the time but has since been largely discredited,[85] the individual development (ontogenesis) of an organism from embryo to adulthood recapitulates in abbreviated form the development of the species (phylogenesis), passing through stages representing the ancestral species. This theory was commonly used in the most diverse fields – anthropology, sociology, criminology, child psychology – to justify all sorts of racial and social prejudices. As the British sexologist Havelock Ellis (1859–1939) explained, for example, the human baby goes through all the stages of humanity in its conquest of the erect posture: "The apes are but imperfect bipeds, with tendencies towards the quadrupedal attitude; the human infant is as imperfect a biped as the ape; savage races do not stand so erect as civilized races. Country people . . . tend to bend forward, and the aristocrat is more erect than the plebeian."[86]

It is to this recapitulation of the "inferior" (low) by the "superior" (high) that Freud alludes when he speaks of abandoned erotogenic zones. As he would write much later in his *Introductory Lectures on Psychoanalysis*, referring to *Love-Life in Nature* by the evolutionary popularizer Wilhelm Bölsche (1861–1919):

> In the case of the development of the libido, [its] phylogenetic origin is, I venture to think, immediately obvious. Consider how in one class of animals the genital apparatus is brought into the closest relation to the mouth, while in another it cannot be distinguished from the excretory apparatus, and in yet others it is linked to the motor organs – all of which you will find attractively set out in W. Bölsche's valuable book. Among animals one can find, so to speak in petrified form, every species of perversion of the sexual organization.[87]

[85] Gould 1977. [86] Ellis 1894, 59. [87] Freud 1916–1917, 354.

(Bölsche, whose book seems to have been an important source of inspiration for Freud, explained for example that the "pederast" is a "zoological reactionary" who "returns to the platypus."[88])

We can better understand now in what sense Freud links repression to the abandonment of erotogenic zones. The repression that occurs in the individual development repeats the abandonment, during the development of the species, of previous forms of sexuality. Behind the psychological repression and "progress in culture, and moral as well as individual development," there is a biological, *organic* repression, which Freud calls elsewhere "primal." We remember that Freud will say it very clearly in "My Views on the Part Played by Sexuality in the Aetiology of the Neuroses," at the moment of evoking the consequences of the abandonment of the seduction theory: "accidental influences have been replaced by constitutional factors, and 'defence' in the purely psychological sense has been replaced by *organic* 'sexual repression.'"[89]

One month after the first mention of the "abandoned erotogenic zones," on January 11, 1897, Freud continues his reasoning by focusing on the nose, an erotogenic zone dear to Fliess:

> Perversions regularly lead to zoophilia and have an animal character ... In this connection one recalls that the principal sense in animals (for sexuality as well) is that of smell, which has been reduced in human beings. As long as smell (or taste) is dominant, urine, feces, and the whole surface of the body, also blood, have a sexually exciting effect.[90]

In short, if perversions are so bestial, it is because they are, so to speak, arrested at the sexuality of the sniffing animal from which we all descend.

However, it was not until the final abandonment of the seduction theory that Freud tied all these themes together in a triumphant "synthesis"[91] that he sent to Fliess on November 14, 1897. It is worth quoting this passage at some length, because of its absolutely decisive, founding character:

> I have often had a suspicion that something organic plays a part in repression; I was able once before to tell you that it was a question of the abandonment of former sexual zones ... the notion was linked to the changed part played by sensations of smell: upright walking, nose raised from the ground, at the same time a number of formerly interesting sensations attached to the earth becoming repulsive – by a process still unknown to me. (He turns up his nose = he regards himself as something

[88] Bölsche 1898–1903, Volume 2, 260–261; see Amouroux 2004.
[89] Freud 1906, 278, my emphasis. [90] Freud 1985, 223. [91] Ibid., 281.

> particularly noble.) Now, the zones which no longer produce a release of sexuality (*Sexualentbindung*) in normal and mature human beings must be the region of the anus and of the mouth and throat. This is to be understood in two ways: first, that seeing and imagining these zones no longer produce an exciting effect, and second, that the internal sensations arising from them make no contribution to the libido, the way the sexual organs proper do. In animals these sexual zones continue in force in both respects; if this persists in human beings too, perversion results. We must assume that in infancy the release of sexuality is not yet so much localized as it is later, so that the zones which are later abandoned (and perhaps the whole surface of the body as well) also instigate something that is analogous to the later release of sexuality.[92]

A little further on, regarding the memory of a perverse sexual attack: "in the same manner as we turn away our sense organ [the head and nose] in disgust, the preconscious and the sense of consciousness turn away from the memory. This is *repression*."[93] Thirty-three years later, Freud will take up exactly the same reasoning in *Civilization and Its Discontents*, this time regarding the taboo of menstruation and the depreciation of excrements imposed by education: "Such a reversal of values would scarcely be possible if the substances that are expelled from the body were not doomed by their strong smells to share the fate which overtook olfactory stimuli after man adopted the erect posture. Anal eroticism, therefore, succumbs in the first instance to the 'organic repression' which paved the way to civilization."[94]

In short, the child goes through a perverse phase during its development, during which the sexual zones abandoned during the evolution of the species continue to produce sensations analogous to adult sexuality, until this infantile sexuality comes up against the sensations of disgust inherited from the upright position of Homo erectus and becomes the object of an organic repression, itself "the affective basis for a multitude of intellectual processes of development, such as morality, shame and the like. Thus the whole of this arises at the expense of extinct (virtual) sexuality," in the form of "successive thrusts in development" (*Entwicklungsschübe*) whose chronology differs in boys and girls.[95] Indeed, whereas the libido of the boy concentrates directly on the genital zone at puberty, the girl must still pass, according to Freud, by an additional organic repression and abandon her "masculine" clitoral zone to the benefit of the "feminine"

92 Ibid., 279. 93 Ibid., 280.

94 Freud 1930, 100; see also session of November 17, 1909 of the Vienna Psychoanalytic Society, Nunberg and Federn 1967.

95 Freud 1985, 280.

vaginal zone. (This last hypothesis, which many have attributed to Victorian prejudices, corresponds in fact to the Fliessian theory of the constitutive bisexuality of the two sexes: at the beginning, there is only one sex.)

From there, several possibilities of development present themselves. Either the organic repression of the perverse infantile (bi)sexuality operates normally, and the individual reaches genital heterosexuality. Or the organic repression fails for one reason or another, in which case the individual remains, so to speak, arrested at this or that perversion – sexual "inversion," anal or urethral eroticism, etc. Or the organic repression is well established, but the memory of an infantile experience concerning the anus or the mouth, etc., requires additional ("secondary," "deferred") repression, in which case the libido "is obliged to proceed in a *regressive* direction (as happens in dreams),"[96] and the result will be a neurosis. To which Freud adds that "the choice of neurosis – the decision whether hysteria or obsessional neurosis emerges – depends on the nature of the thrust (that is to say, its chronological placing)" in the ontogenetic recapitulation of phylogenesis (an idea that will later find a grandiose development in the *Overview of the Transference Neuroses* of 1915[97]).

"Three Essays on the Theory of Sexuality"

We have here, without exception, all the elements of the theory developed seven years later in the "Three Essays on the Theory of Sexuality." As is well known, it was in this famous work, which was initially to be entitled *Human Bisexuality* and which Freud offered Fliess to co-write with him, that Freud first publicly put forward the idea of a polymorphous perverse infantile sexuality. In summary:

- Human sexuality cannot be reduced to heterosexual copulation. As adult perversions show, the sexual drive can perfectly well be directed towards another "object" than the opposite sex (homosexuality, pedophilia, zoophilia) and have another "aim" than genital union (sodomy, cunnilingus, fellatio, exhibitionism, voyeurism, urolagnia, fetishism, coprophilia, sadism, masochism, etc.).
- If it is so, it is because human sexuality is originally perverse and becomes genital-heterosexual only at puberty. From the first months, the child derives a properly sexual pleasure from "erotogenic zones" of

[96] Ibid., 281. [97] Freud 1915c, 9 ff.

the body from which emanates a tension (a "drive," *Trieb*) that it discharges by way of masturbatory type, "auto-erotic" stimulation ("auto-erotism" is a term borrowed from Havelock Ellis, with whom Freud had begun a correspondence in 1898).

- Among these "sources" of the drive, Freud mentions in particular the oral zone, which the child stimulates-satisfies by way of voluptuous sucking (*Lutschen*, *Ludeln*), or the anal and urethral zones that it stimulates-satisfies by way of retention of the fecal mass or urine followed by excretion (enuresis). But any bodily zone (skin, mucous membrane, musculature) can be the source of a "partial drive," this one first "attaching" itself to a vital function/drive to then deviate from it sexually – miction leading to genital masturbation, the scopic drive (*Schautrieb*) leading to voyeurism, the drive for mastery (*Bemächtigungstrieb*) leading to sadism, etc. Infantile sexuality is not only perverse-deviant but also polymorphous-anarchic.
- This sexuality is also bisexual, in the sense that the auto-erotic activity is the same in boys and girls. The masturbation of the little girl, for example, is exclusively clitoral, "masculine," and only becomes properly "feminine" when the clitoral zone is abandoned-repressed in favor of the vaginal zone at puberty (here, in the 1905 edition, Freud significantly adds: "Since I have become acquainted with [Wilhelm Fliess'] notion of bisexuality, I have regarded it as the decisive factor, and without taking bisexuality into account, I think it would scarcely be possible to arrive at an understanding of the sexual manifestations that are actually to be observed in men and women."[98]).
- Auto-erotic, infantile sexuality is nevertheless not completely without an external object: "A child's intercourse with anyone responsible for his care affords him an unending source of sexual excitation and satisfaction from his erotogenic zones,"[99] hence the uniform appearance of "sexual impulses towards its parents, which are as a rule already differentiated owing to the attraction of the opposite sex – the son being drawn towards his mother and the daughter towards her father."[100] Infantile sexuality is incestuous.
- Around the fifth year, this phase of pregenital sexual activity is followed by a "period of sexual latency" (a term that Freud declares in a footnote to have borrowed from Fliess) during which sexuality seems to die out. In reality, the energy of the partial drives is diverted, by a process called "sublimation," to the benefit of "the mental forces which are later to

[98] Freud 1905a, 220. [99] Ibid., 223. [100] Ibid., 227.

impede the course of the sexual instinct and, like dams, restrict its flow – disgust, feelings of shame and the claims of aesthetic and moral ideals. One gets an impression from civilized children that the construction of these dams is a product of education, and no doubt education has much to do with it. But in reality this development is organically determined and fixed by heredity, and it can occasionally occur without any help at all from education. Education will not be trespassing beyond its appropriate domain if it limits itself to following the lines which have already been laid down organically and to impressing them somewhat more clearly and deeply."[101] Among other dams erected during this latency period, the "barrier against incest" prevents sexual drives from continuing to be directed towards the parent of the same sex, thus favoring exogamy and the creation of social units larger than the incestuous family unit.[102]

- At the time of puberty, one attends a return in force of the libido, but channeled this time by the socio-organic "dams" towards the heterosexual object in view of the sexual reproduction. On the one hand, the partial-perverse drives are unified under the primacy of the genital-copulatory goal: the voluptuous tension obtained from the former erogenous zones now serves as "fore-pleasure" (*Vorlust*) to the "end-pleasure" (*Endlust*) provoked by the "discharge/draining" (*Entleerung*) of sexual substances[103] (one will note, here again, the hydraulic metaphor, as well as the very masculine character of this description of sexual pleasure). On the other hand, the incestuous object of the infantile libido is replaced by another object (another person) that resembles it.
- This normal evolution of the libido can undergo all sorts of vicissitudes and developmental arrests. The "organic repression" of the latency period can fail or this or that partial drive proves to be stronger than the "dams" of disgust and shame, in which case we have a frank perversion: the pervert is a sexual fossil who has remained "fixed" at a stage normally out of date in evolution (this is what Darwin called an "arrest of development"). Or else the genital libido is frustrated for one reason or another, in which case it refluxes (regresses) to a previous perverse stage and requires increased, pathogenic repression: this is the neurosis as a "negative of perversion." The neurotic is a sexual fossil that ignores itself (an idea nowhere to be found in Darwin and other evolutionary thinkers).

[101] Ibid., 177. [102] Ibid., 225. [103] Ibid., 210.

Sexual Biology

In later editions of the *Three Essays*, Freud would make all sorts of additions and modifications to this description of human sexuality over the course of his multiple theoretical reworkings: subdivision of the pregenital phase into oral-cannibalistic, sadistic-anal, and phallic phases; addition of a "castration complex" and of a "penis envy" (in girls); differentiation of an ego-(narcissistic)libido and of an object-libido. However, if we stick for the moment to the state of the theory presented in 1905, it is clear that it is a very faithful amplification of the hypotheses shared with Fliess during the years 1896–1897 – the child's (bi)sexual "thrusts" and "drives" or "impulses," their pregenital and incestuous character, the "organic repression" of animal erotogenic zones, etc. At the foundation of the Freudian theory of sexuality, there is the metabiological speculation of the Fliess years.

If it took so long to realize this, it is partly because Freud's first readers could not have been aware of his correspondence with Fliess (it only appeared, in a largely truncated form, in 1950), but also because he presented his theory as the fruit of his clinical experience. In the preface to the third edition (1914), we read that "the exposition to be found in the following pages is based entirely upon everyday medical observation," to which Freud adds, after evoking Haeckel's biogenetic law:

> I must, however, emphasize that the present work is characterized not only by being completely based upon psycho-analytic research but also by being deliberately independent of the findings of biology. I have carefully avoided introducing my scientific anticipations (*wissenschaftliche Erwartungen*), whether derived from general sexual biology or from that of particular animal species, into this study – a study which is concerned with the sexual functions of human beings and which is made possible through the technique of psycho-analysis. Indeed, my aim has rather been to discover how far psychological investigation can throw light upon the biology of the sexual life of man.[104]

In private, Freud was even more explicit. To his Berlin disciple Karl Abraham (1877–1925), who maintained relations with Fliess despite the rupture between them, Freud wrote: "The subjection of our Ψα [psychoanalysis] to a Fliessian sexual biology would be no less a disaster than its subjection to any system of ethics, metaphysics, or anything of the sort."[105]

[104] Ibid., 130–131, translation modified.

[105] Freud and Abraham 2002, 229.

We must understand, however, that the "everyday medical observation[s]" to which Freud refers were anything but empirical observations. Unlike Darwin and other evolutionary researchers such as James Mark Baldwin (1861–1934) or William Preyer (1841–1897), Freud did not study the day-to-day development of his own children. As he himself explains in several places, his theory of sexuality was based on "psycho-analytic observations"[106] made on neurotic adults: "When the account which I have given above of infantile sexuality was first published in 1905, it was founded for the most part on the results of psycho-analytic research upon adults."[107] It was, in other words, results obtained by way of interpretation and construction, as Freud explicitly states in the twentieth *Introductory Lecture on Psycho-Analysis*: "You yourselves will easily perceive that the sexual activities of infants in arms are mostly a matter of interpretation ... These interpretations are arrived at on the basis of analytic examinations made by tracing from the symptoms backwards."[108] Or again, one lecture further on: "It was only with the help of the psycho-analytic investigation of the neuroses that it became possible to discern the still earlier phases of the development of the libido. These are nothing but constructions, to be sure, but, if you carry out psycho-analyses in practice, you will find that they are necessary and useful constructions."[109]

But why, after all, is it necessary to proceed in this way? Why can't we observe children directly or rely on the testimony of nonneurotic adults about their first sexual stirrings? (This was the method used by Havelock Ellis, for example, and by Freud himself at the time of his brief self-analysis.) To this question, Freud always answered by invoking the impossibility of accessing the early years because of infantile amnesia, a phenomenon that he explained by the repression of perverse sexuality that occurred at the time of the latency period: "There can, therefore, be no question [in infantile amnesia] of any real abolition of the impressions of childhood, but rather of an amnesia similar to that which neurotics exhibit for later events, and of which the essence consists in a simple withholding of these impressions from consciousness, viz., in their repression."[110]

But we, who have at our disposal the correspondence with Fliess, now know that this organic repression that was supposed to occur around the fifth year was itself a hypothetical construction on Freud's part, so that the justification of an indirect approach to infantile sexuality rests once again on a circular reasoning. The necessity of psychoanalytic retrodiction is

[106] Freud 1905a, 130. [107] Ibid., 193. [108] Freud 1916–1917, 313. [109] Ibid., 326.
[110] Freud 1905a, 175.

based on a construction that presupposes what is to be proved, namely, the presence of a perverse sexuality from the first months of life. For without the hypothesis of an organic repression, there would, of course, be nothing to repress, nor anything to interpret either. Here, as elsewhere, the repression scheme allowed Freud to legitimize the psychoanalytical interpretation by evoking the existence of "things hidden since the foundation of the world" (Matthew 13:35), where there was perhaps simply nothing.

The idea of a perverse-polymorphous infantile sexuality, suggestive as it is, was not the product of clinical observations patiently gathered by the researcher. What we have in fact are results obtained thanks to interpretations of dreams and neurotic symptoms, themselves based on biological speculations that preceded and oriented them from the beginning. Freud thus reverses the *ordo cognoscendi* when he states in "The Claims of Psycho-Analysis to Scientific Interest": "We have found it necessary to hold aloof from biological considerations during our psycho-analytic work and to refrain from using them for heuristic purposes, so that we may not be misled in our impartial judgement of the psycho-analytic facts before us."[111] It is not for nothing that Freud was hailed in his time as the "Darwin of the mind":[112] psychoanalysis is a "cryptobiology,"[113] a biology that takes on the guise of clinical psychology in order to better conceal its highly speculative character. Above all, let it not be said that all this could be nothing but a biological philosophy or metaphysics – a *Naturphilosophie*!

This goes to the heart of the strange and at the time very scandalous Freudian theory of sexuality. For in the end, on what basis does Freud characterize the "organ pleasure" obtained by the child from certain bodily areas and functions as a *sexual* pleasure? On what grounds does he compare the infant's satiation at the breast to an "orgasm" and the sucking of the thumb to masturbation?[114] In what way is the painful sensation resulting from the accumulation of the fecal mass in the anal area a "voluptuous sensation" (*Wolllustempfindung*[115]) comparable to that of penetration by the penis?[116] Why would the bed-wetting of children be a form of onanistic "nocturnal emission"?[117] Freud himself asks the question in the twenty-first *Introductory Lecture on Psycho-Analysis*, but the only answer he gives in the end is that adults can derive erotic pleasure from these oral, anal, or urethral zones, and that there is therefore nothing to prevent us

111 Freud 1913a, 181–182. 112 Jones 1913, xii. 113 Ibid. 114 Freud 1905a, 180.
115 Ibid., 186, translation modified. 116 Freud 1917b, 131. 117 Freud 1905a, 190.

from extending "the description of being 'sexual' to the activities of early childhood, too, which strive for organ-pleasure."[118]

The real reason is elsewhere, as we have seen. If these areas and these organ pleasures are qualified as sexual, it is because such was the implication of Fliess' theories on the periodic "thrusts" of sexuality in the small child and those of Freud on the ontogenetic recapitulation of forms of sexuality abandoned during the evolution of the species. Only Haeckel's biogenetic law ultimately justifies the description of the child as a bestial adult. Far from being based on empirical investigation, the Freudian theory of sexuality was the product of deduction from abstract metabiological principles, which Freud then confirmed by means of a clinical method that allowed no verification or refutation since any objection or contradictory data was automatically interpreted as resistance or as the effect of an ancestral repression. If it is true, as Freud writes, that "psycho-analysis stands or falls with the recognition of the sexual partial drives, of the erotogenic zones and of the extension thus made possible of the concept of a 'sexual function' in contrast to the narrower 'genital function,'"[119] then this theory that has exerted such a great influence in the course of the twentieth century is very literally *improbable*, unprovable.

"Little Hans" and the Castration Complex

Freud would have protested vigorously, of course. In his later recapitulations of the theory of sexuality presented in the *Three Essays*, he never fails to point out that it had been confirmed after the fact by the observation of young children. He congratulated himself on this as early as 1910 in a note added to the second edition: "It is gratifying to be able to report that direct observation has fully confirmed the conclusions arrived at by psycho-analysis – which is incidentally good evidence of the trustworthiness of that method of research."[120] And in the twentieth *Introductory Lecture on Psycho-Analysis*, after having recalled that the interpretation of neurotic symptoms regularly led back to infantile sexuality: "What we inferred from these analyses was later confirmed point by point by direct observations of children."[121] Far from speculating in a vacuum, psychoanalysis would therefore have successfully conformed to the most rigorous hypothetical-deductive approach: first one formulates heuristic hypotheses (Mach's

[118] Freud 1916–1917, 324. [119] Freud 1913c, 323, translation modified.
[120] Freud 1905a, 193. [121] Freud 1916–1917, 310.

"provisional fictions"), then one tries to confirm/disprove them through observation or experimentation.

The "direct observation" to which Freud refers is that of the famous "little Hans," the involuntary subject of the "Analysis of a Phobia in a Five-Year-Old Boy."[122] "Hans" was actually four and a half years old at the time of this analysis, and his real name was Herbert Graf. His parents, Olga Hönig and the musicologist Max Graf, were both aficionados of psychoanalysis, the former as a patient, the latter as a disciple and fellow traveler. After the publication of the *Three Essays*, Freud had asked his students with young children to gather data that would confirm his theories on infantile sexuality (in short, to do what he himself had neglected to do during the Fliess years). Max Graf was particularly well placed for this task, and so he conscientiously informed Freud of the slightest signs of erotic activity in his son, born on April 10, 1903.

In his 1907 article "The Sexual Enlightenment of Children," Freud mentioned "a delightful little boy, now four years old" whose understanding parents did not repress (and no doubt encouraged) the expression of his sexuality. Now, this "little Herbert" was already showing a keen interest in his "widdler" (*Wiwimacher*) and in that of the people around him before he was three years old. Herbert, Freud noted, was not, however, "a sensual child or at all pathologically disposed. The fact is simply, I think, that, not having been intimidated or oppressed with a sense of guilt, he gives expression quite ingenuously to what he thinks."[123] The idea was therefore that one could have *direct* access to infantile sexuality, before its amnesiac repression during the latency period. The sexual truth comes out of the mouths of babes; all it takes is for adults not to hinder its expression.

In the "Analysis of a Phobia in a Five-Year-Old Boy," where Freud takes up and amplifies these first observations, he specifies that Herbert (renamed "Hans" for the occasion) generously attributed a widdler to all the animals and human beings around him, including his mother and his little sister Hanna. Moreover, his interest in the subject was accompanied by repeated touching of said widdler: "When he was three and a half, his mother found him with his hand on his penis. She threatened him in these words: 'If you do that, I shall send for Dr. A[dler] to cut off your widdler.'"[124] This, then, is the humble starting point of what Freud will universalize fifteen years later under the name of "phallic phase," supposed to insert itself between the oral and anal stages and the latency period. During this sexual stage, the child "knows only one kind of genital: the

[122] Freud 1909. [123] Freud 1907a, 135. [124] Freud 1909, 7.

male one,"[125] and as a consequence, the child enters into the orbit of the "castration complex," the little boy fearing to be castrated and the little girl being distressed at having already been (penis envy).

But we are not there yet. In 1908, when he collates these observations that Max Graf forwards to him, Freud is content with stating that little Herbert was going through a homosexual – meaning *mono*sexual or, more exactly, bisexual with a male dominance – phase: "Hans was a homosexual (as all children may very well be), quite consistently with the fact, which must always be kept in mind, that *he was acquainted with only one kind of genital organ* – a genital organ like his own."[126]

All this is, of course, consistent with the theory put forward in 1905 in the *Three Essays* and before that in the letters to Fliess: boys and girls are originally bisexual and their auto-erotic and masturbatory manifestations have a uniformly masculine character, the erotogenic zone of the girls being first of all located in this miniature penis that is the clitoris.[127] In this sense, the naive phallocentrism professed by little Herbert seemed to confirm the Freudo-Fliessian theory of bisexuality. (The primacy of the phallus in psychoanalysis is the direct heir of this biological postulate: as Freud wrote again in 1924, quoting Karl Abraham, phallocentrism "has a biological prototype in the embryo's undifferentiated genital disposition, which is the same for both sexes."[128]) Moreover, the confirmation thus provided was indeed based on "direct observations" of the little Herbert, even if one can obviously think that the latter's "infantile sexual theory" was in fact due to his ignorance of sexual facts rather than to a hypothetical homo- and/or bisexuality.

On the other hand, the same cannot be said of the rest of the case history, which is based not on observations but on *interpretations* of the child's behavior and statements. It is not for nothing that the title chosen by Freud is "Analysis of a Phobia in a Five-Year-Old Boy": whereas the "little Herbert" of the article "The Sexual Enlightenment of Children" was expressly described as a happy and not "pathologically disposed" child, the "little Hans" of the case history is presented, on the contrary, as a "very youthful *patient*" suffering from an infantile neurosis.[129] What had happened between the two essays to explain such a reversal?

One day when Herbert and his father were in the public garden, Herbert was frightened by a horse-drawn carriage that was stopped in

[125] Freud 1905a, 200 (footnote added in 1924). [126] Freud 1909, 110.
[127] Freud 1905a, 220 ff. [128] Ibid., 200 (footnote added in 1924).
[129] Freud 1909, 5, my emphasis.

front of the park entrance. Max Graf did not pay much attention to this,[130] but soon afterwards, at the beginning of 1908, Herbert did not want to leave the house because he was afraid that one of the many horses trotting through the streets of Vienna would bite him.[131] As Graf was to learn three months later from his son, this fear was in fact the result of an omnibus accident that Herbert had witnessed, in which a horse had fallen over backwards with a loud roar of neighing and hooves hitting the pavement. Stenographic transcript of April 5, 1908:

I: "You had your nonsense already at that time?" (This was how, at Freud's suggestion, father and son had agreed to call the fear of horses.)
HANS: "No. I only got it then. When the horse in the bus fell down, it gave me such a fright, really! That was when I got the nonsense."
I: "But the nonsense was that you thought a horse would bite you. And now you say you were afraid a horse would fall down."
HANS: "Fall down and bite."
I: "Why did it give you such a fright?"
HANS: "Because the horse went like this with its feet. (He lay down on the ground and showed me how it kicked about.) It gave me a fright because it made a row with its feet."[132]

So Herbert had excellent reasons to fear horses, and his anxiety was no more "nonsensical" than those of countless other children terrorized by dogs, wasps, or storms. As for his fear of being bitten by a horse, it referred to an episode from the previous summer. Max Graf's transcript of March 1, 1908: "'When Lizzi had to go away, there was a cart with a white horse in front of her house, to take her luggage to the station.' (Lizzi, he tells me, was a little girl who lived in a neighboring house.) Her father was standing near the horse, and the horse turned its head round (to touch him), and he said to Lizzi: '*Don't put your finger to the white horse or it'll bite you.*'"[133] All the more reason to run away from these dangerous animals and to stay nice and warm at home and cuddle with his mother.[134] From the point of view of a four-and-a-half-year-old boy, this avoidance strategy was perfectly rational.

For Freud and Graf, on the other hand, there was no doubt: it was a *phobia*, in other words, a hysterical symptom that must necessarily hide some repressed desire. One could no longer be satisfied with leaving the field open to the child's naive speech, as in the 1907 article "The Sexual Enlightenment of Children." It was now necessary to suspect it, to decipher it, to hermeneutize it, exactly like the enigmatic symptoms of adult neurotics. This, then, was the first child psychoanalysis in history,

[130] Graf 1952. [131] Freud 1909, 24. [132] Ibid., 50. [133] Ibid., 29. [134] Ibid., 24.

very different in this respect from an ethological observation of child development. Graf asked his son questions following Freud's instructions, and Freud rewrote the notes he gave him, amplifying them with theoretical comments of his own. Apart from a short visit to Freud at the end of March 1908, Herbert was thus essentially analyzed by his father.

At the end of this psychoanalytical investigation, we learn that little Herbert's anxieties were linked to his jealousy towards his little sister, to hostile desires towards his father whom he wanted to replace with the mother, as well as to his fear of being punished by castration for these illicit wishes. Summary:

1. In accordance with the program set forth in the *Three Essays*, Herbert's auto-erotic and "homosexual" libido found its way to object love and first to the mother, the primary dispenser of erotic pleasure. "The boy had found his way to object-love in the usual manner from the care he had received when he was an infant": he wants, very literally, to sleep with his mother and cuddle with her.[135]
2. He therefore nourishes death wishes towards his little sister and his father, who "both took his mummy away from him."[136]
3. These parricidal and sororicidal wishes running up against repression, the incestuous libido directed towards the mother reverses and is "set free" in the form of a diffuse, floating anguish.[137] Herbert does not know why and of what he is afraid, because he is forbidden to know that he fears being castrated by his father to punish his incestuous and parricidal desires. Behind his anguish, there is the "castration complex,"[138] a new theoretical piece that is now added to the Oedipus complex.
4. Finally, the anguish fixes itself more or less arbitrarily on the horse-who-bites-the-fingers, substitute of the father-who-cuts-off-the-widdler. The result is a phobia, a particular form of "anxiety-hysteria."

Freud's conclusion: "Strictly speaking, I learnt nothing new from this analysis, nothing that I had not already been able to discover (though often less distinctly and more indirectly) from other patients analysed at a more advanced age";[139] "In his attitude towards his father and mother, Hans confirms in the most concrete and uncompromising manner what I have said in my *Interpretation of Dreams* and in my *Three Essays* with regard to the sexual relations of a child to his parents."[140]

[135] Ibid., 111. [136] Ibid., 114. [137] Ibid., 115. [138] Ibid., 7. [139] Ibid., 147.
[140] Ibid., 111.

Let us ask ourselves, however, how Freud obtained this confirmation of the Oedipal theory advanced in the letters to Fliess. It was obviously not through "direct observation" of little Herbert, since the latter, by hypothesis, was supposed to be completely unaware of the incestuous-parricidal desires that were hidden behind his fear of horses. The boy himself insists on this several times. When the father asks him why he is jealous when Mummy gives a kiss to Daddy, he answers: "I don't know."[141] Same answer when the father insists on making him admit that he imagines himself to be Daddy when he is in bed with Mommy:

I: "And then you felt afraid of Daddy?"
HANS: "*You know everything. I didn't know anything.*"[142]

One night, Hans comes to disturb his parents to tell them an obscure story about a "big giraffe" and a "crumpled giraffe" that he sat on:

I: "Why did you come into our room?"
HE: "I don't know myself."[143]

The father tells him that he writes all this to the Professor (Freud) who will cure him from his "nonsense":

I: "Yes. But he won't understand how you can think that a giraffe can be crumpled up."
HE: "Just tell him I don't know myself, and then he won't ask."[144]

But Daddy and the Professor keep asking a lot of questions. As Freud explains at the beginning of the theoretical part of the case history, one cannot avoid giving patients "anticipatory ideas" (*Erwartungsvorstellungen*) in the course of psychoanalysis to enable them to say what they do not know. The same applies to Herbert: "It is true that during the analysis Hans had to be told many things that he could not say himself, that he had to be presented with thoughts which he had so far shown no signs of possessing, and that his attention had to be turned in the direction from which his father was expecting something to come."[145]

Is there not a risk, then, Freud wonders, of influencing him, of "suggestionizing" him as Bernheim would say? This was one of the most constant criticisms leveled at Freud by his peers at the time: "You read your theories in the minds of patients; you suggest to them the answers you need to support them."[146] Doesn't this apply, all the more so, to a

[141] Ibid., 89. [142] Ibid., 90. [143] Ibid., 37. [144] Ibid., 38. [145] Ibid., 104.
[146] Gaupp 1900, 234; Aschaffenburg 1906, 1797; Forel 1906, 214; Putnam 1906, 40; Moll 1909, 254; etc.

four-year-old child anxiously scrutinized by his parents for the slightest confirmation of the Professor's theories? As Freud rhetorically objects,

> A child, it will be said, is necessarily highly suggestible, and in regard to no one, perhaps, more than to his own father; he will allow anything to be forced upon him, out of gratitude to his father for taking so much notice of him; none of his assertions can have any evidential value, and everything he produces in the way of associations, phantasies, and dreams will naturally take the direction into which they are being urged by every possible means.[147]

But two pages later, Freud sweeps away the objection: "even during the analysis, the small patient gave evidence of enough independence to acquit him upon the charge of 'suggestion.'"[148] In other words, the little fellow was perfectly capable of contradicting his father when his interpretations were erroneous (a variant of the Tally Argument). Is this really the case, however? As countless miscarriages of justice have shown, interrogating young children is likely to guide their testimony. In the case of Herbert, it is clear from Max Graf's transcripts that analysis had become a kind of game for him in which he would throw the ball back to his father: "Let's play Oedipus, shall we?" The father would suggest, and Herbert would follow:

I: "Did you often get into bed with Mummy at Gmunden?"
HANS: "Yes."
I: "And you used to think to yourself you were Daddy?"
HANS: "Yes."

...

I: "When Fritzl fell down you thought: 'If only Daddy would fall down like that!' ... You thought then that if only Daddy were to die you'd be Daddy."
HANS: "Yes."

...

I: "Would you like to be married to Mummy?"
HANS: "Oh yes."[149]

Or again, about the little sister Hanna:

I: "That was why you thought when Mummy was giving her bath, if only she'd let go, Hanna would fall into the water ..."
HANS (taking me up): "... and die."[150]

[147] Freud 1909, 102. [148] Ibid., 105. [149] Ibid., 90–92. [150] Ibid., 72.

The same assent, though a little more nuanced, when the father suggests to Herbert that he identify him with the horse that had fallen (implied, died):

I: "When the horse fell down, did you think of your daddy?"
HANS: "Perhaps. Yes. It's possible."[151]

In any case, the analysis game is very funny: "When I got up from the table after breakfast Hans said: 'Daddy, don't trot away from me!' I was struck by his saying 'trot' instead of 'run,' and replied: 'Oho! So you're afraid of the horse trotting away from you.' Upon which he laughed."[152]

On the other hand, when Herbert shows independence and proposes other interpretations (other "moves" in the game), he is not listened to. Transcript from March 1, about Gmunden's white horse, which Herbert had learned would bite if you brought your fingers close:

> [Lizzi's] father was standing near the horse, and the horse turned its head round (to touch him), and he said to Lizzi: "Don't put your finger to the white horse or it'll bite you." Upon this I said: "I say, it strikes me that it isn't a horse you mean, but a widdler, that one mustn't put one's hand to."

HE: "But a widdler doesn't bite."
I: "Perhaps it does, though."[153]

Another exchange:

I: "Are you fond of Daddy?"
HANS: "Oh yes."
I: "Or perhaps not."[154]

Yet another exchange, this time about the story of the two giraffes, the big one and the crumpled one. According to Max Graf,

> the big giraffe is myself, or rather my big penis (the long neck), and the crumpled giraffe is my wife, or rather her genital organ ... In the train I explained the giraffe phantasy to him, upon which he said: "Yes, that's right." And when I said to him that I was the big giraffe, and that its long neck had reminded him of a widdler, he said: "Mummy has a neck like a giraffe, too. I saw, when she was washing her white neck."[155]

In a footnote, Freud acknowledges that Herbert was implicitly refuting the sexual symbolism advanced by the father, but he continues: "This symbolism was probably correct, but we really cannot ask more of Hans."[156]

[151] Ibid., 51. [152] Ibid., 45. [153] Ibid., 29. [154] Ibid., 88. [155] Ibid., 39–40.
[156] Ibid., 40–41.

So, whether Herbert agrees with his analyst or resists him, the result is always the same since the analyst knows better than he does what is hidden in his unconscious. As Havelock Ellis was to remark perfidiously a few years later, in this game, the psychoanalyst is always the winner: "Heads I win, tails you lose."[157]

This "Analysis of a Phobia in a Five-Year-Old Boy" was in the end no different from an adult psychoanalysis, and the confirmations Freud found there were obtained in exactly the same way – not by the impartial listening of a naive and innocent word, but by an interpretative questioning constantly oriented by conceptual "constructions" and pre-formed "anticipatory ideas." If Herbert's babbling corroborated the Professor's sexual theories so well, it was because the latter knew in advance what he was looking for and guided him where he wanted to go. It was Freud who confirmed his own theories, not Herbert, whose role was reduced to that of a simple megaphone.

The psychoanalyst Jean Laplanche generously qualifies "little Hans" as "discoverer of the castration complex." That's saying a lot. In fact, it was from Freud that Herbert Graf learned that he was afraid of being punished by his father for wanting to sleep with his mother. Before that, he knew nothing about it. It was Monday, March 30, 1908, in the Professor's office: "The consultation was a short one," Freud tells us.

> I then disclosed to him that he was afraid of his father, precisely because he was so fond of his mother . . . his father was fond of him in spite of it, and he might admit everything to him without any fear. Long before he was in the world, I went on, I had known that a little Hans would come who would be so fond of his mother that he would be bound to feel afraid of his father because of it; and I had told his father this.[158]

Herbert was perplexed. "'Does the Professor talk to God,' Hans asked his father on the way home, 'as he can tell all that beforehand?'"[159]

[157] Ellis 1915, 102. [158] Freud 1909, 42. [159] Ibid.

CHAPTER 4

Drives

After the biological turn of the Fliess years, the key word in psychoanalysis is no longer "trauma" but "drive." The ultimate cause of neurotic disorders is no longer to be found in an external accident but in what Freud often calls an internal, constitutional "disposition" (*Disposition*). As a result, everything that was previously described in neuro-physio-psychological terms (shock, dissociation, inhibition, repression, etc.) is now re-described in biological, i.e., "metapsychological" terms. This new concept, which Freud introduced for the first time in 1896, clearly refers to the biological hypotheses that he shared with Fliess at the time. Talking to Fliess about his book in progress on dreams, he wrote in March 1898:

> It seems to me that the theory of wishfulfillment has brought only the psychological solution and not the biological – or rather metapsychical (*metapsychische*) – one. (I am going to ask you seriously, by the way, whether I may use the name metapsychology for my psychology that leads behind consciousness.) Biologically, dream life seems to me to derive entirely from the residues of the prehistoric period of life (between the ages of one and three) – the same period which is the source of the unconscious and alone contains the etiology of all the psychoneuroses, the period normally characterized by an amnesia analogous to hysterical amnesia.[1]

Metapsychology and Metabiology

It is obviously not by chance that Freud qualifies the first perverse-polymorphous years as a "prehistoric" period. In *The Interpretation of Dreams*, he explains his reasoning:

> Behind this childhood of the individual we are promised a picture of a phylogenetic childhood – a picture of the development of the human race, of which the individual's development is in fact an abbreviated

[1] Freud 1985, 301–302.

> recapitulation influenced by the chance circumstances of life . . . and we may expect that the analysis of dreams will lead us to a knowledge of man's archaic heritage, of what is psychically innate in him. Dreams and neuroses seem to have preserved more mental antiquities than we could have imagined possible.[2]

The prehistory that metapsychology deals with and that leads behind consciousness refers to the biological past of the species. What Freud, at the other end of the work, calls the "bedrock" of the biological: "for the psychical field, the biological field does in fact play the part of the underlying bedrock."[3]

Jean Laplanche and Jean-Bertrand Pontalis, in a famous article, suggested viewing the psychological (according to them, "structural") theory of the Oedipus complex as "that which, already reached in a 'wild' way in the theory of seduction, was nearly lost with it in favor of a biological realism."[4] The opposite is true. Not only does the Oedipus complex appear from the outset in the letters to Fliess in the form of endogenous "impulses" (*Impulse*), but the biological realism that Laplanche and Pontalis deplored will remain until the end at the very foundation of Freudian metapsychology. Once the theory of traumatic seduction was definitively abandoned, psychoanalysis became a psychobiology, itself anchored in an evolutionary metabiology. Admittedly, Freud continues to use psychological terminology – conscious, unconscious, ego, repression, representation, desire, fantasy, love, hate, etc. – but all this is now based on a play of various forces that he calls "drives" (*Triebe*) and that he roots in the history of the species.

Just as the study of dreams is supposed to allow us to go back in time in the history of the "human race," the psychic conflicts of patients in analysis are supposed to echo ancestral forces and events, in a sort of vast biological gigantomachy. The "individual truth," writes Freud in the twenty-third *Introductory Lecture on Psycho-Analysis*, reflects the "prehistoric truth": "I have repeatedly been led to suspect that the psychology of the neuroses has stored up in it more of the antiquities of human development than any other source."[5] Better than the paleontologist, the psychoanalyst is therefore in a position to reconstitute the evolution of the species and even of life in general from the symptoms of his/her clients.

The result in Freud is a constant back and forth between clinical hermeneutics and biological speculation. On the one hand, the

[2] Freud 1900, 548–549. [3] Freud 1937a, 252. [4] Laplanche and Pontalis 1964, 1845.
[5] Freud 1916–1917, 371.

metabiological hypotheses on the development of the libido guide the analyst's interpretations, as we have seen with the analysis of the young Herbert Graf. On the other hand, the difficulties and novelties encountered in the clinic are immediately retranslated and explained in biological terms, prompting each time a reformulation of the theory of drives (*Trieblehre*) and their development. This is often described as a virtuous process of rectification/expansion of the metapsychological theory under the impact of experience. This is forgetting that the clinical "facts" here are interpretations already informed by the theory of drives, so the whole process rather resembles a circle or a feedback loop where the theory is self-generating, self-correcting, and self-confirming without ever encountering any real resistance. A contemporary of Freud, the psychiatrist Emil Kraepelin (1856–1926), described it this way: "Here we meet everywhere the characteristic fundamental features of the Freudian trend of investigation, the presentation of arbitrary assumptions and conjectures as assured facts that are used without hesitation for the building up of always new castles in the air (*Luftschlösser*) ever towering higher, and the tendency to generalization beyond measure from single observations."[6]

This explains the layered structure of Freudian metapsychology, each new conceptual layer being superimposed on the previous one without modifying or supplanting it. Read, for example, the *Three Essays*, constantly augmented with new chapters and passages at almost every reissue (1910, 1915, 1920, 1924): Freud never abandons a theory; he simply adds new ones to it according to the difficulties encountered in the clinic or to the criticisms expressed by his peers. There are thus no less than three successive theories of drives in Freud's work, each time more openly speculative in character. Kraepelin evoked a stacking up of castles in the air; Freud gamely retorted that they were psychoanalytical "myths": "The theory of drives is so to say our mythology. Drives are mythical entities, grandiose (*großartig*) in their indefiniteness."[7]

Sexual Drives, Ego-Drives

The first theory of drives, as it was formalized in the years 1910 to 1915, corresponds to the Freudian turn of the end of the 1890s, and it consists, in short, in a biologization of the neuro-psycho-physiological scheme from which Freud had initially started.

[6] Kraepelin 1913, 938. [7] Freud 1933a, 95, translation modified.

We remember that in the "Project for a Scientific Psychology" and *The Interpretation of Dreams*, the psychical apparatus was structured on the model of the reflex arc: a nerve impulse runs through the system in order to lead as quickly as possible to a motor action supposed to eliminate the tension. As Freud reminds us at the beginning of the essay "Instincts and Their Vicissitudes," physiology "has given us the concept of a 'stimulus' and the pattern of the reflex arc, according to which a stimulus applied to living tissue (nervous substance) from the outside is discharged by action to the outside."[8] As for the drive, it tends similarly to a reflex-automatic action, except that it is an internal and continuous excitation that cannot be escaped as easily and quickly as an external stimulus. This is what the "Project" of 1895 already called (with respect to the "drives" at the origin of the will) an "endogenous stimulus,"[9] i.e., a tension coming from inside the body. Freud expands on this idea in the *Three Essays*:

> By a "drive" (*Trieb*) is provisionally to be understood the psychical representative of an endosomatic, continuously flowing source of stimulation, as contrasted with a "stimulus" (*Reiz*), which is set up by single excitations coming from without. The source (*Quelle*) of a drive is a process of excitation occurring in an organ and the immediate aim (*Ziel*) of the drive lies in the removal of this organic stimulus [through an object (*Objekt*)].[10]

This internal pressure (*Drang*), coming from the body, has therefore all the characteristics of an instinct (*instinctus* originally means "that which stings, instigates from within"). As a matter of fact, the terms *Trieb* and *Instinkt* are interchangeable in German, even if at the time, biologists and philosophers tended to reserve the first for humans and the second for animals.[11] It is an instinctual, biologically determined behavior to which Freud's contemporaries referred when using the term *Trieb*. Breuer, for example, evokes indifferently the "aggressive instinct (*Instinkt*)" and the "sexual drive (*Sexualtrieb*)," as well as "the organism's major physiological needs and drives (*Triebe*): need for oxygen, craving for food, and thirst."[12] Similarly, when Fliess speaks of the sucking drive (*Trieb zum Lutschen oder Ludeln*) of young children, he means an impulse or "thrust" (*Schub*) corresponding to a biological cycle.[13]

The Freudian *Trieb* too is a thrust (the term comes from *treiben*, to push), and it is similarly anchored in biological cycles. As we have seen, the

[8] Freud 1915a, 118. [9] Freud 1895, 317.
[10] Freud 1905a, 168 (added in 1915), translation modified. [11] Shamdasani 2003, 191.
[12] Breuer and Freud 1895, 199–201, translation modified. [13] Fliess 1897, 198.

partial drives of the pregenital stage are supposed to recapitulate, to *repeat* sexual behaviors abandoned during the evolution of the species. It is this implacable biogenetic law that accounts in Freud for the "pushing," irresistible, and irrepressible character of the drives. Every drive is a repetition, a compulsion to repeat behaviors inherited from our ancestors. In "Instincts and Their Vicissitudes," Freud explains that drives are "precipitates" of muscular movements that, in the course of evolution, became "a hereditary disposition" – in other words, innate reflexes – by virtue of being the most appropriate for controlling external excitations. Even if internal impulsive excitations cannot be liquidated in the same way as external excitations and if "the simple pattern of the physiological reflex is [thus] complicated by the introduction of drives ... there is naturally nothing to prevent our supposing that the drives themselves are, at least in part, precipitates of the effects of external stimulation, which in the course of phylogenesis have brought about modifications in the living substance."[14] In short, internal drives are repetitions of reflex movements originally intended to react to external excitations. Same automatism here and there, same compulsive repetition.

It is therefore somewhat futile to try to "de-biologize" the Freudian drive by distinguishing it from any form of instinct, as a French interpretive tradition inspired by the psychoanalyst Jacques Lacan (1901–1981) would have it. The drive is a behavioral stereotypy programmed in the body and transmitted by hereditary means, which is what we usually mean by instinct. Where the Freudian drive differs from the common concept of instinct, however, is in that it is theorized simultaneously in terms of nervous excitation, of energy charge. Faithful to the neurophysiological physicalism of his beginnings, Freud describes this excitation as a current asking to be discharged in order to bring the tension inside the psychical apparatus "to the lowest possible level."[15] Breuer, in the theoretical part of *Studies on Hysteria*, spoke of it fairly classically as an electric current.[16] Freud, for his part, imagines it rather in the form of a liquid current that can be flushed out by "the locks [*die Schleusen*] to motor activity,"[17] but can also run up against "dams"[18] and flow back towards collateral channels. This is how, we remember, perversion and neurosis were explained in the *Three Essays*. When the sexual drive is prevented from unbunging itself normally in the form of genital "end pleasure," it regresses to older sexual phases (perversion) and then moves to symptomatic substitutes under the

[14] Freud 1915a, 120, translation modified. [15] Ibid. [16] Breuer and Freud 1895, 193.
[17] Freud 1900, 537, translation modified. [18] Freud 1905a, 177.

influence of repression (neurosis): "the libido behaves like a stream whose main bed has become blocked. It proceeds to fill up collateral channels which may hitherto have been empty."[19]

This hydraulic metaphor makes sense if we are talking about a quantity of excitation seeking to discharge itself by any means. It is, however, absurd if we are talking about an instinct in the biological sense. An instinct is invariable; it changes neither its nature nor its object. And above all, it does not regress to previous stages of evolution, as Freud would like us to believe, invoking the Haeckelian theory of the recapitulation of phylogenesis by ontogenesis. For Haeckel, the recapitulations of previous morphologies in the course of ontogenetic development are transitory and replaced by later forms. In that sense, there can certainly be pathological arrests in development (Freud's "fixations") but in no way a regression from the final form (can one imagine an adult reverting to a ten-year-old, a five-year-old, or an eight-month-old child?). Freud recognizes this in *Civilization and Its Discontents*: in morphology, "the earlier phases of development are in no sense still preserved; they have been absorbed into the later phases for which they have supplied the material. The embryo cannot be discovered in the adult ... The fact remains that *only in the mind* is such a preservation of all the earlier stages alongside of the final form possible."[20] Here, "nothing which has once been formed can perish ... everything is somehow preserved and ... in suitable circumstances (when, for instance, regression goes back far enough) it can once more be brought to light."[21] "With neurotics it is as though we were in a prehistoric landscape – for instance, in the Jurassic. The great saurians are still running about; the horsetails grow as high as palms."[22]

Rather than an instinct, strictly speaking, the Freudian drive is thus a kind of mobile energy or "pressure" likely to activate any ancestral instinct preserved in the psyche, depending on repressions, regressions, and fixations. The drive translates into *drives*, in the plural, and into *vicissitudes* of drive (*Triebschicksale*). Regarding sexual drives, which visibly orient his description of the drive in general, Freud writes that "They are distinguished by possessing the capacity to act vicariously for one another to a wide extent and by being able to change their objects readily. In consequence of the latter properties they are capable of functions which are far removed from their original purposive actions."[23] A sexual aim can thus be exchanged for a nonsexual one (sublimation); an active aim (sadism,

[19] Ibid., 170. [20] Freud 1930, 71, my emphasis. [21] Ibid., 69. [22] Freud 1938a, 299.
[23] Freud 1915a, 126.

voyeurism) can be reversed into a passive one (masochism, exhibitionism); a genital object can be replaced by a nongenital one; a drive (love) can be transformed into another one (hate), and so on.

It is easy to see why Freud feels the need to make the drive variable. It is not because it would be by nature different from a biological instinct (all drives are, in the last instance, "hereditary dispositions"). It is because the biology of instincts must follow the meanderings of psychoanalytical interpretation, even if it means turning it into an opportunistic speculation. The drive must be mutable, commutable, in order to provide a biological foundation for the permutations and substitutions alleged by the analyst: "Your hatred, Sir, hides a deep love"; "Your masochism is really a sadistic aggression." Once again, psychological hermeneutics and biological speculation support and legitimize each other. Freud explains it very well himself: "Bearing in mind that there are motive forces which work against a drive's being carried through in an unmodified form, we may also regard these vicissitudes as modes of *defence* against the drives."[24] In other words, if the drives (instincts) do not directly reach their goals and objects, it is because of repression that prevents their conscious expression.

Now, repression is a psychic process; it concerns thoughts, fantasies, illicit desires that it removes from the conscious. This is why Freud always takes care to define the drive as the "*psychical* representative" of a somatic excitation.[25] The drive is not the quantity of excitation itself; it represents (*repräsentiert*) it to the psyche in the form of either ideas, "ideational representatives" (*Vorstellungsrepräsentanten*), or feelings, affects:[26] "A 'drive' appears to us as a concept on the frontier (*Grenzbegriff*) between the mental and the somatic."[27] The drive being thus posed as a psycho-corporal mix, Freud gives himself the means to cross the border between the two domains in both directions and to present the repressions, substitutions, and displacements of representations alleged by the analyst as "vicissitudes" of true biological instincts.

In the same way, patients' psychic conflicts (desire/defense, will/counter-will, etc.) are henceforth interpreted as conflicts between drives: "We have discovered that every drive tries to make itself effective by activating ideas that are in keeping with its aims. These drives are not always compatible with one another; their interests often come into conflict. *Opposition between ideas* (Vorstellungen) *is only an expression of struggles*

[24] Ibid., 127, translation modified. [25] Freud 1905a, 168; Freud 1915a, 127, my emphasis.
[26] Freud 1915f, 177. [27] Freud 1915a, 122, translation modified.

between the various drives."[28] Behind the repression of the ideational representatives of this or that sexual drive, there are other drives just as pushing, powerful, and instinctual. When we oppose a drive, it is to satisfy another drive. Nietzsche already said it, which Freud probably did not ignore: "While 'we' believe we are complaining about the *vehemence* of a drive, at bottom it is one drive *which is complaining about another.*"[29]

The drives at work behind the repression of sexual drives Freud calls "ego-drives," since it is the ego that is supposed to be the agent of defense against thoughts irreconcilable with the requirements of reality and society. The ego traditionally designates the autonomous, voluntary, and conscious person (Charcot, as we have seen above, spoke of "that vast collection of personal ideas, accumulated and organized long ago, which constitutes consciousness properly so called, the *ego*"[30]). Translated in evolutionary terms, it is the individual as it distinguishes itself from its environment and fights for its survival (the Darwinian "survival of the fittest"). The ego-drives, in this sense, correspond to the instinct of self-preservation. There is, writes Freud, an "undeniable opposition between the drives which subserve sexuality, the attainment of sexual pleasure, and those other drives, which have as their aim the self-preservation of the individual – the ego-drives. As the poet has said, all the organic drives that operate in our mind may be classified as 'hunger' or 'love.'"[31]

Freud quotes Schiller, but as Frank Sulloway points out, he could just as well have quoted Darwin.[32] In *The Descent of Man, and Selection in Relation to Sex* (1871), Darwin showed how the sexual selection that presides over reproduction differs from the action of natural selection while complementing it: from an evolutionary point of view, it does not matter that the fittest survives if it does not reproduce. The idea of a fundamental dualism of the sexual and self-preservation instincts was thus already established before Freud, and, in fact, most of his contemporaries (Krafft-Ebing and Moll, among others) commonly referred to it. Freud's relative originality lies in the fact that he conceives this dualism as a real antagonism, by raising the psychic conflict between the ego and its sexual desires to the status of a biogenetic struggle between self-preservation drives and sexual drives. Just as desires and fantasies represent a threat to the individual ego and its "interests" (*Ichinteresse*), sexual drives are now conceived as pursuing a goal incompatible with self-preservation drives.

[28] Freud 1910d, 213, my emphasis. [29] Nietzsche 1881, § 109. [30] Charcot 1887, 290.
[31] Freud 1910d, 215. [32] Sulloway 1992, 251–253.

The latter aim at the survival of the individual, whereas sexual drives aim only at the reproduction of the species, beyond the individual.

The idea does not come from Darwin but from the neo-Darwinian biologist August Weismann (1834–1914) and his famous distinction between the mortal "soma" (our modern phenotype) and the immortal "germ-plasm," support of heredity (our genotype).[33] Freud implicitly refers to it in his article "On Narcissism: An Introduction," when justifying his own distinction between sexual drives and ego-drives by "biological considerations":

> The individual does actually carry on a twofold existence: one to serve his own purposes and the other as a link in a chain, which he serves against his will, or at least involuntarily. The individual himself regards sexuality as one of his own ends; whereas from another point of view, he is an appendage to his germ-plasm, at whose disposal he puts his energies in return for a bonus of pleasure. He is the mortal vehicle of a (possibly) immortal substance – like the inheritor of an entailed property, who is only the temporary holder of an estate which survives him. The separation of the sexual drives from the ego-drives would simply reflect this twofold function of the individual.[34]

Here it is then: sexual drives, spurred on by an immediate enjoyment (pleasure principle), push towards reproduction to the detriment of the individual, while ego-drives seek to delay, inhibit, repress this disappearance of the individual (reality principle). Behind the clinic, behind the couch and its miserable secrets of the bedchamber, is replayed the incessant, immense fight of the self and of the species. As Freud recognizes for once in the following paragraph, "the hypothesis of separate ego-drives and sexual drives (that is to say, the libido theory) rests scarcely at all upon a psychological basis, but instead derives its principal support from biology."[35] Psychoanalysis is a psychobiomachy.

Narcissism

The passages just quoted are part of an essay in which Freud simultaneously introduces another dualism, that of the object-libido and the *ego-libido*. In a nutshell: the ego would not only be what is opposed to the sexual libido, it would be itself source and object of the libido, source and object of a sexual drive that Freud calls *narcissistic*.

Scholars speak in this regard of a "second theory of drives," but in reality, this one overlaps chronologically with the first one and coexists in a

[33] Weismann 1892. [34] Freud 1914c, 78, translation modified. [35] Ibid., 79.

more or less contradictory way with it, in the mode of the conceptual layering mentioned above. The term "narcissism" appears, in fact, in Freud's writing as early as 1910, concerning the supposed homosexuality of Leonardo da Vinci: the homosexual

> takes his own person as a model (*Vorbild*) in whose likeness he chooses the new objects of his love ... He finds the objects of his love along the path of narcissism, as we say; for Narcissus, according to the Greek legend, was a youth who preferred his own reflection (*Spiegelbild*) to everything else and who was changed into the lovely flower of that name.[36]

This first theorization of narcissism is still only a variant of the genesis of homosexuality proposed the year before in the case of little Hans, where Freud already explained that every child goes through a homosexual phase during which "*he was acquainted with only one kind of genital organ* – a genital organ like his own," before turning to the mother, the first love object: "Homosexuals, then, are persons who, owing to the erotogenic importance of their own genitals, cannot do without a similar feature in their sexual object. In the course of their development from auto-erotism to object-love, they have remained at a point of fixation between the two."[37] As we can see, what Freud calls narcissism in 1910 is still poorly distinguished from the auto-erotism he was talking about in 1909 (this was already true in Havelock Ellis, from whom he borrows both terms). Basically, it is only a transitory, transitional phase between the auto-erotic pleasure taken on the own body and what Freud calls object love, directed towards a "not-me" body or body part. It was not until the following year (the Schreber case) that Freud clearly separated the narcissistic stage from the auto-erotic stage, and 1914 ("On Narcissism: An Introduction") that he thematized the new ego/narcissistic libido.

This introduction of narcissism into the theory of drives corresponds to Freud's desire to account for psychoses. As a "nerve doctor," he had until then confined himself essentially to the study of neuroses (of "neuro-psychoses of defense"), even if he did not refrain from making theoretical forays into paranoia.[38] However, once he came into contact with the Swiss psychiatrist Eugen Bleuler and his assistant Carl Gustav Jung, he boldly set out to "conquer psychiatry."[39] He recalls it at the beginning of "On Narcissism": "A pressing motive for occupying ourselves with the conception of a primary and normal narcissism arose when the attempt was made

[36] Freud 1910c, 100; see also Freud 1905a, 145 (footnote added in 1910). [37] Freud 1909, 109.
[38] Freud 1985, 390; Freud 1896c, 174–185.
[39] Letter to Bleuler of January 30, 1906, cited in Bleuler 1979, 21.

to subsume what we know of dementia praecox (Kraepelin) or schizophrenia (Bleuler) under the hypothesis of the libido theory."[40]

Jung, with his clinical experience as a psychiatrist, was Freud's main interlocutor (rather than ally) in this undertaking of theoretical conquest. It was in this spirit that Jung had made Freud read the fascinating *Memoirs of My Nervous Illness* by Daniel Paul Schreber, a magistrate who had developed a paranoid delusion shortly after being appointed president (*Senatspräsident*) of the Dresden Court of Appeals.[41] Schreber was convinced that he had been chosen by God to save the world and restore happiness to it. To this end, God would bring about the end of the world and change Schreber into a woman so as to create a race of "new human beings out of Schreber's spirit" by means of the emission of "rays of God." Schreber also claimed that his divine election was the reason for the incessant persecution he suffered at the hands of the psychiatrist who treated him, Professor Paul Emil Flechsig (1847–1929).

Freud, in the "Psycho-Analytic Notes" that he devoted in 1911 to this "autobiographical account of a case of paranoia," retained essentially two features in Schreber's abundant delirium: emasculation or feminization (*Entmannung*), which he attributed to a passive homosexual desire, and megalomania, which he attributed to a regression of the libido towards the ego caused by the repression (or, more exactly, the rejection, *Verwerfung*) of the homosexual object. "The basis of Schreber's illness," he writes, "was the outburst of a homosexual impulse" at the time of the "climateric" of his fifties.[42] It is this homosexuality that Schreber had vehemently rejected and that had then resurfaced from the outside in the inverted, grimacing form of male persecutors. Generalizing from Schreber's case, Freud then proposes to understand all the major types of paranoid delusions as ways of contradicting one and the same homosexual proposition: *I (a man) love him (a man)*. The example given is that of man, but the theory is equally valid for woman:

- The delusion of persecution denies the verb (*I do not love him*, projected as *because he hates me*).
- The delirium of jealousy permutes the subject (*it is she who loves him*).
- The erotomanic delusion contests the complement (*I love her*, projected as *because she loves me*).
- The megalomaniac delusion rejects the whole proposition (*I love no one; I love only myself*).[43]

[40] Freud 1914c, 74. [41] Schreber 1903. [42] Freud 1911, 45–46. [43] Ibid., 63–65.

These four statements, let us note, are not of the same level, and they are not generated in the same way. The first three are a matter of logic, so to speak: Freud deduces them by exhausting the different ways of denying (of repressing, rejecting) the homosexual proposition. The last one, on the other hand, relies once again on biogenetic hypotheses. Indeed, if the delusion of grandeur also consists in a negation of homosexuality (which, after all, is not logically evident: the megalomaniac rejects *any* object), it is because the stage to which it regresses due to repression is supposed to immediately precede the homosexual stage in the normal development of the *libido sexualis*.

Freud reminds us of this by referring to his essay on Leonardo da Vinci:

> Recent investigations have directed our attention to a stage in the development of the libido which it passes through on the way from auto-erotism to object-love. This stage has been given the name of narcissism. What happens is this. There comes a time in the development of the individual at which he unifies his sexual drives (which have hitherto been engaged in auto-erotic activities) in order to obtain a love-object; and he begins by taking himself, his own body, as his love-object ... What is of chief importance in the self (*Selbst*) thus chosen as a love object may already be the genitals. The line of development then leads on to the choice of an external object with similar genitals – that is, to homosexual object-choice – and thence to heterosexuality.[44]

To which Freud adds, and this is new:

> After the stage of heterosexual object-choice has been reached, the homosexual tendencies are not, as might be supposed, done away with or brought to a stop; they are merely deflected from their sexual aim and applied to fresh uses. They now combine with portions of the ego-drives (*Ichtriebe*) and, as "attached" components, help to constitute the social drives (*die sozialen Triebe*), thus making a contribution of eroticism to friendship and comradeship, to *esprit de corps* and to the love of mankind in general.[45]

Any objectality, any relation to the other, would thus be originally (biogenetically) homosexual, whether it is the heterosexual relation or the social relation. Everywhere, we would have reflections, copies, doubles of the narcissistic ego. It is this evolution going from the narcissistic ego to the homosocial alter ego that the paranoid would then traverse in the opposite direction, regressively:

[44] Ibid., 60–61, translation modified. [45] Ibid., 61, translation modified.

> People who have not freed themselves completely from the stage of narcissism – who, that is to say, have at that point a fixation which may operate as a disposition to a later illness (*Krankheitsdisposition*) – are exposed to the danger that some unusually intense high tide (*Hochflut*) of libido, finding no other outflow (*Ablauf*), may lead to a sexualization of their social drives and so undo the sublimations which they had achieved in the course of their development.[46]

Once again using the hydraulic metaphor, Freud imagines that this libidinal "current" (*Strömung*)

> bursts through the dam (*Damm*) at the weakest point. As our analyses show that paranoiacs strive to protect themselves against such a sexualization of their social drive cathexes, we are led to suppose that the weakest point of their development is to be sought somewhere between the stages of auto-eroticism, narcissism, and homosexuality, and that their disposition to illness (which would perhaps be susceptible of a more precise definition) must be situated in this region.[47]

Two things should be noted:

1. The point from which the libido refluxes/regresses is not the sexual sphere strictly speaking but that of social relations. Paranoia is a matter of sublimated, social homosexuality: "it can be assumed that paranoiacs have brought with them a fixation on the stage of narcissism, and it can be said that the length of the retreat from sublimated homosexuality to narcissism is a measure of the amount of regression characteristic of paranoia."[48]
2. The stage at which the libido refluxes/regresses is not auto-eroticism but narcissism. Freud clearly distinguishes the respective destinies of the libido in paranoia and Kraepelin's dementia praecox (schizophrenia, we would say today). In dementia praecox, "the regression extends not only to narcissism (which manifests itself in the form of megalomania) but to the complete abandonment of object love and the return to infantile auto-eroticism. The dispositional fixation must therefore lie further back than in paranoia, and be somewhere at the beginning of the course of development from auto-eroticism to object love."[49]

It is clear from this passage that megalomania is not the same thing for Freud as auto-eroticism and anobjectality (the absence of any relation to the "not-me"). Yet this was the case a few years earlier when he confided to

[46] Ibid., 61. [47] Ibid., 62, translation modified. [48] Ibid., 72. [49] Ibid., 77.

Jung his first views on paranoia. Shortly after their first contact, Freud had sent Jung working notes entitled "Theoretical Opinions on Paranoia." It said:

> In paranoia, the libido is withdrawn from the object ... Where the libido has gone is indicated by the *hostility to the object*, found in paranoia. This is an endogenous perception of libido withdrawal. In view of the relation of compensation between object-cathexis and ego-cathexis, it seems likely that the cathexis withdrawn from the object has returned to the ego, i.e., has become auto-erotic. The paranoid ego is consequently hypercathected, egoistic, meglomaniac.[50]

We see that the scheme that is set up here is exactly the one that Freud will adopt four years later in his comments on the Schreber case, except that two essential pieces are still missing from the picture: megalomaniac narcissism, distinguished from auto-eroticism, and social-sublimated homosexuality. What is it, then, that necessitated their introduction into the theory?

To understand this, we must bring in the objections that Jung raised throughout his correspondence with Freud. Jung, from the outset, was hardly convinced by the all-encompassing application of the libido theory to mental disorders and, in particular, to psychoses. On February 20, 1908, he already submitted to Freud a polite reformulation of his theory of paranoia in terms of nonsexual drives:

> Your views on paranoia have not lain fallow. I have been able to confirm them many times over. Only the thing is not yet ripe. I have therefore kept silent about it so far. The detachment of libido, its regression to autoerotic forms, is probably well explained by the self-assertion, the psychological self-preservation of the individual. Hysteria keeps to the plane of "preservation of the species," paranoia (Dem[entia] pr[aecox]) to the plane of self-preservation, i.e., auto-erotism ... The psychoses (the incurable ones) should probably be regarded as defensive encapsulations that have misfired, or rather, have been carried to extremes.[51]

When we know how firmly Freud assimilated self-preservation to the ego-drives, as opposed to the sexual drives delegated to the "preservation of the species," it is clear that a formula such as "the plane of self-preservation, i.e., auto-erotism" was a pure provocation on the part of Jung. Whereas Freud attributed the megalomaniac "self-assertion" to a withdrawal of the libido on the own auto-erotic body, Jung proposed, on

[50] Freud and Jung 1974, 39. [51] Ibid., 123–124.

the contrary, to see in it a self-assertion of the repressing ego, a "psychological self-preservation of the individual" in his *social, nonsexual* relations with others. By thus making right to a specifically egoic, egoistical pathology, Jung did not only blur the Freudian dualism of sexual drives and self-preservation drives, he also pointed the finger at the indeterminacy of the concept of ego (*Ich*) manipulated by Freud. For when he spoke of a withdrawal of the libido into the ego, Freud was obviously thinking of the degradation of relations with others in paranoia ("hostility to the object," misanthropy, delusions of persecution, etc.). But could he seriously hold this ego to be identical to the auto-erotic body? The megalomaniac is certainly fascinated by his/her ego to the detriment of the "objects" (of the others), but it is to proclaim his/her unheard-of singularity, his/her incomparable solitude, his/her absolute autonomy and centrality. What is the relationship with auto-eroticism, infantile sexuality, the polymorphous perversion of the quadruped in us?

One thing leading to another, Jung came to question the sexual etiology of mental disorders in general. Can one not fall sick from conflicts in the sphere of the social interests of the ego, from sublimation, he asks Freud on August 19, 1907: "I would now like to ask you for an explanation: Do you regard sexuality as the mother of all feelings? . . . Are there not hysterical symptoms which, though co-determined by the sexual complex, are predominently conditioned by a sublimation or by a non-sexual complex (profession, job, etc.)?"[52] Freud's answer by return of post: "When we see people made ill by their work, etc., that is not conclusive, for the sexual (in the male, homosexual) component can easily be demonstrated in analysis."[53] A few months later, Freud takes up the same idea by evoking his rupture with Fliess, which had been marked by a very professional quarrel of priority and accusations of plagiarism: "The paranoid form [of psychosis] is probably conditioned by restriction to the homosexual component . . . My one-time friend Fliess developed a dreadful case of paranoia after throwing off his affection for me, which was undoubtedly considerable. I owe this idea to him, i.e., to his behaviour . . . The breaking down of sublimations in paranoia belongs to the same context."[54]

All this forbids us to be surprised by the appearance of the joint themes of narcissism and sublimated homosexuality in the theory of paranoia proposed in the Schreber case. These are obviously concessions made to Jung but formulated in such a way as to maintain the sexual etiology of paranoia in spite of everything. *Yes . . . but*, Freud seems to say. *Yes*, the ego

[52] Ibid., 79. [53] Ibid., 80. [54] Ibid., 121.

of the megalomaniac delirium is something else than the anarchic and fragmented body of auto-eroticism; it is the unified image (*Bild*) that the individual has of itself. *But* this narcissistic ego *loves* itself madly; its delusions of grandeur are "*a sexual overvaluation of the ego*";[55] "A return is thus made to the stage of narcissism (known to us from the development of the libido), in which a person's only sexual object is his own ego."[56] Narcissism, in other words, is a libidinal, sexual stage. And *yes*, the paranoid delusion does evolve in the sphere of social relations to others; *but* this sociality is of an erotic nature; it is a homosociality that "sublimates" a fundamental homosexuality. The social other is a mirror image (*Spiegelbild*) in which the narcissistic ego continues to desire itself.

Hence, the coda of the essay on Schreber:

> Lastly, I cannot conclude the present work ... without foreshadowing the two chief theses towards the establishment of which the libido theory of the neuroses and psychoses is advancing: namely, that the neuroses arise in the main from a conflict between the ego and the sexual drive, and that the forms which the neuroses assume retain the imprint of the course of development followed by the libido – and by the ego.[57]

Quod erat demonstrandum.

Object-Libido, Ego-Libido

As we can see, the insertion of the new narcissistic "phase" into the development of the libido is based neither on clinical observation (Freud never met Schreber in person, let alone Leonardo da Vinci) nor on any biological reality. Freud does not even try to justify it by evolutionary considerations, as he had done for the perverse stages of infantile sexuality. It is an ad hoc theoretical accommodation that makes it possible to reconcile the sexual etiology of the "neuro-psychoses of defense" with the egoic, nonsexual etiology proposed by Jung. Freud leaves the ground of the clinic and even of biology to engage in purely dialectical reorganizations and syntheses, like any philosopher confronted with contradictions. Narcissism, a kind of conceptual joker, is now everything and its opposite, sexual and nonsexual, egoistic and social, libidinous and sublimated, repressed and repressing, pathological and normal.

As a result, the introduction of narcissism can be read in all senses, both as a confirmation and enlargement of the libido theory, and as its

[55] Freud 1911, 65. [56] Ibid., 79. [57] Ibid., 79, translation modified.

questioning. After all, does narcissism represent a *sexualization*, a "pansexual" extension of the domain of the libido to that of the ego and social interests? Or, on the contrary, an implicit *desexualization* of the libido? This is what Jung affirmed in the second part of his *Transformations and Symbols of the Libido*.[58] Citing the essay on Schreber, Jung noted that Freud himself had expanded the concept of libido with the idea of narcissism and consequently proposed to apply the term to any form of instinct, whether it be the preservation instinct of the species (*Instinkt der Arterhaltung*) or the self-preservation instinct (*Instinkt der Selbsterhaltung*). Under Jung's pen, libido became synonymous with psychic energy in general, with life drive (*Lebenstrieb*), with Schopenhauerian will to live (*Willen zum Dasein*), with Bergsonian *élan vital*.[59]

Freud obviously could not accept such a reformulation, which amounted to diluting the drive dualism on which his own theory of repression and psychic conflict was based. In "On Narcissism," which is a response to Jung's "speculations,"[60] he therefore forcefully reaffirms the ultimate, irreducible character of the opposition between sexual drives and self-preservation/ego-drives, by invoking the "biological considerations" that we know. Far from coinciding purely and simply with the ego-drives, narcissism would only *add* to them, coloring them, so to speak, from the outside. We remember that in the essay on Schreber, Freud already affirmed that the homosexual drives "attach" themselves to the ego-drives to make "a contribution (*Beitrag*) of eroticism to friendship and comradeship," etc. Similarly, here, he writes that narcissism is "the libidinal complement (*Ergänzung*) to the egoism of the self-preservation drive, a measure of which may justifiably be attributed to every living creature."[61]

Anxious to avoid any confusion or conceptual contamination, Freud then proposes to speak of an "ego-*libido*" distinct from the ego-drives. On the one hand, we would have the self-preservation drives and the social "interests" of the ego, and, on the other hand, the sexual drives, themselves divided into object-libido and ego- or narcissistic libido. Either the libido is directed towards an external object, different from the person itself, and we have the object-libido, or it is directed towards the person itself, and we have the ego-libido. In any case, the libido remains in both cases a *libido sexualis*, notwithstanding Jung, and the robust dualism of the two great drives is maintained.

[58] Jung 1912. [59] Shamdasani 2003, 220 ff. [60] Freud 1914c, 79.
[61] Ibid., 74, translation modified.

This is at least, what one would have to say, if Freud, at the same time, did not "narcissize" the libido, to the point of making its sexual character deeply problematic. Until then, narcissism named an intermediate stage in the libidinal development going from auto-eroticism to object love and homosociality. But Freud now postulates a "primary narcissism," by which he means both a primary and a fundamental narcissism. In this new sense, narcissism no longer qualifies as a libidinal stage among others, but rather as the general regime of the libido: *any* libidinal investment is henceforth considered as fundamentally narcissistic, whether it is an object love or a self-love.

Taking up with great constancy his hydraulic description of the drive, Freud imagines the ego and the objects as communicating vessels between which flows and refluxes an essentially narcissistic libido:

> Thus we form the idea of there being an original libidinal cathexis of the ego, from which some is later given off to objects, but which fundamentally persists and is related to the object-cathexes much as the body of an amoeba is related to the pseudopodia which it puts out ... We see also, broadly speaking, an antithesis between ego-libido and object-libido. The more of the one is employed, the more the other becomes depleted. The highest phase of development of which object-libido is capable is seen in the state of being in love, when the subject seems to give up his own personality in favour of an object-cathexis; while we have the opposite condition in the paranoic's phantasy (or self-perception) of the "end of the world."[62]

Same language in the section on "The Theory of Libido" added the following year to the third edition of the *Three Essays*:

> Narcissistic or ego-libido seems to be the great reservoir (*das große Reservoir*) from which the object-cathexes are sent out and into which they are withdrawn once more; the narcissistic libidinal cathexis of the ego is the original state of things, realized in earliest childhood, and is merely covered by the later extrusions of libido, but in essentials persists behind them.[63]

A little like the emanations of the Plotinian One, the emissions of the ego are not distinguished from what they are emitted from and they thus never cease to be narcissistic even when they are yielded, or rather lent to, the objects. When I love, it is still myself that I love: the object-libido is only a vicissitude of the ego-libido inside an economy of the (self-)Same where nothing is lost nor given without return.

[62] Ibid., 75. [63] Freud 1905a, 218.

This is verified in the second section of "On Narcissism," where Freud tries in a rather confused way to distinguish two forms of object love, according to whether the object is chosen in line with the "narcissistic type (*Narzissmustypus*)" or the "attachment type (*Anlehnungstypus*)," where it "attaches" itself to, or more literally "leans" on, the functions of self-preservation (feeding, care, protection of the child). "A person may love," says Freud:

I) According to the narcissistic type:
   a) what he himself is (i.e., himself);
   b) what he himself was;
   c) what he himself would like to be;
   d) someone who was once part of himself.

II) According to the attachment type:
   a) the woman who feeds him;
   b) the man who protects him, and the succession of substitutes who take their place.[64]

The objects of type I are all clearly narcissistic: either one takes oneself as an object (Freud gives the example of the narcissistic woman), or one loves a copy of oneself (homosexuality), or one desires oneself in and as an "ideal ego" (*Idealich*), or one finds oneself in a detached part of oneself (the narcissistic child, "His Majesty the Baby"). But this is no less true of type II objects, in whom one will have recognized the two love objects of the Oedipus complex, models of all later heterosexual objects: the mother who nourishes and the father who protects. One could, indeed, expect that men who choose their object by attachment to the functions of self-preservation would love maternal-nourishing women and that women, conversely, would love paternal-protective men. But Freud tells us that

> complete object-love of the attachment type is, properly speaking, characteristic of the male. It displays the marked sexual overvaluation which is doubtless derived from the child's original narcissism and thus corresponds to a transference of that narcissism to the sexual object. This sexual overvaluation is the origin of the peculiar state of being in love (*Verliebtheit*) ... which is thus traceable to an impoverishment of the ego as regards libido in favour of the love-object.[65]

The overestimation in love typical of the man's "complete object-love" and of which Freud says elsewhere that it "reveals unmistakably the maternal

[64] Freud 1914c, 90, translation modified. [65] Ibid., 88.

prototype of the object-choice"[66] thus ultimately turns out to be narcissistic!

It is the same for "the type of female most frequently met with, which is probably the purest and truest one." Puberty, Freud tells us, causes in most women

> an intensification of the original narcissism, and this is unfavourable to the development of a true object-choice with its accompanying sexual over-valuation. Strictly speaking, it is only themselves that such women love with an intensity comparable to that of the man's love for them. Nor does their need lie in the direction of loving, but of being loved; and *the man who fulfils this condition is the one who finds favour with them.*[67]

The male object is thus not chosen on the model of the protective father but rather as a mirror in which the woman finds her image. Hence the unfortunate "incongruence" (*Inkongruenz*) of female and male object choices, since the woman loves a man in whom she can continue to love herself, while the man loves himself in a narcissistic woman who does not love him.[68]

We shouldn't be surprised if this love fight resembles much more the struggle of the consciences described by Hegel in his famous master–slave dialectic than a courtship ritual in preparation for mating. This narcissistic libido that is lost and found in its objects has nothing erotic or sexual to it anymore; it is an egoistic desire (a self-love) that looks for itself in the other and wants to be for itself, close to itself in the gaze or the recognition of the other. A huge concession to Jung: there is indeed, inherent in the promotion of the metabiological concept of primary narcissism, an implicit desexualization of the libido in general, whether it is the so-called ego-libido or the so-called object-libido.

This is so true that Freud repeatedly indicates that primary narcissism is not fundamentally distinct from the ego-drives. No sooner has he introduced the idea of "an original libidinal cathexis of the ego" than he continues:

> Finally, as regards the differentiation of psychical energies, we are led to the conclusion that to begin with, during the state of narcissism (*im Zustande des Narzißmus*), they exist together and that they are indistinguishable (*ununterscheidbar*) for our coarse analysis; not until there is object-cathexis is it possible to discriminate a sexual energy – the libido – from an energy of the ego-drives.[69]

[66] Freud 1910e, 169. [67] Freud 1914c, 88–89, my emphasis.
[68] Ibid., 89, translation modified. [69] Ibid., 76, translation modified.

Further on, regarding the castration complex and the "masculine protest" that his ex-ally Alfred Adler founded "not on a narcissistic, and therefore still a libidinal, trend, but on a social valuation":

> Psycho-analytic research ordinarily enables us to trace the vicissitudes undergone by the libidinal drives when these, isolated from the ego-drives, are placed in opposition to them; but in the particular field of the castration complex, it allows us to infer the existence of an epoch and a psychical situation in which the two groups of drives, still operating in unison and inseparably mingled, make their appearance as narcissistic interests.[70]

And in the 1915 edition of the *Three Essays*:

> Th[e] ego-libido is, however, only conveniently accessible to analytic study when it has been put to the use of cathecting sexual objects, that is, when it has become *object-libido* ... psycho-analysis for the moment affords us assured information only on the transformations that take place in the object-libido, but is unable to make any immediate distinction between the ego-libido and the other forms of energy operating in the ego.[71]

Either these passages do not mean anything or they mean that sexual drives and ego-drives are initially confused in the "great reservoir" of primary narcissism and that the first ones become effectively libidinal only in a second time, when the original mix emits narcissistic pseudopods towards the objects (ego- and object-libido). We are clearly in the vicinity of Jung's monism and of his "psychic energy" mixing sexuality and self-preservation, preservation of the species and preservation of the self.

The Oral-Cannibalistic Stage

We have yet another sign of this with the introduction in 1915 of an additional stage in the already rather complex history of the libido: the oral-cannibalistic incorporation. Love, we read in "Instincts and Their Vicissitudes,"

> is originally narcissistic, then passes over on to objects, which have been incorporated into the extended ego ... Preliminary stages of love emerge as provisional sexual aims while the sexual drives are passing through their complicated development. As the first of these aims we recognize the phase of *incorporating or devouring* – a type of love which is consistent with abolishing the object's separate existence.[72]

[70] Ibid., 92. [71] Freud 1905a, 217–218. [72] Freud 1915a, 138.

The first sexual-amorous relationship would thus be narcissistic in that it suppresses the object in its otherness and is confused with food ingestion.

One would think one was reading Hegel's definition of self-consciousness as desire ("Desire in its satisfaction is strictly speaking *destructive* and in its content is likewise *in-search-of-itself*";[73] "[desire's] impulse urges it just precisely to destroy this independence and freedom of external things, and to show that they are only there to be destroyed and consumed"[74]). In reality, Freud is here thinking of the pseudopods that allow Haeckel's protists to phagocytize food, as well as of the description that Wilhelm Bölsche gave of this process: "With the firstlings of life there was no opposition between eating and love; eating was a purely logical condition of love";[75] "Love by the fusion of two individuals for the purpose of producing a third is merely a refined form of feeding."[76]

It is this very literally fusional and all-consuming love of our unicellular ancestors that the first oral-cannibalistic stage of the libido is supposed to reproduce at the ontogenetic level. In a section added that same year, 1915, to the *Three Essays*, Freud sees in this phase and in the one that follows it, the sadistic-anal phase, a

> harking back to early animal forms of life. The first of these is the oral or, as it might be called, cannibalistic pregenital sexual organization. Here sexual activity has not yet been separated from the ingestion of food; nor are opposite currents within the activity differentiated. The object of both activities is the same; the sexual aim consists in the *incorporation* of the object – the prototype of a process which, in the form of *identification*, is later to play such an important psychological part.[77]

Originally, there was not opposition but *identity* of the self-preservation drives and the sexual drives, narcissistic *identification* of the ego and the love object. Freud will repeat it later regarding the maternal breast, in a very famous posthumous note: "'The breast is a part of me, I am the breast.' Only later: 'I have it' – that is, 'I am not it.'"[78] Clearly, Freud is confronting here venerable philosophical questions – the Same and the Other, identity and difference, subject and object, self and other – but giving them a biogenetic formulation and solution. The problem, from his own point of view, is that this solution is monistic. Before any "attachment" of the sexual object on the ego's vital functions, before any secondary "contribution" of the libido to the social relations to others, the

[73] Hegel 1830, § 428, translation modified. [74] Hegel 1835, 41.
[75] Bölsche 1926, Volume 1 (1898), 262. [76] Ibid., 138. [77] Freud 1905a, 198.
[78] Freud 1938a, 299.

sexual drives and the drives of self-preservation are indeed posited as originally "indistinguishable," undifferentiated. How then to explain their later conflict? How, above all, to maintain in its central position the mechanism of repression, "the cornerstone on which the whole of psychoanalysis rests"?[79]

The Ego-Ideal

As long as the theory of drives remained clearly dualistic, the situation was simple: the ego, the representative of self-preservation and of the interests of the individual, repressed in the unconscious the ideational representatives of the dangerous sexual drives. *Ego contra Libido*, defense against expenditure, dam against flood. But if the two types of drive spring in fact from the same big narcissistic reservoir? But if the ego is itself source and object of libido? Why, in this case, does the ego repress the libido if it is no longer to preserve itself from an antagonistic drive? Why, in short, does it repress *itself*?

For love of self. This is the surprising answer given by Freud in the last section of "On Narcissism": "Repression, we have said, proceeds from the ego; we might say with greater precision that it proceeds from the self-respect (*Selbstachtung*) of the ego."[80] We remember that Freud mentioned previously, among the different choices of narcissistic object, "what [one oneself] would like to be."[81] This is what he calls here "ideal ego" (*Idealich*) or "ego-ideal" (*Ichideal*):

> This ideal ego is now the target of the self-love (*Selbstliebe*) which was enjoyed in childhood by the actual ego. The subject's narcissism makes its appearance displaced on to this new ideal ego, which, like the infantile ego, finds itself possessed of every perfection that is of value. As always where the libido is concerned, man has here again shown himself incapable of giving up a satisfaction he had once enjoyed . . . What he projects before him as his ideal is the substitute for the lost narcissism of his childhood in which he was his own ideal . . . In this way large amounts of libido of an essentially homosexual kind are drawn into the formation of the narcissistic ego ideal and find outlet and satisfaction in maintaining it.[82]

The ego loves and desires itself in an ideal image of itself, and it is what leads it to repress what does not correspond with this image. Repression, in this respect, is not so much a matter of self-preservation and rational interest as of vanity, of self-love. Notwithstanding Kant, the moral

[79] Freud 1914a, 16. [80] Freud 1914c, 93. [81] Ibid., 90. [82] Ibid., 94–96.

conscience and its imperatives are profoundly irrational because ultimately libidinal in nature:

> It would not surprise us if we were to find a special psychical agency which performs the task of seeing that narcissistic satisfaction from the ego ideal is ensured and which, with this end in view, constantly watches the actual ego and measures it by that ideal. If such an agency does exist, we cannot possibly come upon it as a discovery – we can only recognize it; for we may reflect that what we call our "*conscience*"(*Gewissen*) has the required characteristics.[83]

The voice of conscience, this self-critical and self-censoring agency that forbids us to let ourselves be led by what Kant calls our "pathological" impulses,[84] this voice is itself pathological, even delirious, as the persecuting voices of the paranoid show according to Freud:

> The institution of conscience was at bottom an embodiment, first of parental criticism, and subsequently of that of society ... The voices, as well as the undefined multitude, are brought into the foreground again by the disease, and so the evolution of conscience is reproduced regressively. But the revolt against this "*censoring agency*" arises out of the subject's desire (in accordance with the fundamental character of his illness) to liberate himself from all these influences ... and out of his withdrawal of homosexual libido from them. His conscience then confronts him in a regressive form as a hostile influence from without.[85]

Now, if the moral conscience comes back regressively in the form of verbal hallucinations, it can only be, in good Freudian doctrine, because it was rejected due to its narcissistic, homosexual character. The ideal ego, the repressing authority, is rooted in what it represses, self-censor and libido turned against itself. Just like the devouring ego of primary narcissism from which it descends, it is thus situated on both sides of the drive dualism. *Which is no longer, therefore, a dualism.*

Freud will end up admitting this later in his encyclopedia article "The Theory of the Libido":

> It thus seemed on the face of it as though the slow process of psychoanalytic research was following in the steps of Jung's speculation about a primal libido, especially because the transformation of object-libido into narcissism necessarily carried along with it a certain degree of desexualization, or abandonment of the specifically sexual aims. Nevertheless, it has to be borne in mind that the fact that the self-preservative drives of the ego are

[83] Ibid., 95. [84] Kant 1788, 49. [85] Freud 1914c, 96.

> recognized as libidinal does not necessarily prove that there are no other drives operating in the ego.[86]

The Compulsion to Repeat

What this last sentence alludes to is the third theory of drives put forward in 1920 in "Beyond the Pleasure Principle." Freud, in this famous writing, intends to restore drive dualism, which had been threatened for a while, by introducing a completely new polarity, that of life drives (*Lebenstriebe*) and death drives (*Todestriebe*):

> Our views have from the very first been dualistic, and to-day they are even more definitely *dualistic* than before – now that we describe the opposition as being, not between ego-drives and sexual drives but between life drives and death drives. Jung's libido theory is on the contrary monistic; the fact that he has called his one drive force "libido" is bound to cause confusion, but need not affect us otherwise. We suspect that drives other than *the libidinal self-preservation drives* operate in the ego.[87]

Below the ego-libido, there is death. Below Eros, Thanatos.

It is generally agreed that the idea of the death drive is a major innovation, whether it is to salute the speculative audacity of an aging Freud or, on the contrary, to deplore the absence of a biological foundation for this new hypothesis. In reality, the third theory of drives is in line with the first two, whose presuppositions it systematizes and generalizes by deploying their ultimate, quasi-"transcendental" (Gilles Deleuze) implications.[88] We may well call this philosophy. Freud says it himself: his essay tackles "ultimate things, the great problems of science and life."[89] In more technical terms, we can say that the third theory of drives is an attempt to link even more closely than before the neurophysiological speculation on the reflex structure of the psychical apparatus and the biological speculation on the development of the libido.

The 1920 writing is presented, more precisely, as a speculation (*Spekulation*) on the "beyond the pleasure principle." We recall what this principle corresponds to for Freud: given a closed psychic system where the quantities of excitation are bound (*gebändigt*) and maintained at a constant level, it will tend to discharge (to unbind, to liberate: *entbinden*) as quickly as possible the excitations flowing in from outside or inside the body, in

[86] Freud 1923a, 257, translation modified.
[87] Freud 1920, 53, translation modified, my emphasis.
[88] Deleuze 1967, 29 (passage omitted in the English translation).
[89] Freud 1920, 59.

the mode of reflex action. The tension increase is felt as unpleasant; the discharge (*Entbindung*) which restores the balance of the system is felt as pleasure, hence the name of the principle. As for the principle of reality that through the ego inhibits, delays, and binds the immediate discharge of the primary processes according to the requirements of self-preservation, it only apparently contravenes the principle of pleasure since the displeasure that it implies is never more than a deferred pleasure, a detour in view of satisfaction (of unbinding). Even the "neurotic unpleasure is of that kind – pleasure that cannot be felt as such."[90] The principle of reality (also called principle of displeasure, *Unlustprinzip*) is a "modification" of the principle of pleasure,[91] not an antagonistic principle.

But here are three phenomena that seem to contradict this dominance of the pleasure principle:

- *Traumatic dreams.* The Great War had seen an epidemic of "war neuroses" caused by the terrible traumas experienced in the trenches (British psychiatrists spoke of "shell shock"). Now, not only is the etiology of these neuroses clearly not sexual but the nightmares of the victims make them constantly relive the triggering trauma (the famous flashbacks of post-traumatic disorders). Doesn't this contradict the theory of the dream as a wish fulfillment and the hegemony of the pleasure principle?
- *The cotton reel game.* Freud observes an eighteen-month-old child (his grandson Ernst) who amuses himself by making a wooden reel disappear and reappear with a piece of string tied around it, punctuating his game with an *o-o-o-o* (*fort*, "gone" in German), followed by a triumphant *da!* ("there it is"). But "the first act, that of departure, was staged as a game in itself and far more frequently than the episode in its entirety, with its pleasurable ending."[92] Why? "How then does his repetition of this distressing experience as a game fit in with the pleasure principle?"[93]
- *The transference.* This is the most disturbing objection: nearly a quarter of a century after the beginnings of psychoanalysis, Freud still cannot cure neurotics. The cures are interminable; the patients obstinately reproduce the same behaviors, the same resistances, the same transferences onto the analyst. Indeed, we remember that Freud interprets any disagreement about his hypotheses as a refusal to heal and a reproduction, in the relationship with the analyst, of previous

[90] Ibid., 11. [91] Ibid. [92] Ibid., 16. [93] Ibid., 15.

conflicts: "The patient cannot remember the whole of what is repressed in him ... He is obliged to *repeat* the repressed material as a contemporary experience instead of, as the physician would prefer to see, *remembering* it as something belonging to the past."[94] Patients remain obstinately ill (Karl Mayreder, Sergius Pankejeff); "they seek to bring about the interruption of the treatment while it is still incomplete" (Ida Bauer, Margarethe Csonka), or, on the contrary, they do everything to make it last (Elfriede Hirschfeld, Anna von Vest, Victor von Dirsztay); they "oblige the physician to speak severely to them and treat them coldly" (Bruno Veneziani).[95] Now, "how is [this] compulsion to repeat (*Wiederholungszwang*) – the manifestation of the power of the repressed – related to the pleasure principle? ... [T]he compulsion to repeat also recalls from the past experiences which include no possibility of pleasure, and which can never, even long ago, have brought satisfaction even to drive impulses which have since been repressed."[96] How to explain this failure of psychoanalytical therapy, this resistance to change and happiness?

Regarding the first two phenomena, which he objects to himself in the manner of an "*advocatus diaboli*,"[97] Freud ends up reintegrating them in spite of everything in the orbit of the pleasure principle. The child, by tossing his reel away from him, certainly repeats an unpleasant experience, but it is to better master it:

> At the outset he was in a passive situation – he was overpowered by the experience; but, by repeating it, unpleasurable though it was, as a game, he took on an active part ... the child may, after all, only have been able to repeat his unpleasant experience in play because the repetition carried along with it a yield of pleasure (*Lustgewinn*) of another sort but none the less a direct one.[98]

Same explanation for the nightmares of war neurotics and other deeply traumatized people. By constantly bringing the dreamer back to the moment of the physical shock, they allow the dreamer to act instead of suffering, by re-establishing the psychic preparation (fear, anxiety) which had been lacking at the time (fright): "These dreams are endeavouring to master the stimulus retrospectively, by developing the anxiety whose omission was the cause of the traumatic neurosis."[99]

[94] Ibid., 18. [95] Ibid., 21; Borch-Jacobsen 2021. [96] Freud 1920, 20, translation modified.
[97] Ibid., 59. [98] Ibid., 16. [99] Ibid., 32.

Extending the discussion to the metapsychological level, Freud imagines that a "protective shield" protects the psychical apparatus by filtering the stimuli coming from the outside world, so as to maintain the quantities of energy inside the system at a constant level. Thus protected, this "system which is itself highly cathected is capable of taking up an additional stream of fresh inflowing energy and of converting it into quiescent cathexis, that is of 'binding' it psychically"[100] in view of a later discharge. This is the normal regime of the pleasure/constancy principle coupled with the reality principle: tension followed by release, binding (*Bindung*) followed by unbinding (*Entbindung*, *Lustentbindung*). Trauma, on the other hand, would correspond to a rupture of the protective shield and to a massive influx of free, unbound (*ungebändigt*) energy, requiring a no less massive counter-cathexis at the level of the breach to slow down, brake, and inhibit the devastating flood. Hence the "fixation" to the trauma[101] and the repetition of the painful experience:

> the pleasure principle is for the moment put out of action. There is no longer any possibility of preventing the mental apparatus from being flooded with large amounts of stimulus, and another problem arises instead – the problem of mastering the amounts of stimulus which have broken in and of binding them, in the psychical sense, so that they can then be disposed of.[102]

It is not by chance that Freud writes that "the pleasure principle is *for the moment* put out of action." For the binding repetition is temporary; it is only a detour towards a properly terminal pleasure, putting an end to the reiteration. It is a little, says Freud in a very significant way, like the quasi-painful rise of sexual excitation (the *Vorlust* of the *Three Essays*) prepares the "pleasure of discharge" (of evacuation, of drainage: *Abfuhrlust*).[103] One must first bind, *binden*, to then discharge. Nothing that contradicts the hydraulics of this (very masculine) pleasure principle – on the contrary:

> We have found that one of the earliest and most important functions of the mental apparatus is to bind the drive impulses which impinge on it, to replace the primary process prevailing in them by the secondary process and convert their freely mobile cathectic energy into a mainly quiescent (tonic) cathexis. While this transformation is taking place no attention can be paid to the development of unpleasure; but this does not imply the suspension of the pleasure principle. On the contrary, the transformation occurs on behalf of the pleasure principle; the binding is a preparatory act which introduces

[100] Ibid., 30. [101] Ibid., 13. [102] Ibid., 29–30. [103] Ibid., 62.

> and assures the dominance of the pleasure principle.[104]

There remains, then, the repetition of the transference. For this one, Freud cannot bring himself to see in it a repetition with a view to a secondary benefit or a subsequent gain in pleasure. It has, he says, a "daemonic" character[105] in that the patients seem to be driven to repeat for the sake of repeating, compulsively, without end or reason. Where does this iterative drive, this compulsion to repeat, come from, then, if it can no longer be accounted for within the neurophysiological economy of the (un)pleasure principle? To understand this, Freud turns once again to the biology of instincts and Haeckel's biogenetic law. All life, he reminds us, is punctuated by cycles, repetitive circles (the "grandiose [*großartig*] conception of Wilhelm Fliess" is not far away[106]). Living beings reproduce from generation to generation; they go through the same evolutionary phases; they are subjected to the same "thrusts," "periods," and Fliessian biorhythms; they return tirelessly to the same places (migratory birds and fish), etc.,

> but we are quickly relieved of the necessity for seeking for further examples by the reflection that the most impressive proofs of there being an organic compulsion to repeat lie in the phenomena of heredity and the facts of embryology. We see how the germ of a living animal is obliged in the course of its development to recapitulate (even if only in a transient and abbreviated fashion) the structures of all the forms from which it is sprung, instead of proceeding quickly by the shortest path to its final shape.[107]

And the development of the libido, let us not forget, repeats the history of the species and of life in general, which itself repeats the history of the earth in its relations with the moon and the sun.[108]

Everything in nature that pushes, pulses, propels forward is therefore simultaneously a re-turn, one more turn bringing us back to the starting point. "Eternal Return of the Same," says Freud, quoting Nietzsche:[109]

> At this point we cannot escape a suspicion that we may have come upon the track of a universal attribute of drives and perhaps of organic life in general which has not hitherto been clearly recognized or at least not explicitly stressed. It seems, then, that *a drive is an urge inherent in organic life to restore an earlier state of things* which the living entity has been obliged to abandon under the pressure of external disturbing forces.[110]

[104] Ibid., translation modified. [105] Ibid., 35–36. [106] Ibid., 45. [107] Ibid., 37.
[108] Ibid., 38. [109] Ibid., 22, translation modified. [110] Ibid., 36, translation modified.

In this sense, *every* drive is a compulsion to repeat, an urge to retrace a cycle initiated by an initial disturbance. To make his point, Freud adopts here the language of the cosmogonies of old:

> Once upon a time (*irgend einmal*) the attributes of life were evoked in inanimate matter by the action of a force of whose nature we can form no conception . . . The tension which then arose in what had hitherto been an inanimate substance endeavoured to cancel itself out. In this way the first drive came into being: the drive to return to the inanimate state.[111]

Translated into metabiological terms, this means that all life returns to death, "for dust you are and to dust you will return" (*Genesis* 3: 17–19): "we shall be compelled to say that '*the aim (Ziel) of life is death*' and, looking backwards, that '*inanimate things existed before living ones.*'"[112] Translated into neurophysiological terms, this means that the energetic tension that defines life and pushes to action ("Every drive is a piece of activity"[113]) tends to return to the absolute zero of tension, a bit like an old battery discharges at the end of its life. Action is in view of inaction, in view of the nirvana that "extinguishes" the cycle of reincarnations. Freud takes up this Buddhist notion popularized by Schopenhauer by making of it a "Nirvana principle,"[114] but it should be noted that the latter is nothing else than an extreme formulation of the pleasure principle: the truly final pleasure towards which the will-to-live tendency is inertia; it is death. *Which is, therefore, not "beyond" the pleasure principle*, since it is precisely that which animates and orients the compulsion (the drive) to repeat.

We have here an ultimate synthesis of the two speculations, the metabiological and the neurophysiological. What binds them together is the notion of binding, *Bindung*. At the neurophysiological level, *Bindung* provides the principle of the establishment of stable, coherent units, with constant investment: it is by binding the free energies flowing from outside and by storing them inside their own limits that, for a moment, these units defer the discharge and return to the zero degree of tension.

At the biological level, *Bindung* provides the principle of life as merging or fusion (*Verschmelzung*) of different units: it is by binding to another organism that living beings acquire the energy necessary to postpone death and start again for a new round. Contrary to August Weismann, who affirmed that unicellular organisms such as paramecia are potentially immortal,[115] Freud invokes the work of other researchers tending to show

[111] Ibid., 38, translation modified. [112] Ibid. [113] Freud 1915a, 122, translation modified.
[114] Freud 1920, 56. [115] Weismann 1882; Weismann 1883.

that protozoans die on their own accord unless they "copulate" with other protists by launching their famous pseudopods or are exposed to external sources of excitation, either chemical or mechanical:[116] "This tallies well with the hypothesis that the life process of the individual leads for internal reasons to an abolition of chemical tensions, that is to say, to death, whereas union with the living substance of a different individual increases those tensions, introducing what may be described as fresh *vital differences* which must then *be lived off*."[117]

Since the arch-traumatic influx of the great "unrepresentable force" that introduced the first vital difference, the living tirelessly repeat this energetic difference in order to be able to reduce it, by binding (to) the other, (to) the outside. They are, says Freud, like the androgyne of Plato's *Symposium*, whose parts separated by Zeus "threw their arms about one another eager to grow into one."[118] This compulsion binds, agglutinates, unifies the separated, but in doing so, it repeats the difference that it seeks to cancel. Instead of letting the separated ones die their own death, alone, it restarts the eternal wheel of life by binding them together to form new units, which in turn, etc. Hence, a continuous lengthening of the drive cycle that leads to death, but also a multiplication of repetitive cycles of different amplitudes, each bound unit wanting to return to the starting point at its own rhythm, without consideration for the superior or inferior units. Thus, the "cellular state" (*Zellenstaat*)[119] formed by the union of two or more cells will be vital-binding with respect to these cells,[120] and lethal-unbinding with respect to the cellular community of which they themselves are a part, a little like the "narcissistic … malignant neoplasms" of cancer.[121] The ego of self-preservation drives, likewise, will be vital with respect to the cells that it aggregates and lethal, narcissistic, and unbinding with respect to the family or love unit of the sexual drives, or even with respect to the super-cellular state that is the crowd, the social mass (*Masse*) "held together" (*zusammengehalten*) by Eros.[122]

The same difference of rhythm, Freud writes, in the case of Weismann's mortal soma and immortal germen:

> It is as though the life of the organism moved with a vacillating rhythm (*Zauderrythmus*). One group of drives rushes forward so as to reach the final aim of life as swiftly as possible; but when a particular stage in the advance

[116] Freud 1920, 48. [117] Ibid., 55. [118] Ibid., 58.

[119] Ibid., 50, translation modified. "*Zellenstaat*" is a term borrowed from Bölsche 1887, 50–59; Bölsche 1926 (1898), 165, 186, etc.

[120] Freud 1920, 50. [121] Ibid., 50. [122] Freud 1921, 92.

> has been reached, the other group jerks back to a certain point to make a fresh start and so prolong the journey.[123]

Life Drive, Death Drive

It is at this precise point that Freud introduces the polarity between two types of drives: those which "exercise pressure towards death" – death drives – and the others, sexual drives, which exercise pressure "towards a prolongation of life" – life drives.[124] As he will summarize later in *Civilization and Its Discontents*:

> Starting from speculations on the beginning of life and from biological parallels, I drew the conclusion that, besides the drive to preserve living substance and to join it into ever larger units, there must exist another, contrary drive seeking to dissolve those units and to bring them back to their primaeval, inorganic state. That is to say, apart from Eros (*außer dem Eros*) there was a death drive.[125]

One often wants to see in this famous pair an antagonism between two opposite forces, such as the one between Dionysus and Apollo in Nietzsche or *Philia* and *Neikos* in Empedocles. This is certainly in line with Freud's avowed intention to refound the theory of drives on a firmly dualistic basis, but it does not correspond to what he himself tells us. Strictly speaking, there cannot be a death drive separate from the life drives, since *every* drive is supposed to return to the inanimate and the zero degree of tension. A drive is always both a life *and* a death drive, a detour *and* a return: it is by living that we all return to dust. In the same way that there is no repetition beyond the pleasure principle, since repetition (binding, tension) is at the very center of this principle, we must say, contradicting Freud, that *there is no death drive either*, if at least we understand by this a dark suicidal desire or an obscure "primary masochism."[126] On the contrary, it is only by persevering in our being, by wanting with all our strength to live (self-preservation drives) and to copulate (sexual drives) that we accomplish the repetitive cycle that brings us back to the starting point.

Freud confused two things when making the difference between drive cycles into a difference in nature, as if there were death drives on one side and life drives on the other. Following his own theory, the conflicts between drives (ego-drives/sexual drives, for example) are in fact only

[123] Freud 1920, 41, translation modified. [124] Ibid., 44.
[125] Freud 1930, 118–119, translation modified. [126] Freud 1924.

due to differences in tempo, being understood that they all repeat the same circular path towards the same final goal at their own rhythm. Freud must have realized this, because he recognizes towards the end of the essay that he has difficulty in finding a death drive that is not at the same time a life drive, a manifestation of "the Eros of the poets and philosophers which holds all living things together."[127] Recapitulating the theory of primary narcissism, he thus proposes to derive

> the narcissistic libido of the ego from the stores of libido by means of which the cells of the soma are attached to one another. But we now find ourselves suddenly faced by another question. If the self-preservative drives too are of a libidinal nature, are there perhaps no other drives whatever but the libidinal ones? At all events there are none other visible.[128]

As far as one would look, one would only see erotic *Bindung*, and one would then risk, Freud objects, falling back into Jung's libidinal monism, by undermining the hypothesis of a death drive opposed to the life drives.

Freud, therefore, wants to find a case of pure death drive in order to re-establish the dualism. But where? Unable to find a truly *auto*-destructive drive, he falls back by default on the *allo*-destructive drive – on sadism:

> Is it not plausible to suppose that this sadism is in fact a death drive which, under the influence of the narcissistic libido, has been forced away from the ego and has consequently only emerged in relation to the object? It now enters the service of the sexual function. During the oral stage of organization of the libido, the act of obtaining erotic mastery over an object coincides with that object's destruction; later, the sadistic instinct separates off, and finally, at the stage of genital primacy, it takes on, for the purposes of reproduction, the function of overpowering the sexual object to the extent necessary for carrying out the sexual act. It might indeed be said that the sadism which has been forced out of the ego has pointed the way for the libidinal components of the sexual drive, and that these follow after it to the object . . . If such an assumption as this is permissible, then we have met the demand that we should produce an example of a death instinct – though, it is true, a displaced one.[129]

Thus, it would be necessary to admit that sadism proves the improvable, improbable death drive. As a matter of fact, hatred and aggressiveness will henceforth keep this status in Freudian theory, to the point that the term destructive drive, *Destruktionstrieb*, will tend more and more to take over from *Todestrieb*. In "The Economic Problem of Masochism," Freud speaks of the "death or destructive drive" and continues two sentences later by

[127] Freud 1920, 50. [128] Ibid., 52. [129] Ibid., 54.

calling it, indifferently, "the destructive drive, the drive for mastery, the *will to power*."[130] But is this sadistic drive an example of the death drive itself? No – nor is it a counterexample of the life drives. Freud recognizes it himself; it is an example of "displaced" death drive, diverted from its path, expelled out of the narcissistic ego, which is to say as well: bound to the object, allied to the life drives. Even when it destroys the object by absorbing it, in the way of a protist phagocyting another cell, the narcissistic ego of the oral-cannibalistic phase unites with it, couples, copulates erotically. This sadism is thus already libidinal, binding, vital. Better still, this projection of the death drive towards the other is, according to Freud, the very thing that inaugurates the relationship to the object and therefore the libidinal binding in general: "the libidinal components of the sexual drive . . . follow after [sadism] to the object." It could not be better said that Eros is finally *nothing other* than Thanatos (or Narcissus), and the reverse. Any drive, whatever it is, is a love *and* a destruction of oneself in the other, a will to live *and* a will to die, a will to power *and* a nihilism.

Freud ends up admitting this half-heartedly in "The Economic Problem of Masochism": "we can only assume that a very extensive fusion and amalgamation, in varying proportions, of the two classes of drives takes place, so that we never have to deal with pure life drives or pure death drives but only with mixtures of them in different amounts." Which does not prevent him from continuing: "Corresponding to a fusion of drives of this kind, there may, as a result of certain influences, be a defusion of them. How large the portions of the death drives are which refuse to be tamed in this way by being bound (*solcher Bändigung durch die Bindung*) to admixtures of libido we cannot at present guess."[131]

We don't know anything about it; we can't see it; we can't hear it (the death drive is "mute"; it "works in silence"[132]), but it is imperative that there be something beyond, *meta* – something transcendental, in other words – in order to justify the drive dualism and the interpretative divination of psychoanalysis. The "beyond the pleasure principle" is nowhere else to be found than in this speculation.

130 Freud 1924, 163, translation modified, my emphasis.
131 Ibid., 164.
132 Freud 1923b, 46; Freud 1925a, 57.

CHAPTER 5

Culture

Very early on, psychoanalysis presented itself as a general psychology and even as the only true human science. Starting with a theory of hysteria and the "neuro-psychoses of defense," Freud gradually extended its field to dreams, slips of the tongue, and parapraxes, to witticisms, art, literature, myths, religions, society, and finally, to a theory of *Kultur* – a German term that means at once culture, civilization, and (*via* Herder) the essence of a community or people. It is in this capacity, and not as a simple psychotherapy of the "nervous," that psychoanalysis conquered the world – the whole world. Freud recalled this in 1925, recapitulating his journey since the publication of *The Interpretation of Dreams* and the *Psychopathology of Everyday Life*:

> Previously psycho-analysis had only been concerned with solving pathological phenomena ... But when it came to dreams, it was no longer dealing with a pathological symptom, but with a phenomenon of normal mental life which might occur in any healthy person. If dreams turned out to be constructed like symptoms, if their explanation required the same assumptions – the repression of impulses, substitutive formation, compromise-formation, the dividing of the conscious and the unconscious into various psychical systems – then psycho-analysis was no longer an auxiliary science in the field of psychopathology, it was rather the starting-point of a new and deeper science of the mind which would be equally indispensable for the understanding of the normal. One could carry over (*übertragen*) its postulates and findings to other regions of mental and spiritual happening (*des seelischen und geistigen Geschehens*); a path lay open to it that led far afield, into spheres of universal interest.[1]

Applied Psychoanalysis

1. Everyone dreams. 2. Dreams are structured *like* the symptoms of neurotics. 3. Therefore everyone can be analyzed *like* neurotics. This is

[1] Freud 1925a, 47, translation modified.

the syllogism of the so-called applied psychoanalysis (*angewandte Psychoanalyse*), which is based on a continuous series of analogies (this is the term Freud always uses, *Analogie*): dream is like neurosis, art is like dream, and then also literature, folklore, mythology, etc. The chronology of Freud's writings reflects this analogical extension of the Freudian field: first, *Studies on Hysteria*; then *The Interpretation of Dreams* (1900); then *Psychopathology of Everyday Life* (1901) and *Jokes and their Relation to the Unconscious* (1905); then the small writings on art and literature (*Delusions and Dreams in Jensen's Gradiva*,[2] "Creative Writers and Day-Dreaming," "Leonardo da Vinci and a Memory of his Childhood," "The Moses of Michelangelo,"[3] etc.); *Totem and Taboo* (1912–1913); "The Uncanny" (1919);[4] *Group Psychology and the Analysis of the Ego* (1921); and finally, the "cultural" texts of the last period, *The Future of an Illusion* (1927), *Civilization and Its Discontents* (1930), "Why War?" (1933), *Moses and Monotheism* (1939).

This indeed gives the impression that Freud was content to "apply" or "carry over" in a mechanical way a model derived from psychopathology to other domains, progressing from one step to another and crushing in the process all the differences between the normal and the pathological, the sublime and the morbid, the social and the individual. But in reality, this blurring of the limits between neurosis and normality was present from the beginning in psychoanalysis, from the biologizing turn of the Fliess years. Let us remember: seeking to explain in an evolutionary way the psychological phenomenon of neurotic repression, Freud theorized that the latter was rooted, in the final analysis, in an "organic" repression of the forms of perverse sexuality abandoned during the evolution of the species. This was to state from the outset that repression is a destiny of humanity, and not only a neurotic mechanism. Freud will repeat this throughout; we all repress, even if we do not all repress in the same way, nor with the same intensity: "the borderline between the normal and the abnormal in nervous matters is a fluid one, and . . . we are all a little neurotic";[5] "a normal ego of this sort is, like normality in general, an ideal fiction";[6] "We have seen that it is not scientifically feasible to draw a line of demarcation between what is psychically normal and abnormal";[7] "since the boundaries between [normal and pathological processes] are not sharply drawn, their mechanisms are to a large extent the same."[8]

[2] Freud 1907b. [3] Freud 1914d. [4] Freud 1919b. [5] Freud 1901, 278.
[6] Freud 1937a, 235. [7] Freud 1938b, 195. [8] Freud 1939, 125.

Everyone is susceptible to analysis (a shoreless extension of the field of the application of analytic psychotherapy), just as is any human activity or production (a shoreless extension of the field of the application of psychoanalytic theory). Psychoanalysis "applies" to everyone and everything, to the sick as well as to the healthy, to symptoms as well as to symbols, to art as well as to dreams or to slips of the tongue. The extraordinary cultural success of psychoanalysis in the twentieth century finds its main reason there. But it is important to understand that it is not psychoanalysis as a theory of neuroses that is applied to other fields, because, strictly speaking, this psychopathological theory is only one of the multiple applications of a general science of man whose "cornerstone" is repression.[9]

Behind the symptom, dream, witticism, slip of the tongue, work of art, or advances in science and technology, we always find the same repression of infantile drives, albeit confronted differently depending on the case. Some succumb to neurosis or psychosis under the effect of too strong libidinal fixations and/or regressions caused by sexual frustrations or traumas. Others manage to successfully repress their perverse and incestuous drives, or they sublimate them by diverting their energy towards nonsexual goals (science, intellectual investigation, "social drives"). Still others manage to make the expression of their drives and fantasies socially accepted by buying the complacency of their public thanks to a purely aesthetic or formal "yield of pleasure" – "incentive bonus" (*Verlockungsprämie*) of the artist, "technique" of the punster.[10]

The application of psychoanalysis is thus not from the restricted theory of psychoneuroses to "normal" and cultural phenomena but from the general theory of repression to the various effects and repercussions of the latter. The fact that Freud began as a clinician and then turned to culture should not mislead us: psychoanalysis is from the beginning a theory of culture, since it is a theory of repression as fons et origo of the civilizing process. We remember Freud's triumphant anticipation when he announced to Fliess: "Another presentiment tells me, as though I already knew – but I know nothing at all – that I shall very soon uncover the source of morality."[11] We also remember how the first formulation of "the idea of abandoned *erotogenic zones*" in the course of evolution was immediately followed by this: "In this . . . [would thus lie] progress in culture, and moral as well as individual development."[12] Psychoanalysis of culture is already completely there in these dazzling hypotheses about the "horror of incest," the erect posture, and the organic repression of the genito-

[9] Freud 1914a, 16. [10] Freud 1905d; Freud 1908. [11] Freud 1985, 249. [12] Ibid., 212.

urethral-anal stench, "the affective basis for a multitude of intellectual processes of development, such as morality, shame and the like."[13] Which will be echoed at the other end of the work: "The fateful process of civilization would thus have set in with man's adoption of an erect posture."[14] At the foundation of psychoanalysis as a theory of the repressed, there is a sociobiological theory of repression, that is to say of *Kultur*, mores, community, authority, social sanction.

Consequently, one should not say that Freud applied the results of individual psychology to what he himself very often calls "collective" or "group psychology" (*Kollektivpsychologie, Massenpsychologie*), because the latter precedes the former, both historically and logically. If the individual represses his/her perverse drives, it is not only because parents, community, society require it. More deeply, it is because at some given moment in the evolution of the human species, our ancestors adopted a vertical posture and abandoned the relevant sexual zones. The psychological, ontogenetic repression is only so compulsive because it repeats the organic, phylogenetic repression. Behind moral law and social prohibition stands Haeckel's biogenetic law. Our individual repression and therefore our unconscious are the recapitulation of a *collective* repression and unconscious: "Man's archaic heritage forms the nucleus of the unconscious mind; and whatever part of that heritage has to be left behind in the advance to later phases of development, because it is unserviceable or incompatible with what is new and harmful to it, falls a victim to the process of repression."[15]

It is true that Freud, in his book on Moses, explicitly refutes the Jungian notion of "collective unconscious": "It is not easy for us to carry over (*übertragen*) the concepts of individual psychology into group psychology (*Psychologie der Massen*); and I do not think we gain anything by introducing the concept of a 'collective' unconscious." But, he continues: "The content of the unconscious, indeed, is in any case a collective, universal property of mankind . . . We find that in a number of important relations our children react, not in a manner corresponding to their own experience, but instinctively (*instinktmässig*), like the animals, in a manner that is only explicable as phylogenetic acquisition."[16] As the philosopher Todd Dufresne aptly notes, Freud does not reject the concept of "collective unconscious" because it is false but because it is redundant (and Jungian).[17] The truth is that Freud and Jung agree on the trans-individual,

[13] Ibid., 280. [14] Freud 1930, 99. [15] Freud 1919a, 204. [16] Freud 1939, 132–133.
[17] Dufresne 2017, 230–231.

because phylogenetic, character of the unconscious, thus translating in psychobiological terms a tradition of romantic thought that goes from the "absolute unconscious" of Carl Gustav Carus (1789–1869) to the "universal consciousness" of André Breton.[18]

Far from cultural forms being explained by analogy with the forms of psychopathology, as the notion of "applied psychoanalysis" suggests, it is culture understood as a supra-individual, sociobiological process that ultimately explains the vicissitudes of individual psychology. If the myths and symbols of humanity are so similar to the dreams of the healthy and the symptoms of the neurotic, it is because dreams and symptoms are themselves individual recapitulations of these collective myths and symbols, "a repetition of the prehistoric and the ancient (*eine Wiederholung der Prähistorik und der Antike*)."[19] This provocative reversal proposed by Jung in his *Transformations and Symbols of the Libido*, with a long quotation from Nietzsche to support it, only makes explicit the biogenetic logic in Freud's work since the very beginning.

The Barrier against Incest

This is why one should not take literally the polemical statement that opens *Totem and Taboo*, subtitled "Some Points of Agreement between the Mental Lives of Savages and Neurotics" and Freud's first work devoted entirely to culture:

> The four essays that follow ... represent a first attempt on my part at applying the point of view and the findings of psycho-analysis to some unsolved problems of the psychology of peoples [*Völkerpsychologie*, a term difficult to translate, popularized by the psychologist Wilhelm Wundt (1832–1920)]. Thus they offer, on the one hand, a methodological contrast to Wilhelm Wundt's extensive work, which applies the hypotheses and working methods of non-analytic psychology to the same purposes, and on the other hand to the writings of the Zurich school of psycho-analysis, which endeavour, on the contrary, to solve the problems of individual psychology with the help of material derived from the psychology of peoples.[20]

Not only is this opposition between individual and collective psychology artificial and forced, from Freud's own point of view, but *Totem and Taboo* can in no way be reduced to a simple dilettante excursion of the

[18] Breton 1924a; see Shamdasani 2003, 235. [19] Jung 1912, 25.
[20] Freud 1912–1913, xii, translation modified.

psychoanalyst into ethnology. Rather, Freud addresses here a fundamental, central problem of psychoanalytic metapsychology itself, namely, the prohibition of incest as the origin of human culture.

Until then, it was the hypothesis of the organic repression of the quadruped-perverse sexuality that provided the cornerstone of the psychoanalytical edifice, by accounting for the appearance of the "cultural" reaction formations at the time of the sexual latency period. Having no more use because of this ontogenetic recapitulation of human "verticalization," the energy of the perverse drives would be directed, said the *Three Essays*, "from sexual aims and their direction to new ones – a process which deserves the name of 'sublimation'" and is the source of "all cultural achievements (*kulturellen Leistungen*)":[21]

> It is during the period of total or only partial latency that are built up the mental forces which are later to impede the course of the sexual drive and, like dams, restrict its flow – disgust, feelings of shame and the claims of aesthetic and moral ideals. One gets an impression from civilized children (*Kulturkinde*) that the construction of these dams is a product of education, and no doubt education has much to do with it. But in reality this development is organically determined and fixed by heredity, and it can occasionally occur without any help at all from education.[22]

Now, this biogenetic theory certainly provides the reason for the repression of the autoerotic-perverse sexuality postulated by Freud, as well as for the passage of each small human animal to civilization and the sublime. But what about the prohibition of incest?

In the *Three Essays* and again in the case history of little Hans, Freud imagined that the object love that follows autoeroticism is first directed (after a narcissistic-homosexual phase) towards the parent of the opposite sex, to then come up against the "barrier against incest" and be directed, after a period of sexual latency, towards substitutes for the incestuous object. However, to which episode of the history of the species can this universal horror of incest correspond? In the letters to Fliess and in the *Three Essays*, Freud invoked the necessity of establishing an exogamic exchange of women within society: "Respect for this barrier [against incest] is essentially a cultural demand (*Kulturforderung*) made by society. Society must (*muß*) defend itself against the danger that the interests which it needs for the establishment of higher social units may be swallowed up by the family."[23]

[21] Freud 1905a, 178, translation modified. [22] Ibid., translation modified. [23] Ibid., 225.

But why does society *have to* do this? Or rather, why *must* there be society and its "cultural demands"? Exogamy can be explained very well once society has been established, but it does not explain the establishment of society itself, its *instauratio*. From the evolutionary point of view which is that of Freud, one does not see why our ancestors would have sacrificed their sexual freedom "*for the benefit of the larger community*."[24] After all, these "Overmen" did not, by assumption, care about the community. Freud often quotes the "remarkable sentence" of Diderot, in *Rameau's Nephew*: "If the little savage were left to himself, preserving all his foolishness and adding to the small sense of a child in the cradle the violent passions of a man of thirty, he would strangle his father and lie with his mother."[25] Why then did the savages forbid themselves, one fine day, to do so?

What Freud finds here at the very heart of his metapsychobiological construction is finally nothing other than the classical question of the passage from the state of nature to the rule of law, such as what Hobbes, Spinoza, Rousseau, and Hegel had already asked themselves. The difference is that, unlike these thinkers, Freud has at his disposal an efficient time machine allowing him to go back in history: Haeckel's biogenetic law. As our present is nothing else than an abbreviated recapitulation of our past, Freud posits that we can reconstitute one from the other. This is how he had traced the evolution of human sexuality starting from those "fossils" that are perverts and children, or again how he had deduced the organic repression of perversions from the psychological repression of neurotics. In *Totem and Taboo*, he adds another fossil to this list, crucial for the reconstruction of the phylogenetic origin of the incest barrier: the savage.

Like so many of his contemporaries (James Sully, Herbert Spencer, G. Stanley Hall, James Mark Baldwin, Cesare Lombroso, Gustave Le Bon), Freud thinks, indeed, that the savage is like the child (or the idiot, or the criminal, or the man of the crowd). They all recapitulate primitive, pre-civilized, prelogical man: same "animism," same narcissism, same magical thinking, same belief in the "omnipotence of thoughts."[26] Spencer stated that "the intellectual traits of the uncivilized are traits recurring in the children of the civilized."[27] Sully wrote that "the lowest races of mankind stand in close proximity to the animal world. The same is

[24] Freud 1985, 252, my emphasis.
[25] Diderot 1762–1773, 178, quoted in Freud 1916–1917, 338; Freud 1931, 251; Freud 1938b, 192.
[26] Freud 1912–1913, 85 ff. [27] Spencer 1895, 89.

true for the infants of civilized races."[28] Freud, likewise, opens *Totem and Taboo* with the affirmation that

> in a certain sense [the prehistoric man] is still our contemporary. There are men still living who, as we believe, stand very near to primitive man, far nearer than we do . . . Such is our view of those whom we describe as savages or half-savages; and their mental life must have a peculiar interest for us if we are right in seeing in it a well-preserved picture of an early stage of our own development.[29]

So if it is true, as Baldwin wrote, that "the embryology of society is open to study in the nursery,"[30] all the more reason to study it in the social and mental lives of these grown children that are the savages, our earlier cousins. Hence this research program that Freud already announced at the end of the study on President Schreber, in direct reference to Jung's work:

> And I am of opinion that the time will soon be ripe for us to make an extension of a thesis which has long been asserted by psycho-analysts, and to complete what has hitherto had only an individual and ontogenetic application by the addition of its anthropological counterpart, which is to be conceived phylogenetically. "In dreams and in neuroses," so our thesis has run, "we come once more upon *the child* and the peculiarities which characterize his modes of thought and his emotional life." "And we come upon the *savage* too," we may now add, "upon the *primitive* man, as he stands revealed to us in the light of the researches of archaeology and of ethnology."[31]

Totem and Taboo

The starting point of the analysis is provided, in *Totem and Taboo*, by the prohibition of incest among Australian aborigines. They are, Freud tells us, the most savage humans on earth, the most devoid of culture, and the closest, therefore, to primitive man, our common ancestor. And yet, "these poor naked cannibals . . . set before themselves with the most scrupulous care and the most painful severity the aim of avoiding incestuous sexual relations."[32] (Why Freud qualifies them as cannibals we will learn in a moment.) These savages are consequently as though at the juncture between nature and culture, already downstream from the prohibition and yet still as close as possible to its establishment. As for the concrete

[28] Sully 1896, 5. [29] Freud 1912–1913, 1. [30] Baldwin 1895, 156. [31] Freud 1911, 82.
[32] Freud 1912–1913, 2.

form of the prohibition, Freud finds it in the famous law of totemic exogamy put forward by the anthropologist James Frazer (1854–1941) in the four volumes of *Totemism and Exogamy.*[33] In this impressive compilation, Frazer described how the aborigines are organized in kins bearing the name of a *totem*, most often an animal or a plant, which they venerate as the ancestor of the group and which is the object of all kinds of sacred prohibitions called *taboos.* Under penalty of punishment, clan members are forbidden to kill, touch, or consume their totem. It is similarly forbidden to have sexual relations with other members of the same totem clan: "In almost every place where we find totems we also find *a law against persons of the same totem having sexual relations with one another and consequently against their marrying.* This, then, is 'exogamy,' an institution related to totemism."[34]

Freud immediately speaks about the "horror of incest" of the savages, making the connection with the child and the neurotic:

> Psycho-analysis has taught us that a boy's earliest choice of objects for his love is incestuous . . . A neurotic . . . invariably exhibits some degree of psychical infantilism. He has either failed to get free from the psychosexual conditions that prevailed in his childhood or he has returned to them – two possibilities which may be summed up as developmental inhibition and regression . . . We have arrived at the point of regarding a child's relation to his parents, dominated as it is by incestuous longings, as the nuclear complex of neurosis.[35]

Hence the equation savage = neurotic, which allows Freud to reason by analogy and to apply to totemic institutions the same psychoanalytical inferences as to neurotic symptoms.

The savages forbid themselves in an extraordinarily severe way totemic "incest"? This must be because they strongly desire it, like the neurotics.[36] Their prohibitions and their taboos are imposed in an unmotivated and "categorical" way, like the Kantian imperative?[37] This is because the real reason for these prohibitions must remain unconscious, like the absurd "ceremonial" of the obsessional.[38] The tabooed thing arouses in them both veneration and terror, respect and repulsion? This is because they are "ambivalent" in relation to it, just as the neurotics are in relation to what tempts them all the more because it is something that they forbid themselves.[39] And finally, the totem animal, ancestor of the clan, shall not be

[33] Frazer 1887–1910. [34] Freud 1912–1913, 3–4. [35] Ibid., 17.
[36] Ibid., 32, 70, 123, etc. [37] Ibid., xiv, 22, 26. [38] Ibid., 27. [39] Ibid., 29, 31.

killed? This is because it represents the hated and loved *father*, just like the anxiety-provoking horse of little Hans' zoophobia.[40]

Expected conclusion:

> If the totem animal is the father, then the two principal ordinances of totemism, the two taboo prohibitions which constitute its core – not to kill the totem and not to have sexual relations with a woman of the same totem – coincide in their content with the two crimes of Oedipus, who killed his father and married his mother, as well as with the two primal wishes of children, the insufficient repression or the re-awakening of which forms the nucleus of perhaps every psychoneurosis.[41]

However, as convincing as they may (or may not) be, these analogies between savages and neurotics still do not tell us anything about the evolutionary, prehistoric origin of the two Oedipal prohibitions. The quasi-neurotic ambivalence of savages towards their totem may inform us about the incestuous and parricidal desires that plague them, but it still does not tell us why they forbid themselves to act on them. Now, Freud's question is: why do these "poor naked cannibals" prevent themselves from strangling their father and lying with their mother? To what phylogenetic event does this universal horror of incest, common to children, savages, and neurotics, refer?

To answer this evolutionary question, Freud first turns to Darwin himself. In *The Descent of Man*, Darwin had indeed tried to explain the origin of exogamy by the jealousy of dominant males within small herds of animals. In support of this theory, Darwin cited an article by Dr. Thomas Staughton Savage (1804–1880) in which he described the habits of the great ape he had discovered in Gabon, *Troglodytes gorilla*: "My informers all agree that but one adult male is seen in a band; when the young male grows up, a contest takes place for mastery, and the strongest, by killing and driving out the others, establishes himself as the head of the community."[42] Darwin deduced from this that "the younger males, being thus expelled and wandering about, would, when at last successful in finding a partner, prevent too close interbreeding within the limits of the same family."[43] This hypothesis was then taken up and amplified by James Jasper Atkinson (–1899) and his cousin Andrew Lang (1844–1912), both of whom saw in totemic exogamy a gradual institutionalization of the sexual jealousy of the dominating male of the primal horde.[44]

[40] Ibid., 126 ff. [41] Ibid., 132. [42] Savage 1847, 423, quoted in Darwin 1871, Volume 2, 362.
[43] Ibid. [44] Lang and Atkinson 1903.

Freud, significantly, is not satisfied with this genesis of exogamy. This is because the Darwin–Atkinson theory does not solve the problem of the passage from force to right, that is to say, to consented authority. It is easy to see why young males are obliged to seek out females outside the horde, but it is not clear why they stop themselves from finding them within it. Atkinson himself explained that after a while, the alpha male had to be killed by the other males who were ganging up on him, after which they would fight among themselves to see who would become the new sexual despot, etc. So why would the cycle of violence ever stop? "Thus," writes Freud, "any new organization of society would be precluded."[45] To explain the emergence of the totemic institution, we must explain how and why the young males (the "sons" or "brothers," in Atkinson's anachronistic terms) came to *internalize* the external violence of the dominant male (of the "tyrannical father"[46]), by renouncing the females of the horde.

Freud summed up the problem – and its solution – in a letter to Jones, while he was writing the last chapter of *Totem and Taboo*:

> The true historical source of repression I hope to touch upon in the last of the 4 papers ... I may as well give you the answer now: Every *internal* repression barrier is the historical outcome of an *external* obstacle. Therefore: internalization (*Verinnerlichung*) of resistances, the history of the human race as deposited in its present innate tendencies to repression.[47]

We note in passing this term "internalization," which comes directly from Nietzsche's *Genealogy of Morals*: "All instincts that do not discharge themselves outwardly *turn inwards* – this is what I call the *internalization* (*Verinnerlichung*) of man ... Hostility, cruelty, joy in persecuting, in attacking, in change, in destruction – all this turned against the possessors of such instincts: *that* is the origin of 'bad conscience.'"[48]

This internalization Freud finds in the cannibalism of the members of the primal horde: "Cannibal savages as they were, it goes without saying that they devoured the one they had killed (*den Getöteten*)."[49] This is why, from the outset, Freud described the Australian aborigines as "poor naked cannibals": it is essential for his thesis that the great apes from which these savage men descend have *ingested*, *incorporated* the jealous male who was an obstacle to their sexual drives. In support of this construction, he invokes the theory of sacrifice proposed by the pastor William Robertson

[45] Freud 1912–1913, 142. [46] Ibid. [47] Freud and Jones 1993, 148
[48] Nietzsche 1887, II, 16. [49] Freud 1912–1913, 142, translation modified.

Smith (1846–1894) in his famous *Lectures on the Religion of the Semites.*[50] Smith, a friend of Frazer's and a prominent biblical scholar, argued that Semitic sacrificial rites represented the remnants of the "totem stage" of the religious development of humanity as a whole. According to him, their original meaning was the affirmation by group members of their commensality with the totemic deity during the ritual consumption of a sacrificial animal. By eating it together, the humans and the god sealed their community of blood: "It was natural, therefore, that the kinsmen and their kindred god should seal and strengthen their fellowship by meeting together from time to time to nourish their common life by a common meal."[51] Freud's paraphrase: "This completely literal way of regarding blood-kinship as identity of substance makes it easy to understand the necessity for renewing it from time to time by the physical process of the sacrificial meal."[52]

Smith, in fact, did not identify the sacrificial animal with the totemic animal. He certainly pointed out in passing that "the totem is sometimes sacrificed at an annual feast" and "eaten as a mystic sacrament," but he added in a note that: "The proof of this has to be put together out of *the fragmentary evidence* which is generally all that we possess on such matters."[53] Freud, in his own summary of Smith's thesis, does not show the same caution: "On the basis of copious evidence (*einer reichen Evidenz*)," he writes, "Robertson Smith identifies the sacrificial animal with the primitive totem animal."[54] One quickly understands why Freud is so keen for the consumed victim to be the totemic animal (the parent) itself. Indeed, the totemic animal having previously been identified as the father via the zoophobia of little Hans, he can now find the father figure behind the sacrificial victim of the totemic meal and finally complete the Darwin–Atkinson hypothesis. How, he asks himself, could the totemic institution have arisen from the Darwinian horde?

> Can this form of organization have developed out of the other one? And if so, along what lines? If we call the celebration of the totem meal to our help, we shall be able to find an answer. One day the brothers who had been driven out came together, killed and *devoured* their father and so made an end of the patriarchal horde.[55]

To eat, absorb, consume, is to commune, to become one with what one ingests and kills in the same movement. One has, of course, recognized the

[50] Smith 1889. [51] Smith 1889, 275. [52] Freud 1912–1913, 137–138.
[53] Smith 1889, 295, my emphasis. [54] Freud 1912–1913, 136. [55] Ibid., 141, my emphasis.

oral-cannibalistic incorporation in which Freud sees the first ambivalent relation to the object, itself conceived as "harking back to early animal forms of life" such as the fusion of the unicellular organisms described by Wilhelm Bölsche.[56] Bölsche, in a passage that could not fail to catch Freud's attention, already brought the loving, "living kind of feeding" of unicellular organisms closer to the animistic beliefs of the savages: "Savage nations still believe that in drinking the blood of a lion something of his character, his courage and his power passes into the man who drinks it."[57] Bölsche called this "character feeding";[58] Freud prefers to speak of "identification":

> The violent primal father had doubtless been the feared and envied model (*Vorbild*) of each one of the company of brothers: and in the act of devouring him they accomplished their identification with him, and each one of them acquired a portion of his strength. The totem meal, which is perhaps mankind's earliest festival, would thus be a repetition and a commemoration of this memorable and criminal deed, which was the beginning of so many things – of social organization, of moral restrictions and of religion.[59]

One will ask: how can a murder be at the origin of law? Freud's answer is that by devouring the still panting and bloody flesh of the model rival, the "poor naked cannibals" internalized the obstacle presented by him in the most literal way: his flesh became their flesh, his blood their blood, his body their body. Freud repeats this in *Moses and Monotheism*: "each of them wished to take his place in reality. We can, if so, understand the cannibalistic act as an attempt to ensure identification with him by incorporating a piece of him."[60] All of Freud's hazardous reasoning rests in the final analysis on this literal, physical identification of the killers and their victim. It alone explains why these wild animals began to respect the beast they had just killed, even though it was no longer there to prevent them from satisfying their desires. Once the corpse had been eaten, the killers became the dead person *themselves* and thus blamed *themselves* for having killed it, what Freud expresses in mythical terms by saying that the "sons" and "brothers," members of the same community of blood, began to retroactively love the one who thus acceded to the status of "father," of common "primal father" (*Urvater*):

[56] Freud 1905a, 198. [57] Bölsche 1926, Volume 1 (1898), 138–139. [58] Ibid., 139.
[59] Freud 1912–1913, 142. [60] Freud 1939, 82.

> They hated their father, who presented such a formidable obstacle to their craving for power and their sexual desires; but they loved and admired him too. After they had got rid of him, had satisfied their hatred and had put into effect their wish to identify themselves with him, the affection which had all this time been pushed under was bound to make itself felt. It did so in the form of remorse. A sense of guilt made its appearance, which in this instance coincided with the remorse felt by the whole group . . . What had up to then been prevented by the dead's actual existence was thenceforward prohibited by the sons themselves, in accordance with the psychological procedure so familiar to us in psycho-analyses under the name of "*deferred obedience*." They revoked their deed by forbidding the killing of the totem, the substitute for their father; and they renounced its fruits by resigning their claim to the women who had now been set free.[61]

It should be noted, however, that it is not the "love" and "affection" for the father that Freud strangely mentions here that can explain the retrospective obedience. For it is only *after* having eliminated the rival, and under the impulse of remorse, that his murderers began to love him as a Father and to commune in this love. In order to love him, they had to start by killing him: "Society was now based on complicity in the common crime."[62] Only the *devouring* and *identifying* love of oral incorporation allows Freud to account for the internal bite of remorse, that is to say, for the transition from what he calls elsewhere "social anxiety" before an external power to "moral anxiety" (*Gewissenangst*) before an internal voice.[63] Without this identification confusing the self and the other, Freud could not justify the passage from outside to inside, from force to right, from naked violence to respect for others. He comes back to it in a note of "Group Psychology and the Analysis of the Ego": identifications

> result among other things in a person limiting his aggressiveness towards those with whom he has identified himself, and in his sparing them and giving them help. The study of such identifications, like those, for instance which lie at the root of clan feeling, led Robertson Smith (*Kinship and Marriage*, 1885) to the surprising discovery that they rest upon the acknowledgement of the possession of a common substance, and may even therefore be created by a meal eaten in common. This feature makes it possible to connect this kind of identification with the early history of the human family which I constructed in *Totem and Taboo*.[64]

The fact remains that this nonaggressive identification was initially murderous and necessarily so, since to put oneself in the place of the "envied model" is to kill it. Respect for the alter ego emerges from its

[61] Freud 1912–1913, 143. [62] Ibid., 146. [63] Freud 1930, 125 ff. [64] Freud 1921, 110.

egoistic, narcissistic elimination, and everything therefore begins in what Freud, taking up a term proposed by Bleuler, calls "emotional ambivalence" (*Gefühlsambivalenz*).[65] As he also writes in "Thoughts for the Time on War and Death," it is "beside the dead body of the loved one" that moral conscience (*Gewissen*) is born: "What came into existence was . . . the earliest ethical commandments. The first and most important prohibition made by the awakening conscience was: 'Thou shalt not kill.' It was acquired in relation to dead people who were loved, as a reaction against the satisfaction of the hatred hidden behind the grief for them."[66] It follows that moral conscience is always an already guilty conscience, since it is always already the result of murder: *Thou hast killed.* Far from the members of the primal horde having felt guilty for having transgressed a previously known and established law, it is in the transgression and the feeling of fault that they were made to know the law of the Father: "They thus created out of their filial sense of guilt the two fundamental taboos of totemism, which for that very reason inevitably corresponded to the two repressed wishes of the Oedipus complex."[67]

Religion

Culture, for Freud, is a fundamentally guilty culture: this is the price to pay for a sociobiological theory which tries to found the civilizing process on the aggressivo-sexual drives that its function is to limit or control. In "Group Psychology and the Analysis of the Ego," Freud characteristically refrains from the easy approach that would consist in rooting the social bond in a positive "herd instinct," as done by Wilfred Trotter (1872–1939).[68] Similarly, he never mentions the Darwinian hypothesis – which he must have known – of an evolutionary advantage provided by altruism and social cooperation.[69] This is because he only considers culture negatively, in the mode of repression and "renunciation of drive" (*Triebversagung*),[70] while simultaneously seeking to root it in that very thing which it denies, renounces, refuses. The paradox of a feeling of original guilt results from these two contradictory requirements. The forbidden, for Freud, is born of its transgression; society, religion, and morality emerge from the crime: "Society was now based on complicity in the common crime; religion was based on the sense of guilt and the

[65] Freud 1912–1913, 18 ff. [66] Freud 1915d, 295. [67] Freud 1912–1913, 143.
[68] Freud 1921, 117 ff. [69] Darwin 1871, Volume 1, 166.
[70] Freud 1927, 7; Freud 1930, 97; Freud 1939, 116 ff, translation modified.

remorse attaching to it; while morality was based partly on the exigencies of this society and partly on the penance demanded by the sense of guilt."[71]

In *Totem and Taboo*, Freud relates the origin of culture to a unique event, adopting the tone of myth: "One day the brothers came together," etc. In *Moses and Monotheism*, on the other hand, he specifies that the same scenario was repeated countless times in the course of prehistory: "the events I am about to describe occurred to all primitive men – that is, to all our ancestors. The story is told in an enormously condensed form, as though it had happened on a single occasion, while in fact it covered thousands of years and was repeated countless times during that long period."[72] Now, either this passage means nothing or it means that there has never been a single event separating once and for all the violent prehistory of humanity from its nonviolent, "cultural" history. It is each time that a male or males killed another male and devoured him to appropriate his strength that the feeling of guilt must have set in, without this apparently preventing the repetition of the murder over countless generations. In other words, the ambivalence of oral incorporation was present *from the start*, on the occasion of any murder, but also *afterwards*, since remorse did not interrupt the cycle of violence.

From there, Freud unfolds a history of culture conceived as a perpetual return of the same prehistory, of the same "archaic heritage," of the same ambivalence. What is striking in this universal history is its repetitive character. In accordance with Haeckel's biogenetic law, all these great organisms that are human societies are supposed to pass again and again by the same evolutionary stage, the same stage of the development of drives. No evolution, no progress, nothing but the compulsive commemoration of the murder of the primal father, with occasional regressions towards the primal horde and the real crime. Ritual, religion, myth, art: all these cultural forms are only a long series of attempts to atone for the original crime while committing it once again. Quick overview:

- *Ritual.* Taking up Robertson Smith's theory, Freud sees in the animal sacrifice the core of the totemic religion, itself conceived as the first religion of humanity. Now, the animal that one solemnly kills to eat it is the father whose death one piously mourns while joyfully celebrating his murder: "Totemic religion not only comprised expressions of

[71] Freud 1912–1913, 146. [72] Freud 1939, 81.

remorse and attempts at atonement, it also served as a remembrance of the triumph over the father."[73]

- *Greek tragedy*. Here, Freud silently corrects Aristotle's *Poetics* and Nietzsche's *The Birth of Tragedy*: "But why had the Hero of tragedy to suffer? and what was the meaning of his 'tragic guilt'? I will cut the discussion short and give a quick reply. He had to suffer because he was the primal father, the Hero of the great primaeval tragedy which was being re-enacted with a tendentious twist; and the tragic guilt was the guilt which he had to take on himself in order to relieve the Chorus from theirs . . . The crime which was thrown on to his shoulders, presumptuousness and rebelliousness against a great authority, was precisely the crime for which the members of the Chorus, the company of brothers, were responsible."[74]
- *Religion*. The god is still the father but now freed in part from the ambivalence of the sacrificial murder. The father is no longer ritually killed in the form of an animal; he becomes a God the Father whom the brothers love in the mode of nostalgia (*Sehnsucht*), an Almighty whom they fear and respect: "Thus after a long lapse of time their bitterness against their father, which had driven them to their deed, grew less, and their longing for him increased; and it became possible for an ideal to emerge which embodied the unlimited power of the primal father against whom they had once fought as well as their readiness to submit to him."[75] Religion is the retrospective illusion (*Illusion*) of a *good* God, kind and loving, powerful and protective (theme of *The Future of an Illusion*).
- *Family*. Once the primal father (who is not yet a father) is eliminated, there is no longer a horde but not yet a family. Freud thus imagines an obscure period during which the repentant brothers would have forbidden themselves all women (but how did they reproduce then?) and where the latter would have "perhaps" established a "mother right," in accordance with the hypotheses of the jurist and philologist Johann Jakob Bachofen (1815–1887).[76] Freud hardly dwells on this original matriarchy, nor on the "mother-goddesses" who would have come from it, because what matters to him is to pass as quickly as possible to the next stage of human society, which is, in fact, a return to the starting point: "With the introduction of father-deities a fatherless society gradually changed into one organized on a patriarchal basis. The family

[73] Freud 1912–1913, 145. [74] Ibid., 156; Freud 1939, 87. [75] Freud 1912–1913, 148.
[76] Ibid., 144, translation modified.

was a restoration of the former primal horde and it gave back to fathers a large portion of their former rights."[77] The essence of the family is patriarchal, Oedipal, with all the ambivalence that that implies.

- *Society*. The same applies to society, a large family or brotherhood dominated by a Father-Chief-Leader. The chief or the king is a man divinized, paternized: "As a result of decisive cultural changes, the original democratic equality that had prevailed among all the individual clansmen became untenable; and there developed at the same time an inclination, based on veneration felt for particular human individuals who stood out from others, to revive the ancient paternal ideal by creating gods. The notion of a man becoming a god . . . strikes us to-day as shockingly presumptuous; but even in classical antiquity there was nothing revolting in it."[78] It is this "great man,"[79] this "great leader personality (*große Führerpersönlichkeit*),"[80] that now holds together the group or crowd (*Masse*) of obedient subjects, as evidenced by the panicked dissolution that his disappearance causes.[81] Hence Freud's following blunt statement, typical of social Darwinism: "One instance of the innate and ineradicable inequality of men is their tendency to fall into the two classes of leaders (*Führer*) and followers. The latter constitute the vast majority; they stand in need of an authority which will make decisions for them and to which they for the most part offer an unqualified submission."[82] No society without a leader (Freud is not a democrat). Under the most organic and differentiated social formations (under democracy), there is the unanimist crowd hypnotized by the *Führer*; and under the crowd, there is the primal horde: "Thus the crowd appears to us as a revival of the primal horde. Just as primitive man survives potentially in every individual, so the primal horde may arise once more out of any random collection . . . He [the 'father of the primal horde'], at the very beginning of the history of mankind, was the 'Overman' whom Nietzsche only expected from the future. Even to-day the members of a crowd stand in need of the illusion that they are equally and justly loved by their *Führer*; but the *Führer* himself need love no one else, he may be of a masterful nature (*Herrennatur*), absolutely narcissistic, self-confident and independent."[83] (The fascism of the 1930s will give a terrifying echo to this description of the social bond.)

[77] Ibid., 149. [78] Ibid., 148–149, translation modified. [79] Freud 1939, 107 ff.
[80] Freud 1930, 141. [81] Freud 1921, 97. [82] Freud 1933b, 212.
[83] Freud 1921, 123, translation modified.

- *Jewish monotheism*. Just as there is hardly any room in this story for female deities, Freud barely mentions polytheism. The *gods* are in his eyes only a deceptive multiplication of *the* original god. The true religion is monotheistic, because paternal: "These male gods of polytheism . . . are numerous, mutually restrictive, and are occasionally subordinated to a superior high god. The next step, however, leads us to the theme with which we are here concerned – to the return of a single father-god of unlimited dominion."[84] It is this "return of the repressed" that is traced in *Moses and Monotheism*, the ultimate reiteration of *Totem and Taboo*. On the basis of an acrobatic scaffolding of historical hypotheses, Freud establishes that: 1. Moses was an Egyptian follower of the monotheistic cult of Aten, which he imposed on Semitic tribes by taking them out of Egypt to found his own empire; 2. One day, the Jews rebelled against him and killed him, just as the brothers of the primal horde had killed the *Urvater* in the past; 3. The cult of Aten was merged with that of Yahweh, a cruel volcanic deity from the Arabian Peninsula, casting into oblivion the Egyptian origin of the god and the murder of his prophet; 4. However, the Jewish prophets kept the obscure memory of the murder of Moses, maintaining an endless feeling of guilt towards the jealous God and demanding from the Jewish people an ever more strict and exacting "ascetic morality" (Nietzsche): "In a fresh rapture of moral asceticism [the Jews] imposed more and more new instinctual renunciations on themselves and in that way reached – in doctrine and precept, at least – ethical heights which had remained inaccessible to the other peoples of antiquity . . . These ethical ideas cannot, however, disavow their origin from the sense of guilt felt on account of a suppressed hostility to God."[85] In summary, the sublime Jewish monotheism is for Freud the religion most faithful to the *ethical* origin of all religions, because the murder of Moses revived in his people the "deferred obedience" of the members of the primal horde towards the dead father.
- *Christianity*. In Christianity, which grew out of Judaism, the original crime of humanity is practically confessed, for if the Son of Man must die in order to deliver humanity from a sin committed against God the Father, it must be, by virtue of the law of retaliation, to redeem a parricide.[86] However, this reconciliation with the Father simultaneously repeats the murder it is supposed to expiate: "But at

[84] Freud 1939, 83. [85] Ibid., 134. [86] Freud 1915d, 292–293.

> that point the inexorable psychological law of ambivalence stepped in." The Son "himself became God, beside, or, more correctly, in place of, the Father. A Son-religion displaced the Father-religion. As a sign of this substitution the ancient totem meal was revived in the form of communion, in which the company of brothers consumed the flesh and blood of the Son – no longer the Father – obtained sanctity thereby and identified themselves with him."[87] Freud, in *Moses and Monotheism*, is very severe towards this religion of the Son, in which he sees "a cultural regression as compared with the older, Jewish one."[88] By redeeming their sin, the Son in fact freed men from the feeling of guilt that had led the Jews to the path of renunciation of drive and intellect (primacy of the Book, iconoclasm, rejection of idols, of magic, and of the belief in the "omnipotence of thoughts").[89] Mired in the cult of images, relics, saints, and Mary, "the Christian religion did not maintain the high level in intellectuality (*Geistigkeit*) to which Judaism had soared."[90] Christianity, in the eyes of Freud, is monotheism for the brutes and the enjoyers. It could not, therefore, reveal the dark ethical truth of culture: "The Father is dead; nothing is allowed any longer!"

Only a "completely godless Jew," as Freud calls himself in a letter of October 9, 1918, to the Lutheran pastor Oskar Pfister (1873–1956),[91] could reveal this truth, only, that is, an heir of the ethical and intellectual tradition of this people that stuck like a "fossil"[92] to the ancient guilt, without ever trying to ease or conceal it: "And even the demand for belief in [God] seems to take a second place in comparison with the seriousness of these ethical requirements."[93] Freud is often criticized, with some justification, for having published his iconoclastic demolition of Moses at the very moment when the latter's people were being massacred by the Nazis. But in Freud's own logic, *Moses and Monotheism* is really an *Apology for Judaism*, a retort to the idolaters and to all those violent brutes for whom "the development of muscular strength is the popular ideal."[94] The psychoanalytical demystification of Moses is supposed to fulfill the very truth of Judaism, a truth superior to all other religions *because it is nonreligious*, without "illusion." This is why, as Freud wrote to Pfister, we had to wait for an atheist Jew to invent psychoanalysis: in him, religion – the Mosaic religion – finally became a science, a disillusioned religion and a science of illusion.

[87] Freud 1912–1913, 154. [88] Freud 1939, 88. [89] Ibid., 111 ff.
[90] Ibid., 88, translation modified. [91] Freud and Pfister 1963, 37 [92] Freud 1939, 88.
[93] Ibid., 119. [94] Ibid., 115.

Group Psychology

Human culture is thus founded on the "renunciation of drive," this ancestral repression of the parricide-incestuous impulses that it repeats and commemorates compulsively in its institutions and its history. One last question remains to be answered: how is the memory of the original fault transmitted, if this crime is to remain hidden, unseen, unconscious? At the end of *Totem and Taboo*, Freud specifies the axiom on which his construction rests:

> No one can have failed to observe, in the first place, that I have taken as the basis of my whole position the existence of a collective mind, in which mental processes occur just as they do in the mind of an individual. In particular, I have supposed that the sense of guilt for an action has persisted for many thousands of years and has remained operative in generations which can have had no knowledge of that action.[95]

The term "collective mind" (*Massenpsyche*) does not come randomly from Freud's pen. It is a concept proposed by Gustave Le Bon (1841–1931) in his famous *Psychology of Crowds (Psychologie des foules)*. Freud quotes this concept extensively in his own *Group Psychology* (*Massenpsychologie*), where he also translates it as *Kollektivseele* or *Massenseele*.[96] According to Le Bon, the psychology of the members of a crowd (their *Massenpsychologie*, in Freud's translation) is different from their individual psychology: "the fact that they have been transformed into a crowd puts them in possession of a sort of collective mind (*âme collective*) which makes them feel, think, and act in a manner quite different from that in which each individual of them would feel, think, and act were he in a state of isolation."[97] They regress to a purely reflex, automatic, uninhibited mode of thinking, comparable to a hypnotic state where any suggestion, even the most criminal, is immediately put into action. To explain this fact, Le Bon recalls (in 1895!):

> the truth established by modern psychology, that unconscious phenomena play an altogether preponderating part not only in organic life, but also in the operations of the intelligence. The conscious life of the mind is of small importance in comparison with its unconscious life . . . Our conscious acts are the outcome of an unconscious substratum created in the mind in the main by hereditary influences. This substratum consists of the innumerable common characteristics handed down from generation to generation, which constitute the mind of the race (*l'âme de la race*) . . . It is more especially

95 Freud 1912–1913, 157. 96 Freud 1921, 73, 97. 97 Le Bon 1895, 7.

> with respect to those unconscious elements which constitute the mind of the race that all the individuals belonging to it resemble each other . . . It is precisely these general qualities of character, governed by forces of which we are unconscious, and possessed by the majority of the normal individuals of a race in much the same degree – it is precisely these qualities, I say, that in crowds become common property. In the collective mind the intellectual aptitudes of the individuals, and in consequence their individuality, are weakened. The heterogeneous is swamped by the homogeneous, and the unconscious qualities obtain the upper hand.[98]

In summary, the collective mind is a trans-individual unconscious, transmitted hereditarily. This is how, Freud continues in *Totem and Taboo*, the memory of the original murder was maintained and reproduced, from generation to generation:

> Without the assumption of a collective mind, which makes it possible to neglect the interruptions of mental acts caused by the extinction of the individual, the psychology of peoples (*Völkerpsychologie*) in general cannot exist . . . The psychology of peoples shows very little interest, on the whole, in the manner in which the required continuity in the mental life of successive generations is established. A part of the problem seems to be met by the inheritance of psychical dispositions which, however, need to be given some sort of impetus in the life of the individual before they can be roused into actual operation.[99]

Apart from its application to the specific problem of crowds, Le Bon's theory of the collective mind was hardly original. The idea of an organic memory of the race was all the more widespread in the second half of the nineteenth century as it was used to explain the mechanism of biological heredity in general, as well as the formation of instincts and reflexes. The argument, based on an analogy between memory and heredity, had been launched in 1870 by the physiologist (and Breuer's mentor) Ewald Hering (1834–1918) and is found in Haeckel as well as in Thomas Laycock, August Forel, Edward Drinker Cope (1840–1897), Samuel Butler (1835–1902), and Théodule Ribot (1839–1916).[100] It can be summarized as follows: memory is like learning; it is increased by repetition over long periods of time; what is first repeated consciously becomes, after a certain time, automatic, reflex, unconscious; innate instincts and reflexes, in the same way, are memories of events repeated in the course of evolution that have been imprinted in living matter (in germ cells) and have since been

[98] Ibid., 7–9, translation modified. [99] Freud 1912–1913, 158, translation modified.
[100] Gould 1977, 96–100; Shamdasani 2003, 184–187.

transmitted from generation to generation. In the words of the paleontologist Alpheus Hyatt (1838–1902), "heredity is a form of unconscious organic memory."[101]

This theory was consistent with the mechanism of the inheritance of acquired characteristics postulated by Jean-Baptiste Lamarck (1744–1829), which was still used at the time to account for heredity: if the legendary giraffe has a long neck, it is because countless previous generations, finding nothing to eat on the ground, stretched it to feed on the trees.[102] The theory of organic memory was also compatible with Haeckel's biogenetic law, because the latter was itself based on Lamarckian principles: ontogeny is the abbreviated recapitulation (organic memory) of the characters acquired in their order of appearance in the course of phylogeny. This interweaving of common presuppositions explains why the proponents of the "unconscious memory of Nature"[103] were all simultaneously Haeckelians and Lamarckians. This also applies to Freud, who was a convinced Lamarckian and had even planned to write a book on "Lamarck and psychoanalysis" in collaboration with Sándor Ferenczi.[104] (The project was abandoned when Freud realized that it was redundant: "My impression is that we are coming completely into line with the psycho-Lamarckists, such as [August] Pauly [1850–1914], and will have little to say that is completely new."[105])

One understands now why Freud, in *Moses and Monotheism*, takes care to specify that the story told in *Totem and Taboo* "in fact covered thousands of years and was repeated countless times during that long period."[106] What he has in mind is the mechanism of organic memory: the murder of the father had to be repeated countless times during prehistory for the trace to be imprinted in the form of an unconscious memory of the human race and to be transmitted compulsively through the generations. Only in this way can one explain why humans have kept the memory of an act forgotten for thousands of years, and why the Jews have continued to repent of a murder of which no written or even oral traces remained: "In my opinion there is an almost complete conformity in this respect between the individual and the group: in the group too an impression of the past is retained in unconscious memory-traces."[107]

It is this collective unconscious, this "mind of the race" as Le Bon used to say, that accounts for ethnic identities and the psychology of peoples, as well as that of crowds:

101 Hyatt 1893, 4. 102 Lamarck 1809, 256. 103 Hering 1870, 31.
104 Freud 1915c, 93 ff. 105 Ibid., 94. 106 Freud 1939, 81. 107 Ibid., 94.

> When I spoke of the survival of a tradition among a people (*Volk*) or of the formation of a people's character (*Volkscharakter*), I had mostly in mind an inherited tradition of this kind and not one transmitted by communication ... If we assume the survival of these memory-traces in the archaic heritage, we have bridged the gulf between individual and group psychology (*Massenpsychologie*): we can deal with peoples as we do with an individual neurotic.[108]

Conclusion: "I have no hesitation in declaring that men have always known (in this special way) that they once possessed a primal father and killed him."[109]

The problem here is that the biological postulates on which this theory of transmission was based had long since been disproved and abandoned, and Freud knew this very well. As early as the beginning of the 1880s, Weismann had demolished the Lamarckian theory of the inheritance of acquired characteristics by introducing the idea of a separation (the famous "Weismann barrier") between the perishable soma and the immutable germ plasm, the only one responsible for the hereditary transmission. This neo-Darwinian theory, based on a strict application of the mechanism of natural selection, had paved the way for the rediscovery at the turn of the century of Gregor Mendel's (1822–1884) laws of genetic transmission. From then on, it was no longer possible to believe in the action of the environment on hereditary transmission, nor, by way of consequence, in Haeckel's biogenetic law and its multiple psychological, anthropological, and racist applications. What had seemed plausible and even obvious to generations of researchers became obsolete, just fit to be thrown into the basket of falsified theories and pseudo-scientific prejudices. This was already true in 1912–1913, when Freud was working on *Totem and Taboo*, and even more so in the late 1930s, when he wrote *Moses and Monotheism*. At that time, only the ideologist Trofim Lysenko (1896–1976) was left in the Soviet Union to defend neo-Lamarckian theses. And Freud.

In his biography of Freud, Ernest Jones tells how he tried to dissuade him from using Lamarckian theory in his *Moses*. In vain:

> I told him he had of course the right to hold any opinion he liked in his own field of psychology, even if it ran counter to all biological principles, but I begged him to omit the passage where he applied it to the whole field of biological evolution, since no responsible biologist regarded it as tenable any longer. All he could say is that they were all wrong and the passage must

[108] Ibid., 99–100. [109] Ibid., 101.

> stay. And he documented this recalcitrance in the book with the following words: "My position, no doubt, is made more difficult by the present attitude of biological science, which refuses to hear of the inheritance of acquired characters by succeeding generations. I must, however, in all modesty confess that nevertheless I cannot do without this factor in biological evolution."[110]

In his own book, Freud continued: "If it is not so, we shall not advance a step further along the path we entered on, either in analysis or in group psychology. The audacity cannot be avoided."[111] Freud was right: without the hypothesis of a hereditary transmission of acquired characters, the whole patiently constructed edifice of psychoanalysis would collapse. Better than Jones, Freud knew perfectly well that psychoanalysis was not just a psychological "speciality" but a metapsychobiological theory based on the biogenetic law and thus, ultimately, on the transmission to descendants of the characters acquired during phylogenesis. This essential piece removed, there was no more perverse-polymorphous infantile sexuality, no more libidinal stages, no more organic repression, no more Oedipus complex, no more barrier against incest, no more renunciation of drive, no more mass psychology, nor even unconscious. There was no more psychoanalysis. Freud had no choice: it was psychoanalysis or science. To the psychiatrist Joseph Wortis (1906–1995), who questioned him in 1934 about his Lamarckism, he replied: "We can't bother with the biologists. We have our own science."[112] Psychoanalysis, an audacious science.

The Id and the Superego

From *Totem and Taboo* onwards, the reconstruction of the history of human culture and repression was now more or less complete and definitive. In Chapter IV of *Civilization and Its Discontents*, Freud summarized it as follows. Our (male) ancestor was an animal walking on all fours and whose sexuality was periodic due to being excited during periods of menstruation by odors coming from the genito-urethral-anal zone. Because of the gradual adoption of the upright position, the corresponding erogenous zones were abandoned, generating an organic repression of the sense of smell and olfactory excitations in favor of the constant visual excitations provoked by the genitals, "which were previously concealed"(?).[113] There followed a disgust for the urethro-anal zone and

[110] Jones 1957, 313. [111] Freud 1939, 100. [112] Wortis 1954, 84. [113] Freud 1939, 99.

excrements, the taboo of menstruation, and "the continuity of [male] sexual excitation":[114] "When this happened, the male acquired a motive for keeping the female, or, speaking more generally, his sexual objects, near him."[115] Hence the formation of small families or hordes headed by a domineering "father,"[116] until the moment when the weaker "brothers" joined forces to kill him, devoured him, felt guilty in retrospect, and internalized the obstacle that he had presented to their impulses until then by instituting the double prohibition of incest and murder, the foundation of human society, etc.

It is this collective history of the species, transmitted in a hereditary way in the form of organic drives and mnemonic traces, that individual development recapitulates, in accordance with the biogenetic law. At first, the child passes through an ambivalent oral-cannibalistic phase, distantly echoing animal forms where sexuality and ingestion (copulation and the destruction of the other) were still confused. Then it is the anal (or sadistic-anal) phase, which repeats the perverse sexuality of our quadruped ancestors, and which is interrupted by modesty and disgust, heirs of the organic repression caused by the "verticalization" of the anthropoid apes. Then comes the phallic-Oedipal phase, which corresponds to the primacy of the visible genital organ (male) and to the aggressive rivalry with the dominant male for the possession of the females. Finally comes the moment of the "decline" or "demolition" of the Oedipus complex, which initiates the period of sexual latency and which reproduces the murderous incorporation of the primal father with its consequences: feelings of guilt, horror of incest, and the search for sexual objects outside the original "family" (exogamy). In some versions, Freud also links the castration complex that marks the terminal phase of the Oedipus complex to a real castration operated in the past by the primal father on his sons.[117] (But how, then, could they have transmitted this acquired character to their descendants?)

It is to the moment of the decline of the Oedipus complex, meant to mark the passage of the little savage human to the civilized state of being, that the 1923 essay "The Ego and the Id" is devoted. In this famous writing, Freud introduces what is called the "second topography" of the psychical apparatus, where the tripartition *Cs*/*Pcs*/*Ucs* (conscious/preconscious/unconscious) is replaced by that of the ego, the id, and the superego. The essay, he assures us in the opening paragraph, is an attempt to link together "various facts of analytic observation ... in the present

[114] Ibid. [115] Ibid. [116] Ibid., 100. [117] Freud 1915c, 17, 79; Freud 1916–1917, 371.

work, however, there are no fresh borrowings from biology, and on that account it stands closer to psycho-analysis than does *Beyond the Pleasure Principle*. It is more in the nature of a synthesis than of a speculation."[118] This presentation, however, is misleading because the conceptual reorganization of "The Ego and the Id" consists in reality of a retroactive alignment of the clinical data on the psychobiohistorical speculation of *Totem and Taboo*. In summary, the superego is a revival of the primal father, and the id in which it plunges is the archaic heritage of humanity.

Freud's starting point in this essay is a paradox, which we are surprised that he took so long to realize. It is, one might say, the paradox of analysis: repression, which creates the unconscious, is itself unconscious (and must be, otherwise it would only be a matter of a Sartrean "bad faith"[119]). The patients in analysis resist the analyst's interpretations, but they do not know anything about it (they are only aware of not agreeing with their therapist). They feel guilty for harboring this or that desire, but again, they ignore it (says the analyst): "as far as the patient is concerned this sense of guilt is dumb; it does not tell him he is guilty; he does not feel guilty, he feels ill. This sense of guilt expresses itself only as a resistance to recovery which it is extremely difficult to overcome" – a phenomenon Freud calls "negative therapeutic reaction."[120] It is, therefore, not only the repressed that is unconscious but also the repressor. Now, Freud had until then localized the operation of repression in the ego, an agency associated, moreover, with moral requirements and consciousness. A double correction was therefore in order:

1. "We have come upon something in the ego itself which is also unconscious, which behaves exactly like the repressed . . . A part of the ego, too – and Heaven knows how important a part – may be *Ucs*, undoubtedly is *Ucs*."[121] This repressing, moralizing, and unconscious part is the narcissistic "ideal ego" that Freud had already mentioned in his essay "On Narcissism." Freud renames it here "superego" (*Überich*).
2. "We recognize that the *Ucs* does not coincide with the repressed," hence "the necessity of postulating," next to the latent *Pcs* and the repressed *Ucs*, "a third *Ucs*, which is not repressed."[122] This nonrepressed unconscious Freud calls "*id*" (in German *Es*, neutral pronoun), borrowing this term from the physician Georg Groddeck

[118] Freud 1923b, 12. [119] Sartre 1943, 93–94. [120] Freud 1923b, 49–50.
[121] Ibid., 17–18. [122] Ibid., 18.

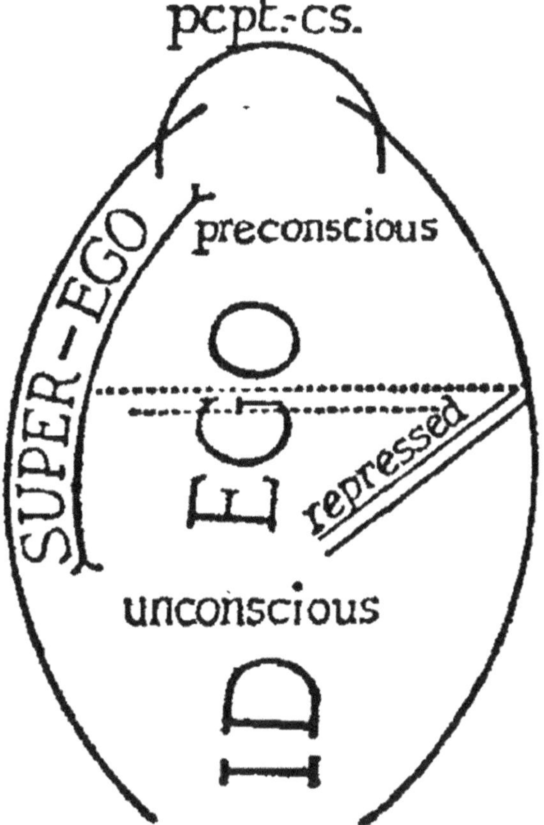

Figure 3. Diagram of the *New Introductory Lectures on Psycho-Analysis*

> (1886–1934) and from Nietzsche, "who habitually used this grammatical term for whatever in our nature is impersonal (*das Unpersönliche*) and, so to speak, subject to natural law."[123]

Hence a new diagram of the psychical apparatus, where the ego communicates with the id via the superego (we use here the drawing of the *New Introductory Lectures on Psycho-Analysis*, more complete than the one proposed in "The Ego and the Id").

[123] Ibid., 23. Freud forgets to mention his colleague and mentor Sigmund Exner, who used the *Es* in a similar fashion. See Gauchet 1992, 121–123, 127 ff.

Freud does not tell us much about the id, but it is quite obvious that this impersonal unconscious, removed from the vicissitudes of individual repression, is none other than the collective and phylogenetic unconscious postulated by him since *Totem and Taboo* to explain the hereditary transmission of humanity's sense of guilt. He states it very clearly in a note of "Group Psychology and the Analysis of the Ego," at the very moment when he tries to distinguish his concept of the unconscious from that of Gustave Le Bon:

> Le Bon's unconscious more especially contains the most deeply buried features of the mind of the race, which as a matter of fact lies outside the scope of individual psycho-analysis. We do not fail to recognize, indeed, that *the ego's nucleus (the id, as I have called it later), which comprises the "archaic heritage" of the human mind*, is unconscious; but in addition to this we distinguish the "unconscious repressed," *which arose from a portion of that heritage*. This concept of the repressed is not to be found in Le Bon.[124]

The id, on the other hand, is a fortiori the same unconscious as that of Le Bon.

As for the superego, this archaic and unconscious core of the ego, Freud describes it in Chapter III of "The Ego and the Id" as the product of consecutive, parental identifications at the exit of the Oedipus complex. The demonstration, intended to explain why "this part of the ego is less firmly connected with consciousness,"[125] is laborious, and it is done in several steps, as if Freud tried several theories before coming to the fact.

Step 1: Freud posits that the ego, or, more exactly, its "character," is a precipitate of identifications with abandoned sexual objects. The mechanism that Freud is thinking of here is that of melancholic depression, which he had theorized in 1917 in "Mourning and Melancholia"[126] and which he now extends to the formation of the self in general: when a libidinal object is lost or abandoned, it is re-erected by way of identification in the ego at the end of a regression to "the individual's primitive oral phase," in which "object-cathexis and identification are no doubt indistinguishable from each other."[127] Unsurprisingly, a footnote refers here to the cannibalism of savages and to the belief that the qualities of the incorporated animal "persist as part of the character of those who eat them."[128]

Step 2: Freud posits that this "part of the ego" that is the superego results, more specifically, from an identification of the ego with the

[124] Freud 1921, 75, translation modified, my emphasis. [125] Freud 1923b, 28.
[126] Freud 1917c. [127] Ibid., 29. [128] Ibid.; see also Freud 1921, 105.

parental objects abandoned at the time of the "demolition" of the Oedipus complex. He first recalls how the child enters the Oedipus complex by taking the example of the little boy. The boy develops an object-cathexis with regard to the mother whom he would like to "have" sexually and an identification with the father whom he would like to "be,"[129] until the moment when the father appears as an "obstacle" to the possession of the mother and "his identification with his father then takes on a hostile coloring ... it seems as if the ambivalence inherent in the identification from the beginning had become manifest."[130] Just as the original oral identification was devouring and destructive, the Oedipal identification with the father (again) becomes murderous, the boy literally wanting to take his place with the mother. Then comes the moment of the demolition of the Oedipus complex, when "the boy's object-cathexis of his mother must be given up."[131] The outcome that is considered as "the most normal," Freud then says, consists in a "strengthening (*Verstärkung*) of his identification with his father," which translates into a consolidation of "the masculinity in a boy's character."[132] Problem: one should have expected the boy to identify regressively with the *mother*, since she is the abandoned object. How, then, can we explain the normal and sexually normative "strengthening" of the identification with the father?

Step 3: Freud resurrects the once forgotten Fliessian bisexuality and assumes now that the little boy who loves his mother and hates his father is simultaneously a little girl who loves her father and hates her mother. The Oedipus complex being thus always double, positive and negative, the renunciation of the two libidinal objects at the moment of the destruction of the complex would result in two regressive identifications, one to the father and the other to the mother. For example (but everything is organized in terms of *this* particular example), the identification with the father that the boy wants to be and replace in the positive complex would be reinforced by a regressive identification with the paternal object lost in the negative complex. The expected advantage of this hypothesis is obviously that it should make it possible to explain why and how the destruction of the Oedipus complex takes place: the hated rival (the father, in this instance) being simultaneously an object of love, the child ceases hostilities and abandons its other object of love to him by identifying pacifically with him. The superego would be the result of "these two identifications in some way united with each other."[133]

[129] Freud 1921, 106. [130] Freud 1923b, 32. [131] Ibid. [132] Ibid., translation modified.
[133] Ibid., 34.

Step 4: Freud does not stop there, however, as the problem just bounces back. Apart from the fact that the intervention of bisexuality does not in any way settle the question of sexual normatization (if the child identifies with both parents, it will necessarily remain masculine *and* feminine), we do not see why identification with the lost object would put an end to Oedipal rivalry. To say that one identifies with the rival (the father) of the positive complex because one loves him in the negative complex is perhaps to account for the strengthening of the identification; it is not to explain why this strengthening would be accompanied by an attenuation of the initial ambivalence. On the contrary, to identify with the beloved father is still to identify with the father rival, to put oneself in his place with the mother and, at the extreme, to "devour" him, to kill him, etc. This is why, Freud continues:

> The superego is, however, not simply a residue of the earliest object-choices of the id; it also represents an energetic reaction-formation against those choices. Its relation to the ego is not exhausted by the precept: "You ought to be like this (like your father)." It also comprises the prohibition: "You may not be like this (like your father) – that is, you may not do all that he does; some things are his prerogative." This double aspect of the ego ideal derives from the fact that the ego ideal had the task of repressing the Oedipus complex; indeed, it is to that revolutionary event that it owes its existence . . . The child's parents, and especially his father, were perceived as the obstacle to a realization of his Oedipus wishes; so, his infantile ego fortified itself (*stärkte sich*) for the carrying out of the repression by erecting this same obstacle within itself. It borrowed strength to do this, so to speak, from the father, and this loan was an extraordinarily momentous act.[134]

In this crucial passage, Freud admits very clearly that bisexual love for the Oedipal rival can in no way explain the pacification of identification and the respect of the "obstacle" he presents: the child (the boy) does not identify with him (the father) *out of* love but *in order to* be able to love him and cease the hostilities. More exactly, *the child identifies with him in order to no longer identify with him*, in order to no longer compete with him for the possession of the mother – to get out of the Oedipus complex, in a word. One will, of course, have recognized here the mechanism of the internalization (*Verinnerlichung*) of the obstacle that Freud put at the principle of the cultural renunciation of the incestuous and parricidal drives in *Totem and Taboo*. Just as the son-brothers of the primal horde had incorporated the father to appropriate his strength and his character,

[134] Ibid., 34.

with the known consequences, so here the child (the boy) "borrowed strength . . . from the father" to obey him. And how? By identifying with him, by incorporating him in the ego in the form of a superego charged with enforcing respect of the prohibition. Freud's study *Thomas Woodrow Wilson* specifies this link with cannibalism:

> Equally unable to kill the father or to submit utterly to him, the little boy finds an escape which approximates removal of his father and nevertheless avoids murder. He identifies with his father. Thereby he satisfies both his tender and hostile desires with respect to his father. He not only expresses his love and admiration for his father but also removes his father by incorporating his father in himself as if by an act of cannibalism . . . This almighty, omniscient, all-virtuous father of childhood, as a result of his incorporation in the child, becomes an internal psychic power which in psychoanalysis we call the ego ideal or the superego.[135]

That the demolition of the Oedipus from which the superego emerges is nothing else than a repetition, at the level of ontogeny, of the original drama of the murder of the primal father is what is confirmed by the rest of "The Ego and the Id." From where, Freud asks himself, does the superego draw "its compulsive character which manifests itself in the form of a categorical imperative"[136] if not from the id?

> Through the forming of the ideal, what biology and the vicissitudes of the human species have created in the id and left behind in it is taken over by the ego and re-experienced in relation to itself as an individual. Owing to the way in which the ego ideal is formed, it has the most abundant links with the phylogenetic acquisition of each individual – his archaic heritage . . . The superego, according to our hypothesis, actually originated from the experiences that led to totemism. The question whether it was the ego or the id that experienced and acquired these things soon comes to nothing . . . The experiences of the ego seem at first to be lost for inheritance; but, when they have been repeated often enough and with sufficient strength in many individuals in successive generations, they transform themselves, so to say, into experiences of the id, the impressions of which are preserved by heredity. Thus in the id, which is capable of being inherited, are harboured residues of the existences of countless egos; and, when the ego forms its superego out of the id, it may perhaps only be reviving shapes of former egos and be bringing them to resurrection.[137]

This is why, Freud writes in *Civilization and Its Discontents*, "experience shows . . . that the severity of the super-ego which a child develops in no way corresponds to the severity of treatment which he has himself met

[135] Freud and Bullitt 1930–1932, 40. [136] Freud 1923b, 35. [137] Ibid., 36–38.

with" from the father of ontogenesis; "when a child reacts to his first great instinctual frustrations with excessively strong aggressiveness and with a correspondingly severe superego, he is following a phylogenetic model (*Vorbild*) and is going beyond the response that would be currently justified; for the father of prehistoric times was undoubtedly terrible, and an extreme amount of aggressiveness may be attributed to him."[138]

Far from resulting from a psychological dialectic of rivalry and love, as Freud seemed to want to demonstrate at first, the exit from the Oedipus complex accomplishes in fact a biological destiny. If around the fifth year we abandon the incestuous object to our rival by identifying ourselves with this obstacle, it is simply because we are programmed to do so, just as we are programmed to lose our milk teeth between the ages of six and twelve and to develop secondary sexual characteristics in adolescence. In "A Child Is Being Beaten," Freud explains that the "incestuous loves" of the Oedipus complex

> are bound to come to grief sooner or later, though we cannot say on what particular stumbling block. Most probably they pass away because their time is over, because the children have entered upon a new phase of development in which they are compelled to recapitulate from the history of mankind the repression of an incestuous object-choice, just as at an earlier stage they were obliged to effect an object-choice of that very sort.[139]

This is what the formula "the superego reaches deep down into the id"[140] means: the individual repression of the Oedipus complex is instinctual; it repeats compulsively, imperatively, the murderous incorporation of the primal father from which the prohibition of incest and culture in general are derived. One leaves the Oedipus complex because culture is rooted in the hereditary heritage of the species.

This means as well that one never leaves the Oedipus complex. What Freud presents as the destruction of the Oedipus complex is really its continuation, its endless repetition. For if the "superegoic" identification with the father of individual history repeats the civilizing identification with the father of collective prehistory, it necessarily also repeats its ambivalence. One recalls that the brothers of the primal horde forbade themselves the women of the father only after having devoured him, by identifying themselves with the obstacle that he presented. The little child (the boy), in the same way, only "gets out" of the identifying rivalry of the Oedipus complex by identifying with the rival who is an obstacle to him,

[138] Freud 1930, 130–131. [139] Freud 1919a, 188. [140] Freud 1923b, 49.

thus, by doing precisely that which is forbidden to him: "You may not be like this (like your father)." Whether in individual history or in the collective history of humanity, the law emerges in its transgression, in a criminal "internalization" of the father.

Hence the ruthlessness of this law, hence the "sadistic" cruelty of the superego: the more one identifies with the father, the more guilty one is; the more one respects the law, the more it punishes one; the more moral and obedient one is, the more intense is the feeling of guilt. The superego, which Freud designates as the place of the moral conscience (*Gewissen*), is simultaneously the place of the Oedipal crime, so that there cannot be a good relation to the law. Whatever the ego does, it will never be up to the voice of its conscience and its paradoxical injunction: "No matter what the ego may actually achieve in life, the superego is never satisfied with the achievement. It admonishes incessantly: You must make the impossible possible! You can accomplish the impossible! You are the Beloved Son of the Father! You are the Father Himself! You are God!"[141] But, obviously, one can only be the Father, the God, by killing him, therefore by disobeying him at the very moment one obeys him. To be moral, civilized, "cultured" is to be guilty. A priori guilty, necessarily guilty.

Civilization and Its Discontents

This is the lesson of this book, which is not called *Civilization and Its Discontents* by chance. There is discomfort, malaise, *Unbehagen* in *Kultur*, because progress necessarily results in an increase of the sense of guilt. Freud summarizes his thesis in the concluding chapter of the book: "my intention [is] to represent the sense of guilt as the most important problem in the development of civilization and to show that the price we pay for our advance in civilization is a loss of happiness through the heightening of the sense of guilt."[142]

Civilization and Its Discontents is Freud's true testament, much more than *Moses and Monotheism* or *An Outline of Psycho-Analysis*. Here, Freud ties together all the great themes of his theory, in the form of a vast recapitulative coda. Nothing new, but everything is there, one last time. *Civilization and Its Discontents* is also one of Freud's most popular books (12,000 copies sold in the year of its publication), and that is no accident. Even better than Nietzsche's *Zarathustra*, it is "a book for everyone and no one" that is addressed to the whole of humanity and not only to colleagues

[141] Freud and Bullitt 1930–1932, 41–42. [142] Freud 1930, 134.

specialized in psychopathology. Freud, the "godless Jew," announces in it the Bad News to the whole of Creation: men, you will never be happy because you have killed the Father, and you will have to atone until the end of time.

How is it, indeed, that we humans are so uncomfortable in existence, so dissatisfied, we humans who, thanks to the progress of civilization (*Kultur*), have nevertheless moved away from "our animal ancestors"[143] and dominate nature like gods?[144] A first answer is this: because "civilization is built up upon a renunciation of drive (*Triebverzicht*)" and "presupposes precisely the non-satisfaction (by suppression, repression or some other means) of powerful drives. This 'cultural frustration' (*Kulturversagung*) dominates the large field of social relationships between human beings,"[145] and it implies the frustration of our animal, asocial, individualistic drives. Civilization begins with living together, which "is only made possible when a majority comes together which is stronger than any separate individual and which remains united against all separate individuals. The power of this community is then set up as 'right' in opposition to the power of the individual, which is condemned as 'brute force.'"[146] If we do not find happiness in the life of culture, it is thus because society forces us to give up our individual freedom, sexual freedom in particular.

However, it is only a first attempt at an answer, as Freud can no longer be satisfied with opposing sexual drives in such a simple way with the interests of society, as represented in the individual by the ego. It is the year 1929, post *Totem and Taboo*, "On Narcissism," "Beyond the Pleasure Principle," and "The Ego and the Id," and at this stage, the social-cultural processes themselves appear as libidinal, erotic, instinctual processes, in the widest sense of the phrase. This is why Freud carries on by declaring that "the development of civilization appears to us as a peculiar process which takes place above mankind (*über die Menschheit*)."[147] By this he means that the *Kulturversagung* responsible for our malaise is part of the evolution of the species and even of the living in general: "both the process of human civilization and of the development of the individual are also vital processes – which is to say that they must share in the most general characteristic of life."[148]

Now, the most general characteristic of life, as we know since "Beyond the Pleasure Principle," is the union, the erotic *Bindung*. From the "cellular state" formed by the fusion of two or more unicellular organisms until

[143] Ibid., 89. [144] Ibid., 91. [145] Ibid., 97, translation modified. [146] Ibid., 95.
[147] Ibid., 96, translation modified; see also 122, 139. [148] Ibid., 139.

human society, we are in the presence of one and the same process of *unification* of individuals, of one and the same concentric expansion of the living. Hence this hypothesis, not far in its evolutionary inspiration from the organicism of Herbert Spencer (1820–1903) and the "biosociology" of Alfred Espinas (1844–1922): "I may now add that civilization is a process in the service of Eros, whose purpose is to combine single human individuals, and after that families, then races, peoples and nations, into one great unity, the unity of mankind."[149]

But why, then, does civilization require a renunciation of sexual freedom, if it is itself an erotic, vital process? Freud first sketches an explanation of an accounting, economic type: in order to unite the members of society, culture "summons up aim-inhibited libido on the largest scale so as to strengthen the communal bond by relations of friendship. In order for these aims to be fulfilled, a restriction upon sexual life is unavoidable."[150] Admittedly, this economy of Eros accounts for the tensions between the individual and society (between the strictly sexual bond and the social bond). But does it really explain why we fail so constantly to be happy? After all, what is lost on one side is gained on the other, so that one could imagine a kind of amicable compromise (a sublimation, for instance) between the individual libido and the being in common. Where is the tragic of civilization in all of this? And, above all, why is it necessary to take libido to fight against libido? Isn't the real question against what is *the libido in general*, the Eros, cultural life, defending itself?

Against the death drive, that is to say disunity, unbinding, destruction. From Chapter V on, the investigation on civilization and happiness is suddenly placed on a completely different ground, that of the immense "battle of the giants"[151] opposing Eros and Thanatos, the life drive and the death drive. The real problem of culture, we now learn, is not sexuality and love; it is violence, aggression, hostility, sadism, hatred. The human animal is not only a fornicating ape, it is also a wolf, *homo homini lupus.*[152] And this wolf spreads everywhere the death that it carries in itself; externalized death drive becomes sadistic destruction drive: "The existence of this inclination to aggression . . . is the factor which disturbs our relations with our neighbour . . . Civilization has to use its utmost efforts in order to set limits to man's aggressive drives and to hold the manifestations of them in check by psychical reaction-formations."[153]

[149] Ibid., 122. [150] Ibid., 109. [151] Ibid., 122. [152] Ibid., 111. [153] Ibid., 112.

But how are these barriers erected? The mechanism of the mobilization of "aim-inhibited libido" obviously does not satisfy Freud, for it is still necessary to account for the inhibition itself. We find again the problem of the passage from the state of nature to the rule of law that obsessed *Totem and Taboo*, but this time brought to the level of the biological speculation on the life and death drives. How does the wolf that we are cease to carry death outside, and how does it forbid itself to kill? "What means does civilization employ in order to inhibit the aggressiveness which opposes it, to make it harmless, to get rid of it, perhaps?"[154] The response: the individual's

> aggressiveness is introjected, internalized (*verinnerlicht*); it is, in point of fact, sent back to where it came from – that is, it is directed towards his own ego. There it is taken over by a portion of the ego, which sets itself over against the rest of the ego as superego, and which now, in the form of "conscience," is ready to put into action against the ego the same harsh aggressiveness that the ego would have liked to satisfy upon other, extraneous individuals.[155]

One will have recognized the mechanism of the *Verinnerlichung* that Nietzsche put at the foundation of bad conscience. Let us quote this passage once again, too close to Freud's for it to be a coincidence: "All instincts that do not discharge themselves outwardly *turn inwards* – this is what I call the *internalization* (*Verinnerlichung*) of man ... Hostility, cruelty, joy in persecuting, in attacking, in change, in destruction – all this turned against the possessors of such instincts: *that* is the origin of 'bad conscience.'"[156] In Freud, likewise, the little wolf that is the child turns the aggressiveness that he nourished towards the father against himself, by identifying himself with him in order to better obey him.[157] Again, this is how the brothers of the animal horde had retrospectively punished themselves for having devoured the father, by turning their own violence against themselves:

> We cannot get away from the assumption that man's sense of guilt springs from the Oedipus complex and was acquired at the killing of the father by the brothers banded together. On that occasion an act of aggression was not suppressed but carried out; but it was the same act of aggression whose suppression in the child is supposed to be the source of his sense of guilt.[158]

[154] Ibid., 123. [155] Ibid. [156] Nietzsche 1887, II, 16. [157] Freud 1930, 129–130.
[158] Ibid., 131.

One understands why Freud irresistibly returns to the murder of the primal father, because only real devouring ultimately makes it possible to explain the first internalization of the destructive drive, *before* the establishment of the paternal ban and of cultural "barriers," in other words, *before* the "repression" of aggression, which "is supposed to be the source of [the] sense of guilt." Originally, the destructive drive had to find its limit within itself, at the end of its own violence, and where, then, if not in the ambivalence of incorporation? Let us remember that the destructive sadism of oral incorporation is not the death drive itself but an alloy, already, of the life drive and death drive, a mixture of union and disunion:

> Is it not plausible to suppose that this sadism is in fact a death drive which, under the influence of the narcissistic libido, has been forced away from the ego and has consequently only emerged in relation to the object? It now enters the service of the sexual function. During the oral stage of organization of the libido, the act of obtaining erotic mastery over an object coincides with that object's destruction.[159]

It is this ambivalence of cannibalistic identification that ultimately accounts for the turning of aggression against oneself, guilty remorse, and the emergence of civilization:

> This remorse was the result of the primordial ambivalence of feeling towards the father. His sons hated him, but they loved him, too. After their hatred had been satisfied by their act of aggression, their love came to the fore in their remorse for the deed. It set up the superego by identification with the father ... And since the inclination to aggressiveness against the father was repeated in the following generations, the sense of guilt, too, persisted, and it was reinforced once more by every piece of aggressiveness that was suppressed and carried over to the super-ego. Now, I think, we can at last grasp two things perfectly clearly: the part played by love in the origin of conscience and the fatal inevitability of the sense of guilt.[160]

Nothing new compared to *Totem and Taboo* and "The Ego and the Id," as we can see, except that the history of human civilization is now reformulated in the terms of the great metabiological speculation of "Beyond the Pleasure Principle." If we are so uncomfortable in civilization, it is because we feel obscurely guilty, even if we have done nothing wrong. And if we feel guilty, it is because "the sense of guilt is an expression of the

[159] Freud 1920, 54, translation modified. [160] Freud 1930, 132.

conflict due to ambivalence, of the eternal struggle between Eros and the death or destructive drive."[161]

The first libidinal bond to another is simultaneously an unbinding, a destructive incorporation, and therefore the more we love, the more we kill, the more we feel guilty. Civilization being nothing other than the continuation of the biological process by which the living agglutinate themselves "erotically" and cohere in order to defer the return to death, it is necessarily always guilt-inducing. In Freud's illusion-free universe, one is guilty of living:

> Since civilization obeys an internal erotic impulsion (*Antrieb*) which causes human beings to unite in a closely-knit group, it can only achieve this aim through an ever-increasing reinforcement of the sense of guilt. What began in relation to the father is completed in relation to the group. If civilization is a necessary course of development from the family to humanity as a whole, then – as a result of the inborn conflict arising from ambivalence, of the eternal struggle between the trends of love and death – there is inextricably bound up with it an increase of the sense of guilt.[162]

In the same way that life in general is a mortal disease, a cyclical return to the inorganic, isn't cultural life, then, a neurosis of humanity, an eternal ambivalent return of the repressed? Freud asks the question rhetorically at the end of his book: "may we not be justified in reaching the diagnosis that, under the influence of cultural urges, some civilizations, or some epochs of civilization – possibly the whole of mankind – have become 'neurotic'?"[163] The answer is obviously "yes," even if Freud hesitates to pose as a Nietzschean "physician of culture" in the lines that follow: "Moreover, the diagnosis of communal neuroses is faced with a special difficulty. In an individual neurosis we take as our starting-point the contrast that distinguishes the patient from his environment, which is assumed to be 'normal.' For a group all of whose members are affected by one and the same disorder no such background could exist."[164] And for good reason, since civilization is the norm – the *sick* norm, therefore, the pathogenic and pathological norm.

What Freud tells us in these truly final lines is that there is no cure for culture, nor for the neurosis that is its individual repetition. No hope, no redemption, no savior, even if it is the psychoanalyst. We are condemned to repression and guilt, because such is our "archaic heritage": "One is reminded of the great poet's [Goethe] moving arraignment of the 'Heavenly Powers':

[161] Ibid., translation modified. [162] Ibid., 133. [163] Ibid., 144. [164] Ibid.

You lead us into life, to stray
Into our destined guilt, and then
Leave us to suffer and to pay
The debt all guilts exact from mortal men."[165]

This is often described as the pessimism of an old man estranged from life and the "fury of healing," but this therapeutic nihilism was in fact inscribed in the theory from the very beginning, from the moment Freud defined neurosis as the effect of repression, i.e., of civilization. For in the end, how to cure civilization? The metabiological theory proposed in *Civilization and Its Discontents* only ratifies the ineluctability of culture and repression by naturalizing them. What began with the "miserable little pile of secrets"[166] of Viennese ladies ends with the eternal struggle of the two heavenly powers, Eros and Thanatos.

[165] Ibid., 133. [166] Malraux 1943, 79.

Conclusion

We asked in the Introduction whether Freud was a philosopher. Obviously, the answer must now be "yes," in spite of the many protests of the main person concerned. Freud claimed to have created a new science based on his clinical experience, but he really did something quite different. Imbued with the physicalism of Brücke and his Viennese masters, he had set out "to furnish a psychology that shall be a natural science: that is, to represent psychical processes as quantitatively determinate states of specifiable material particles," as he wrote at the opening of the *Project* of 1895.[1] In the end, he proposed a *Naturphilosophie* embracing the history of the planet, of human life and culture from the great polarity of Eros and Thanatos, of Love and Hate – precisely the kind of romantic mixture of science and philosophy that Brücke and his friends Hermann von Helmholtz (1821–1894) and Emil Du Bois-Reymond (1818–1896) had vowed to abandon once and for all.

Frank Sulloway describes Freudian psychoanalysis as a cryptobiology, meaning that it is a biological theory presented in the form of psychology. It should be added that this cryptobiology is even more profoundly a cryptophilosophy, a speculative philosophy of nature built from evolutionary postulates borrowed from the biology of the time and cloaked in a psychotherapy of neuroses. It is not just that Freud based his psychological concepts on a biological foundation, which, after all, was a legitimate project (it is still today that of evolutionary psychology and, more generally, of neuroscience). Much more damning is the fact that from a certain point onwards, he used these Lamarcko-Haeckelian presuppositions in an entirely a priori way, in order to guarantee the internal coherence of the true "system of nature" that he was building. This is what Kraepelin reproached him for when he spoke of the "castles in the air" of psychoanalysis: these castles are magnificent; one likes to walk around in them

[1] Freud 1895, 295.

endlessly, but they rest on nothing but themselves. Concepts such as narcissism, death drive, id, superego, oral incorporation, identification, affective ambivalence, etc. were not introduced to account for clinical data, whatever Freud may say. They were internal adjustments intended to make the theory more consistent, more encompassing, more resistant to contradiction, in a word, more systematic.

We must, therefore, reverse the relationship established by Freud between theory and clinic. As the sexologist Albert Moll already said in 1909, Freud did not base his theories on the impartial listening of his neurotic patients; he made them find these theories in their "unconscious," with the help of an irresistible hermeneutic: "These clinical histories ... rather produce the impression that much of the alleged histories have been introduced by the suggestive questioning of the examiner ... The impression produced in my mind is that the theory of Freud ... suffices to account for the clinical histories, not that the clinical histories suffice to prove the truth of the theory."[2] Besides, the primary objective of an analysis has never been clinical observation, nor even healing (which is impossible anyway, if we are to believe the last Freud). What Freud asked of his patients was to validate the theories he had elaborated elsewhere by confirming the interpretations he proposed to them. As he wrote to Pastor Pfister regarding one of his patients, Elfriede Hirschfeld, although she had "no chance of getting cured ... at least psychoanalysis should learn from her case and profit by her."[3]

The psychoanalytic cure is not a therapy, nor even a method to access self-knowledge. It is a philosophical initiation during which patients are invited to find in themselves the truths taught by the master, in short, to become disciples. Henri Ellenberger (1905–1993), the great historian of psychotherapy, compared psychoanalysis to the philosophical schools of antiquity: "Psychoanalysis, is it a science? It does not meet the criteria (unified science, defined domain and methodology). It corresponds to the traits of a philosophical sect (closed organisation, highly personal initiation, a doctrine which is changeable but defined by its official adoption, cult and legend of the founder)."[4]

Ellenberger did not mean this as a compliment, but perhaps this was, after all, what Freud wanted from the beginning: to be a master of truth, to

[2] Moll 1909, 190.

[3] Unpublished letter to Oskar Pfister of January 2, 1912; Sigmund Freud Collection, Box 38, Folders 23–28, Manuscript Division, Library of Congress, Washington, DC, 1909–1940.

[4] "Les incertitudes de la psychanalyse" (The uncertainties of psychoanalysis), typed notes, Centre Henri Ellenberger, Hôpital Sainte-Anne, Paris.

deal with "ultimate things, the great problems of science and life,"[5] to speculate freely without having to be bothered with proof. "We cannot do," he wrote to Fliess, "without people who have the courage to think something new before they can demonstrate it."[6] Such philosophical audacity is grandiose, *großartig*, as Freud also said of Fliess' theory and of his own theory of drives. It has impressed many.

[5] Freud 1920, 59. [6] Freud 1985, 155.

Bibliography

Amouroux, Rémy (2004), "'Le précieux livre de W. Bölsche.' Freud et la culture évolutionniste allemande du début du XXe siècle," *Gesnerus*, 61, 24–36.

Aristotelis Opera edidit Academia Regia Borussica (1831–1870), 5 vols., ed. Immanuelis Bekkeri, Berlin: Georgium Reimerum.

Aschaffenburg, Gustav (1906), "Die Beziehung des sexuellen Lebens zur Entstehung von Nerven – und Geistes Krankheiten," *Münchener medizinische Wochenschrift*, 53, September 11, 1793–1798.

Baldwin, James Mark (1895), *Mental Development in the Child and the Race: Methods and Processes*, New York: Macmillan.

Bellamy, Edward (1880), *Dr. Heidenhoff's Process*, New York: D. Appleton.

Bernheim, Hippolyte (1888), *De la suggestion et de ses applications à la thérapeutique*, Paris: Octave Doin (2nd revised ed. of the volume published in 1886).

(1891), *Hypnotisme, suggestion, psychothérapie*, Paris: Fayard, 1991 (reprint of 2nd ed. of 1903).

Binswanger, Ludwig (1957), *Sigmund Freud: Reminiscences of a Friendship*, trans. Norbert Guterman, New York: Grune & Stratton.

Bleuler, Manfred (ed.) (1979), *Beiträge zur Schizophrenielehre der Zürcher Psychiatrischen Universitätsklinik Burghölzli (1902–1971)*, Darmstadt: Wissenschaftliche Buchgesellschaft.

Bölsche, Wilhelm (1887), *Die naturwissenschaftlichen Grundlagen der Poesie: Prolegomena einer realistischen Aesthetik*, Leipzig: Carl Reissner.

(1898–1903), *Das Liebesleben in der Natur: Eine Entwicklungsgeschichte der Liebe*, 3 vols. (1898, 1900, 1903), Leipzig: Eugen Diederichs.

(1926), *Love-Life in Nature: The Story of the Evolution of Love*, 2 vols., trans. Cyril Brown, New York: Albert & Charles Boni.

Borch-Jacobsen, Mikkel (2021), *Freud's Patients: A Book of Lives*, trans. Andrew Brown, London: Reaktion Books.

Bourneville, Désiré-Magloire, and Regnard, Paul (1878), *Iconographie photographique de la Salpêtrière: Service de M. Charcot*, Paris: Progrès Médical and V. Adrien Delahaye & Cie.

Braid, James (1843), *Neurhypnology; Or, the Rationale of Nervous Sleep, Considered in Relation with Animal Magnetism*, London: John Churchill.

Brentano, Franz (1874/1973), *Psychology from an Empirical Standpoint*, trans. Antos C. Rancurello, D. B. Terrell, and Linda L. McAlister, London: Routledge.

Breton, André (1924a/1969), *Les Pas perdus*, Paris: Gallimard.

(1924b/1972), "*Manifesto of Surrealism*," in *Manifestoes of Surrealism*, trans. Richard Seaver and Helen R. Lane, Ann Arbor: The University of Michigan.

Breuer, Josef, and Freud, Sigmund (1895), "Studies on Hysteria," *SE*, 2, 1–306.

Charcot, Jean-Martin (1887/1991), *Clinical Lectures on Diseases of the Nervous System*, Vol. 3, ed. Ruth Harris, trans. Thomas Savill, London: Tavistock/ Routledge.

Charteris, Hugo (1960), "Dr Jung Looks Back and On," *Daily Telegraph*, January 21.

Darwin, Charles Robert (1871), *The Descent of Man, and Selection in Relation to Sex*, 2 vols., London: John Murray.

(1877), "A Biographical Sketch of an Infant," *Mind*, 2, 285–294.

Delboeuf, Joseph (1885/1993), *Le Sommeil et les rêves, et autres textes*, Paris: Fayard.

Deleuze, Gilles (1967), *Présentation de Sacher-Masoch*, Paris: Minuit.

Descartes, René (1644/1989), *Discourse on Method and the Meditations*, trans. John Veitch, Buffalo, NY: Prometheus Books.

Diderot, Denis (1762–1773/1975), "Le Neveu de Rameau," in *Oeuvres complètes*, Vol. XII, eds. Herbert Dieckmann and Jean Varloot, Paris: Hermann.

Dufresne, Todd (2017), *The Late Sigmund Freud: Or, The Last Word on Psychoanalysis, Society, and All the Riddles of Life*, Cambridge: Cambridge University Press.

Eissler, Kurt R. (1952), Letter to Anna Freud of August 20, 1952, Anna Freud Papers, Box 19, Manuscript Division, Library of Congress, Washington, DC.

Ellis, Havelock (1894), *Man and Woman*, New York: Charles Scribner's Sons.

(1915), *Studies in the Psychology of Sex*, Vol. 2, 3rd ed., Philadelphia: F. A. Davis.

Feuerbach, Ludwig (1841/1957), *The Essence of Christianity*, trans. George Eliot, New York: Harper.

Fliess, Wilhelm (1897), *Die Beziehung zwischen Nase und weiblichen Geschlechtsorganen. In ihrer biologischen Bedeutungen dargestellt*, Leipzig: Franz Deuticke.

Flournoy, Théodore (1896), *Notice sur le laboratoire de psychologie de l'université de Genève*, Geneva: Eggiman.

Forel, August (1889), *Der Hypnotismus: Seine Bedeutung und seine Handhabung*, Stuttgart: Ferdinand Enke.

(1906), *Hypnotism; Or, Suggestion and Psychotherapy*, trans. Henry William Armit, London: Rebman (based on the 5th revised ed. of Forel 1889).

(1910), "La psychologie et la psychothérapie à l'université," *Journal für Psychologie und Neurologie*, 17, Ergänzungsheft, 307–317.

(1968), *August Forel: Briefe/Correspondance 1864–1927*, Bern: Hans Huber.

Frazer, James George (1887–1910), *Totemism and Exogamy: A Treatise on Certain Early Forms of Superstition and Society*, 4 vols., London: Macmillan.

Freud, Sigmund (1888a), "Hysteria," *SE*, 1, 37–59.

(1888b), "Gehirn," in *Handwörterbuch der Gesamten Medizin*, Stuttgart: Ferdinand Enke Verlag, 1888–1891, 1, 684–697.

(1889), "Review of August Forel's *Hypnotism*," *SE*, 1, 89–102.

(1890), "Psychical (or Mental) Treatment," *SE*, 7, 281–302.

(1891), "Hypnosis," *SE*, 1, 103–114.

(1892/1987), "Bericht über einen Vortrag 'Über Hypnose und Suggestion'," in *Gesammelte Werke, Nachtragsband*, eds. Angela Richards and Ilse Grubrich-Simitis, Frankfurt am Main: S. Fischer Verlag, 165–178.

(1892–1893), "A Case of Successful Treatment by Hypnosis. With Some Remarks on the Origin of Hysterical Symptoms through 'Counter-Will'," *SE*, 1, 115–128.

(1895), "Project for a Scientific Psychology," *SE*, 1, 281–397.

(1896a), "Heredity and the Aetiology of the Neuroses," *SE*, 3, 141–156.

(1896b), "The Aetiology of Hysteria," *SE*, 3, 189–221.

(1896c), "Further Remarks on the Neuro-Psychoses of Defence," *SE*, 3, 157–185.

(1899), "Screen Memories," *SE*, 3, 301–322.

(1900), "The Interpretation of Dreams," *SE*, 4–5.

(1901), "The Psychopathology of Everyday Life," *SE*, 6.

(1905a), "Three Essays on the Theory of Sexuality," *SE*, 7, 121–245.

(1905b), "On Psychotherapy," *SE*, 7, 257–268.

(1905c), "Fragment of an Analysis of a Case of Hysteria," *SE*, 7, 3–122.

(1905d), "Jokes and their Relation to the Unconscious," *SE*, 8.

(1906), "My Views on the Part Played by Sexuality in the Aetiology of the Neuroses," *SE*, 7, 269–279.

(1907a), "The Sexual Enlightenment of Children. An Open Letter to Dr. M. Fürst," *SE*, 9, 129–140.

(1907b), "Delusions and Dreams in Jensen's Gradiva," *SE*, 9, 3–96.

(1908), "Creative Writers and Day-Dreaming," *SE*, 9, 141–153.

(1909), "Analysis of a Phobia in a Five-Year-Old Boy," *SE*, 10, 3–149.

(1910a), "Five Lectures on Psycho-Analysis," *SE*, 11, 1–56.

(1910b), "The Future Prospects of Psycho-Analytic Therapy," *SE*, 11, 139–151.

(1910c), "Leonardo da Vinci and a Memory of his Childhood," *SE*, 11, 59–137.

(1910d), "The Psycho-Analytic View of Psychogenic Disturbance of Vision," *SE*, 11, 209–218.

(1910e), "A Special Type of Choice of Object Made by Men (Contributions to the Psychology of Love I)," *SE*, 11, 163–176.

(1911), "Psycho-Analytic Notes on an Autobiographical Account of a Case of Paranoia (Dementia Paranoides)," *SE*, 12, 9–84.

(1912), "Recommendations to Physicians Practising Psycho-Analysis," *SE*, 12, 109–120.

(1912–1913), "Totem and Taboo," *SE*, 13, 1–161.
(1913a), "The Claims of Psycho-Analysis to Scientific Interest," *SE*, 13, 165–190.
(1913b), "On Beginning the Treatment (Further Recommendations on the Technique of Psycho-Analysis II)," *SE*, 12, 121–144.
(1913c), "The Disposition to Obsessional Neurosis," *SE*, 12, 317–326.
(1914a), "On the History of the Psycho-Analytic Movement," *SE*, 14, 7–66.
(1914b), "Remembering, Repeating and Working-Through. (Further Recommendations on the Technique of Psycho-Analysis)," *SE*, 12, 145–156.
(1914c), "On Narcissism: An Introduction," *SE*, 14, 67–102.
(1914d), "The Moses of Michelangelo," *SE*, 13, 209–238.
(1915a), "Instincts and Their Vicissitudes," *SE*, 14, 109–140.
(1915b), "Observations on Transference-Love," *SE*, 12, 157–171.
(1915c), *A Phylogenetic Fantasy: Overview of the Transference Neuroses*, Ilse Grubrich-Simitis, trans. Axel Hoffer and Peter T. Hoffer, Cambridge, MA: The Belknap Press of Harvard University Press.
(1915d), "Thoughts for the Time on War and Death," *SE*, 14, 273–302.
(1915e), "Repression," *SE*, 14, 141–158.
(1915f), "The Unconscious," *SE*, 14, 159–215.
(1916–1917), "Introductory Lectures on Psycho-Analysis," *SE*, 15–16.
(1917a), "A Difficulty on the Path of Psycho-Analysis," *SE*, 17, 135–144.
(1917b), "On Transformations of Instinct as Exemplified in Anal Erotism," *SE*, 17, 125–134.
(1917c), "Mourning and Melancholia," *SE*, 14, 237–258.
(1919a), "'A Child Is Being Beaten': A Contribution to the Study of the Origin of Sexual Perversions," *SE*, 17, 165–204.
(1919b), "The Uncanny," *SE*, 17, 217–256.
(1920), "Beyond the Pleasure Principle," *SE*, 18, 3–64.
(1921), "Group Psychology and the Analysis of the Ego," *SE*, 18, 65–144.
(1923a), "Two Encyclopedia Articles," *SE*, 18, 233–260.
(1923b), "The Ego and the Id," *SE*, 19, 12–68.
(1923c), "Remarks on the Theory and Practice of Dream-Interpretation," *SE*, 19, 109–124.
(1924), "The Economic Problem of Masochism," *SE*, 19, 157–172.
(1925a), "An Autobiographical Study," *SE*, 20, 1–74.
(1925b), "The Resistances to Psycho-Analysis," *SE*, 19, 213–222.
(1926a), "The Question of Lay Analysis: Conversations with an Impartial Person," *SE*, 20, 179–258.
(1926b), "Inhibition, Symptoms and Anxiety," *SE*, 20, 77–178.
(1927), "The Future of an Illusion," *SE*, 21, 3–58.
(1930), "Civilization and Its Discontents," *SE*, 21, 64–148.
(1931), "The Expert Opinion in the Halsmann Case," *SE*, 21, 251–253.
(1933a), "New Introductory Lectures on Psycho-Analysis," *SE*, 22, 1–182.
(1933b), "Why War?," *SE*, 22, 203–218.

(1937a), "Analysis Terminable and Interminable," *SE*, 23, 20–53.
(1937b), "Constructions in Analysis," *SE*, 23, 255–269.
(1938a), "Findings, Ideas, Problems," *SE*, 23, 299–300.
(1938b), "An Outline of Psycho-Analysis," *SE*, 23, 141–208.
(1939), "Moses and Monotheism," *SE*, 23, 3–140.
(1960), *Letters of Sigmund Freud, 1873–1939*, ed. Ernst L. Freud, trans. Tania and James Stern, London: Hogarth Press.
(1985), *The Complete Letters of Sigmund Freud to Wilhelm Fliess 1887–1904*, ed. Jeffrey Moussaief Masson, Cambridge, MA, and London: The Belknap Press of Harvard University Press.

Freud, Sigmund, and Bullitt, William C. (1930–1932/1967), *Thomas Woodrow Wilson: A Psychological Study*, Boston: Houghton Mifflin.

Freud, Sigmund, and Pfister, Oskar (1963), *Psychoanalysis and Faith: The Letters of Sigmund Freud and Oskar Pfister*, eds. Heinrich Meng and Ernst L. Freud, trans. Eric Mosbacher, New York: Basic Books.

Freud, Sigmund, and Jung, Carl Gustav (1974), *The Freud/Jung Letters; the Correspondence between Sigmund Freud and C. G. Jung*, ed. William McGuire, trans. Ralph Manheim and R. F. C. Hull, Princeton, NJ: Princeton University Press.

Freud, Sigmund, and Ferenczi, Sándor (1993), *The Correspondence of Sigmund Freud and Sándor Ferenczi*, Vol. I: 1908–1914, eds. Eva Brabant, Ernst Falzeder, and Patrizia Giampieri-Deutsch, introd. André Haynal, trans. Peter Hoffer, Cambridge, MA: Harvard University Press.

Freud, Sigmund, and Jones, Ernest (1993), *The Complete Correspondence of Sigmund Freud and Ernest Jones, 1908–1939*, ed. R. Andrews Paskauskas, Cambridge, MA: Harvard University Press.

Freud, Sigmund, and Abraham, Karl (2002), *The Complete Correspondence of Sigmund Freud to Karl Abraham, 1907–1925, Completed Edition*, ed. Ernst Falzeder, London: Karnac.

Gauchet, Marcel (1992), *L'Inconscient cérébral*, Paris: Seuil.

Gaupp, Robert (1900), "Review of Freud (1899)," *Zeitschrift für Psychologie und Physiologie der Sinnesorgane*, 23, 233–234.

Gould, Stephen Jay (1977), *Ontogeny and Phylogeny*, Cambridge: The Belknap Press of Harvard University Press.

Graf, Max (1952), Interview with Kurt Eissler, Sigmund Freud Collection, Box 115, Folder 13, Manuscript Division, Library of Congress, Washington, DC.

Grünbaum, Adolf (1985), *The Foundations of Psychoanalysis: A Philosophical Critique*, Berkeley, Los Angeles, and London: University of California Press.

Haeckel, Ernst (1874), *Anthropogenie oder Entwickelungsgeschichte des Menschen: Keimes- und Stammes-Geschichte*, Leipzig: Wilhelm Engelmann.

Hart, Bernard (1929), *Psychopathology: Its Development and Its Place in Medicine*, Cambridge: Cambridge University Press.

Hegel, Georg Wilhelm Friedrich (1830/1971), *Hegel's Philosophy of Mind: Being Part Three of the Encyclopaedia of Philosophical Sciences*, trans. W. Wallace, Oxford: Clarendon Press.

(1835/1993), *Introductory Lectures on Aesthetics*, trans. B. Bosanquet, London: Penguin Books.
Heidenhain, Rudolf (1880), *Der sogenannte thierische Magnetismus. Physiologische Beobachtungen*, Leipzig: Breitkopf und Hartel.
Hering, Ewald (1870), "Über das Gedächtnis als allgemeine Funktion der organisirte Materie. Vortrag, gehalten in Wien 30. Mai 1870," Leipzig, Akademische Verlagsgesellschaft, 1921.
Hyatt, Alpheus (1893), ""Phylogeny of an Acquired Characteristic," *Proceedings of the American Philosophical Society*, 32, 349–647.
Janet, Pierre (1913), "Psycho-Analysis," in *XVIIth International Congress of Medicine*, London: Section XII, Psychiatry I, 1–52.
Jones, Ernest (1913), *Papers on Psycho-Analysis*, London: Baillière, Tindall & Cox.
(1953), *The Life and Work of Sigmund Freud*, Vol. 1, New York: Basic Books.
(1955), *The Life and Work of Sigmund Freud*, Vol. 2, New York: Basic Books.
(1957), *The Life and Work of Sigmund Freud*, Vol. 3, New York: Basic Books.
Jung, Carl Gustav (1912), *Wandlungen und Symbole der Libido. Ein Beitrag zur Entwicklungsgeschichte des Denkens*, 1st ed., Leipzig – Wien: Franz Deuticke.
Kant, Immanuel (1781), *Critique of Pure Reason*, trans. J. M. D. Meiklejohn, Buffalo – New York: Prometheus Books.
(1788/2002), *Critique of Practical Reason*, trans. W. S. Pluhar, Indianapolis – Cambridge: Hackett Publishing.
Kraepelin, Emil (1913), *Psychiatrie: Ein Lehrbuch für Studierende und Ärzte, III. Band, Klinische Psychiatrie, II. Teil*, Leipzig: J. A. Barth.
Lamarck, Jean-Baptiste (1809), *Philosophie zoologique, ou Exposition des considérations relatives à l'histoire des animaux*, Paris: Dentu.
Lang, Andrew, and Atkinson, James Jasper (1903), *Social Origins*, includes J. J. Atkinson, *Primal Law*, London, New York, Bombay: Longmans, Green, & Co.
Lang, Andrew (1905), *The Secret of the Totem*, London, New York, Bombay: Longmans, Green, & Co.
Laplanche, Jean, and Pontalis, Jean-Bertrand (1964), "Fantasme originaire, fantasme des origines, origine du fantasme," *Les Temps Modernes*, 19:215, 1833–1868.
Laycock, Thomas (1840), *Treatise on the Nervous Diseases of Women: Comprising an Inquiry into the Nature, Causes, and Treatment of Spinal and Hysterical Diseases*, London: Longman.
(1845), "On the Reflex Function of the Brain," *British and Foreign Medical Journal*, 19, 298–311.
(1876), "Reflex, Automatic and Unconscious Cerebration; A History and a Criticism," *The Journal of Mental Science*, 21, 477–498.
Le Bon, Gustave (1895/1896), *The Crowd: A Study of the Popular Mind*, New York: The Macmillan Co.
Mach, Ernst (1905/1976), *Knowledge and Error: Sketches on the Psychology of Enquiry*, ed. Brian McGuinness, trans. Thomas J. McCormack and Paul Foulkes, Dordrecht and Boston: D. Reidel.

Malcolm, Norman (1958), *Ludwig Wittgenstein: A Memoir*, London: Oxford University Press.

Malraux, André (1943/1997), *Les Noyers de l'Altenburg*, Paris: Gallimard.

Maudsley, Henry (1867), *The Physiology and Pathology of the Mind*, New York: D. Appleton.

Mayer, Andreas (2001), "L'hypnotisme introspectif et l'auto-analyse de Freud. Les procédés d'auto-observation dans la pratique clinique," *Revue d'histoire des sciences humaines*, 5, 171–196.

Moll, Albert (1909/1913), *The Sexual Life of the Child*, trans. Eden Paul, New York: Macmillan.

Nietzsche, Friedrich (1881/1982), *Daybreak*, trans. Reginald John Hollingdale, Cambridge: Cambridge University Press.

(1881–1882/1973), "Nachgelassene Fragmente Frühjahr 1881–Sommer 1882," in *Nietzsche Werke. Kritische Gesamtausgabe*, Vol. 2, eds. Giorgio Colli and Mazzino Montinari, Berlin: Walter de Gruyter.

(1887/1967), *On the Genealogy of Morals*, trans. Walter Kaufmann and Reginald John Hollingdale, New York: Random House.

Nunberg, Herman, and Federn, Ernst (eds.) (1967), *Minutes of the Vienna Psychoanalytic Society*, Vol. 2: 1908–1910, trans. Margarethe Nunberg, New York: International Universities Press.

Popper, Karl (1963), *Conjectures and Refutations: The Growth of Scientific Knowledge*, London: Routledge and Kegan Paul.

Putman, James Jackson (1906), "Recent Experiences in the Study and Treatment of Hysteria at Massachusetts General Hospital," *Journal of Abnormal Psychology*, 1, 26–41.

Sartre, Jean-Paul (1943/1984), *Being and Nothingness*, trans. H. Barnes, New York: Washington Square Press.

Savage, Thomas Staughton (1847), "Notice of the External Characters and Habits of Troglodytes Gorilla, a New Species of Orang from the Gaboon River," *Boston Journal of Natural History*, 5:4, Art. XXXIV, 417–443.

Schreber, Daniel Paul (1903/1988), *Memoirs of My Nervous Illness*, eds. and trans. Ida Macalpine and Richard A. Hunter, Cambridge, MA and London: Harvard University Press.

Shamdasani, Sonu (2003), *Jung and the Making of Modern Psychology*, Cambridge: Cambridge University Press.

Smith, William Robertson (1889/1894), *Lectures on the Religion of the Semites*, London: Adam and Charles Black.

Spencer, Herbert (1895), *The Principles of Sociology*, 3rd ed., New York: D. Appleton.

Sulloway, Frank J. (1992), *Freud, Biologist of the Mind*, 2nd revised ed., Cambridge, MA: Harvard University Press.

Sully, James (1896), *Studies of Childhood*, New York: D. Appleton.

Swales, Peter J. (1983), "Freud, Krafft-Ebing, and the Witches: The Role of Krafft-Ebing in Freud's Flight into Fantasy," New York: privately published by the author.

Treichl, Heinrich (2003), *Fast ein Jahrhundert. Erinnerungen*, Wien: Zsolnay.

Von Krafft-Ebing, Richard (1894), *Psychopathia sexualis, mit besonderer Berücksichtigung der conträre Sexualempfindung: eine klinisch-forensische Studie*, 9th ed., Stuttgart: Ferdinand Enke.

Von Strümpell, Adolf (1896), "Review of J. Breuer and S. Freud's Studies on Hysteria," *Deutsche Zeitschrift für Nervenheilkunde*, 8, 159–161.

Weismann, August (1882), *Ueber die Dauer des Lebens; ein Vortrag*, Jena: G. Fischer.

(1883), *Ueber Leben und Tot. Eine biologische Untersuchung*, Jena, G. Fischer, 1884.

(1892/1893), *The Germ Plasm: A Theory of Heredity*, trans. William Newton Parker and Harriet Rönnfeldt, London: The Contemporary Science Series.

Wortis, Joseph (1954), *Fragments of an Analysis with Freud*, New York: Viking Press.

Wittgenstein, Ludwig (1966), *Lectures and Conversations on Aesthetic, Psychology, and Religious Belief*, ed. Cyril Berrett, Berkeley: University of California Press.

Woodworth, R. S. (1917), "Some Criticisms of the Freudian Psychology," *Journal of Abnormal Psychology*, 12, 174–194.

Index

For EU product safety concerns, contact us at Calle de José Abascal, 56–1°, 28003 Madrid, Spain or eugpsr@cambridge.org.

www.ingramcontent.com/pod-product-compliance
Ingram Content Group UK Ltd.
Pitfield, Milton Keynes, MK11 3LW, UK
UKHW022132080726
473066UK00009B/511

* 9 7 8 1 0 0 9 3 7 1 1 4 8 *